CHRISTOPHER HARDER

THROUGH THE LEGAL LOOKING GLASS

Inspiration

"Our deepest fear is not that we are inadequate. Our deepest fear is that we are powerful beyond measure. It is our light, not our darkness that frightens us. We ask ourselves, who am I to be brilliant, gorgeous, talented and fabulous? Actually who are you not to be? You are a child of God. Your playing small doesn't serve the world. There's nothing enlightened about shrinking so that other people won't feel insecure around you. We are all meant to shine, as children do. We were born to make manifest the glory of God that is within us. It's not just in some of us: it's in everyone. And as we let our own light shine, we unconsciously give other people permission to do the same. As we are liberated from our own fear, our presence automatically liberates others."

*Nelson Mandela President of South Africa,
in his 1994 inaugural speech.*

This edition published by
Howling At The Moon Publishing Ltd
PO Box 302-188
North Harbour
Auckland

http://www.howlingatthemoon.com

(c) Copyright Christopher Harder, 2002

Christopher Harder asserts the moral right to be acknowledged as the author of this work. All rights reserved

Through The Legal Looking Glass is copyright. Except for the purpose of fair reviewing, no part of this publication may be copied, reproduced or transmitted in any form or by any means, including via technology either already in existence or developed subsequent to publication, without the express written permission of the copyright holders.

ISBN: 0-9582054-9-3
Book design: Howling At The Moon Publishing

Dedication,

To my wife, Philippa, forever patient and long-suffering, I dedicate this book. And to Justice David Morris for helping to make it all as fascinating as it has been.

Acknowledgements

My gratitude and profound thanks to the following people who made this book possible and helped in bringing it to fruition.   Camille Wills, Roger Wakefield, & Justin Von Tunzelman.

& Special Thanks

To my talented colleague, Melanie Coxon for winning my Privacy Appeal against the Proceedings Commissioner.
To Anecia Williams, one of God's angels.
To the late Stuart Ennor for his 'line of thinking'

BY THE SAME AUTHOR:

Guns of Lautoka
Mercy, Mistress, Mercy

Contents

7	Abstract: Gridiron Vs Rugby
9	Early Childhood to age 21
28	Bus Strike Injunction case
40	My 1st case, A Heroin Import
55	Cannabis vs Japanese Maple
58	A Hot Gun and Drugs on the Fire
65	Mr. Justice Speight
68	A Pocket Knife and a Severed Ear
72	The Prostitute/Secretary Rape Case
76	The Parnell Panther Rape Case
87	Jail for Me, and an Arms Amnesty in Fiji
104	The Lawyers' Golden Rule
109	Rainbow Warrior Spies in Washington DC
135	The Plumley-Walker B and D Murder Saga
169	A Knife in the Heart Manslaughter
173	The Shower Nozzle Case
177	Donnelly '7 Shots in the Back Murder'
187	Whangape Maori Protest
193	The Papal Knight Drug case Gone Wrong
198	Hong Kong Triad Kidnapping case
207	Donnelly Re-Trial (Pt 2)
210	Bennett Body in the Woods (Pt 1) Nov 1993
225	Collie Rape Appeals: August 1994
228	The Bennett Body in the Wood trial (Pt2)
239	Legal Sunscreen 1997
244	The Baby L Saga 1998
249	The Long Rape case
260	Sami Rape Appeal
264	Where My Heart Is

Epilogue: Judges
Fees

Preface

These are my recollections of events, made without prejudice, fear or favour. The cases are well documented and most of them a matter of public record. To protect the innocent (and some of the guilty) I have changed some names and details where appropriate or prudent. Name suppression orders have been honoured.

Abstract: Gridiron vs Rugby

Willie Fleming, an African American, was, in his time, the best Gridiron (North American football) player in Canada I had ever had the pleasure to watch run with a football. He played for the British Columbia Lions who played their home games at Empire Stadium in Vancouver.

Whenever Wiseman trophy winning quarterback Joe Knapp tossed the ball to Fleming, Fleming would tuck it tight under his arm, then duck and dive his way through the opposition ranks, like poetry in motion, in search of the next touchdown. If I had to, I would compare him with New Zealand's All Black Tana Umaga for speed and lightness of foot and never taking his eye off the ball for a moment.

Many times when the B.C. Lions were behind in the game with the ball on their own goal line and seconds only remaining on the clock, the legendary quarterback would throw the football high in the air and as far as he could in the direction of Willie Fleming who was running fast towards the opposition goal line. This is called the long bomb or the 'Hail Mary' pass. Often Joe Knapp would just throw the ball high and far, saying a Hail Mary in the hope that the football would be caught by the likes of 'magic dancer', Willie Fleming. More often than not Fleming would pluck the ball out of the air as he was running towards the opposition goal line, skirting the remaining players and scoring the winning touchdown just as the time on the clock ran out and the referee fired his starters pistol to signal that the game was over.

The most significant difference between North American Gridiron football and New Zealand rugby I find, is that no forward passes are allowed in rugby and a player has to physically get past all the opposing team members with ball in hand, in order to score a try where in gridiron you can run through the opposition, or you can go over the opposition heads throwing the long bomb to your targeted receiver.

I guess that's what I've been doing most of my professional life in New Zealand.... playing Gridiron rules instead of Rugby rules, thereby breaking all the Old Boy network codes and delivering those long bomb, forward, 'Hail Mary' passes from time to time. No wonder my battle for acceptance has been so bruising, brutalising and simply unbearable at times.

Having had to appear before the Disciplinary tribunal 4 times in the last 10 years has taken its toll on me and worn me down to the point where I thought I might well lose the game. Fortunately I have succeeded in living by an old adage Peter Williams QC told me many years ago. 'Never let the bastards get you down!'

To that end and in the hope of finally winning the game, I have written this book. It is the story of my eventful and often dramatic journey navigating life and law. It is my last long bomb, 'Hail Mary' pass in this game, from deep in my own end zone with time fast running out on the clock, in search of one final winning touchdown!

Early Childhood To 21

I was the first of twin boys born, at five forty-five In the evening of September 27, 1948. Named Christopher Lloyd (Lloyd after my father) Harder. My fraternal twin brother named Gregory Wilson (my mother's maiden name) Harder arrived some twenty-five minutes later weighing in at a respectable six pounds. By comparison I weighed just on four pounds. Clearly I was the runt of the two.

Our father, Lloyd Jacob Harder, was a travelling salesman in Vancouver, British Columbia and was only home six months out of twelve. He met my mother in London during the war. She was a Wren. My father, a Canadian airforceman, was full of charm. He promised that they would marry after the war. My mother was of Scottish descent and born in Edinburgh. Her name, Elma, is short for Elizabeth Marion. Prior to our birth she worked for the *Vancouver Sun* newspaper as a telephonist.

When my brother and I were just young crawlers, still unable to walk, our family lived in a two-bedroom apartment on Fourth Avenue in Vancouver not far from the Kitsilano beach. Even then it would appear that I had a predilection to push boundaries.

My father tells a story about when my brother and I were around ten months old. Back then Gregory, nicknamed Barnie Pots, and I, nicknamed Blondie, would with regular routine be put in our highchairs and fed the standard Heinz baby food regime of mashed carrots or brains then a dessert of stewed apple or peach. Before our parents sat down to eat my father would set us down on the rug in the middle of the living room and tell us to stay on the rug while they ate their meal.

Apparently, I'd appear to listen to everything he said but just as soon as I thought nobody was watching I would crawl to the edge of the rug and poke my foot over. Quickly I would pull it back watching or listening for any consequence or response. If nothing happened - that is, father didn't growl - then often I would go further, next time dangling a whole limb over the edge. It would seem even back then I would throw caution to the wind and with no fear, make a break for freedom by crawling off the rug, and disappearing around the hallway corner at speed. When caught, as I inevitably was, I would be put back on the rug with further admonishment. For persistent re-offending of this kind I would be removed to the bedroom where I would be put behind my crib bars. I can't actually recall these episodes but with a recurring history of rebellion in my 53 years I would say it's true.

When I was young I seemed to have a talent for getting myself into trouble. On one occasion my inquisitiveness nearly caused my brother and me our lives. I found what I thought was candy in my father's coat pocket. I snuck upstairs to our bedroom where my brother soon joined me. There we gorged ourselves on the 'candy'. In very short order following discovery, my father, amid great panic, rushed us to hospital where our stomachs were pumped – because the 'candy' had in fact been rat poison. My father, to deal with a couple of the tailed variety that had invaded the laundry room out back, where the household garbage was kept, had purchased it that day. Obviously the Harder twins inherited a strong constitution because we're both still around today.

One day I was outside playing on the lawn of our ground level apartment on Fourth Avenue, by myself. I was kicking a soccer ball around the yard when I banged the ball with my foot sending it flying into the prohibited zone beyond the green stringed fence netting surrounding a patch of newly sown grass. Obviously I knew I wasn't supposed to go onto that grass, that's why it was fenced off, but my ball was inside the netting and I wanted it back. It didn't take me long to decide what I was going to do. I stepped back, and then took a running jump in an effort to leap over the fence. It was not only my ball handling that was a bit off. So was the timing of my jump. Instead of jumping over the fence – I landed directly on top of the fence which rebounded like an oversized elastic band, flinging me backwards where I landed on my head. This story finishes with my bleeding head wrapped in towels, and another trip to hospital. Although I don't specifically recall, I am certain that this episode taught me that in future I would just have to learn to jump higher.

I remember the day I broke my front teeth. Oh how my mother cried. My brother and I were ten. We were getting ready for a piano recital the two of us were to play in. My brother was having a bath before he got dressed for this great occasion. I was waiting outside the bathroom door in the hallway for my turn.

Mother had our neighbour Mrs Teeple and her five-year old daughter Ruthie over for a cup of tea. Mrs Teeple's teenage son Jeff had dammed the babbling brook that ran between our properties the summer before and now we had a pond to play on and ducks to feed. We eventually had a punt built by Silas Huckleback, to pole around the water looking for frogs and duck eggs when we had nothing better to do.

As a youngster I often did things on impulse not considering the possible consequences first. This was one of those occasions. As my twin came out of the bathroom I hid around the corner waiting. Young Ruthie was walking down the hall in our direction. Greg was wearing a white towel as he walked by, or he was until I ripped it off him in front of our young neighbour, exposing him in front of a girl. Dumb move Chris! Boy did my brother ever get angry.

He retaliated instantly, giving me an almighty push and I fell to the floor face down. Suffering such humiliation severely provoked Greg, who jumped on the back of my head and broke my front teeth to the eternal anguish of my mother. The piano recital was a disaster my mother never forgot. It hurt like hell, especially when I sucked a breath of air over the raw exposed nerves of my broken teeth. Now I had an inverted V where my front teeth sat, and a lisp. This necessitated years of elocution lessons practicing how to say the likes of 'The brown cow jumped over the moon!' When I joined the military at 16 I finally got my teeth fixed.

I first met Melvin Burritt alias Silas Huckleback when I was around eight or nine. He sported a Wild Bill Hickock styled moustache and beard and he was a communist. Silas was a character out of another dimension. He wore buckskin leather pants and jacket and he had a pinto pony he used to ride in the annual Lynn Valley Day parade. Silas Huckleback would lead the parade on his prancing brown and black spotted pinto pony. In one hand he would wave around an old Davy Crockett style flintlock rifle. In the other hand he would hold his faded white cowboy hat aloft then give the pony a little nudge with his spurs, let out a great big war yelp like a banshee and race across the playing field like a bat out of hell.

Every day after school I would hurry to Silas Huckleback's to hear his stories. He always had time to listen to me despite the fact I was a non-stop chatterbox always asking him questions. Silas built a little shed out the back of the log cabin he had built for his 'missus'. He had a whisky still in one corner and a barrel of mash in the other. The shed always had an aroma about it.

Silas could make his whisky, or do whatever he wanted including an occasional smoke of his Prairie 'loco weed' and his wife would not interfere. He refused to pay the Revenuer, as he called the tax department, its exorbitant tax on government-taxed liquor. That was why Silas had a little whisky still in the corner of the room where he would make his Lynn Valley 'moonshine'.

Silas was an eccentric individual who liked to tell great tales of when he was a cowboy in the early 1900s. He would show me his black and white picture (dated 1914) of him riding a bucking bronco wearing a buckskin jacket and clutching his cowboy hat tight in his right hand flung high in the air in typical bronco busting style.

Silas Huckleback was a creative person and a very interesting individual to a young boy growing up, to talk to and to be influenced by. Every day after school I would visit my mentor. He would tell me of his great overseas adventures. How in 1956 he decided he wanted to travel to the USSR (Russia) to see for himself if communism really worked. It took him two years to get a visa and in 1958 he flew to Moscow for six weeks in the middle of the cold war.

When Silas returned from Russia he told me tales and answered my questions about his adventure for six months. He confided in me that the communism he observed in Russia had not lived up to his expectations.

Three years later in 1961 Silas travelled to Cuba. Fidel Castro and Che Guevara had led a successful revolution in 1958 against Fulgencio Batista, the Cuban dictator most communists hated with a vengeance. When Silas returned from Cuba he showed me a picture of himself standing between Che Guevara and Fidel Castro on the front steps of the Palace of the Revolution in Havana, Cuba. He was so proud of that picture. I soaked up his overseas adventures and tales of revolution like a thirsty puppy!

I listened to all of Silas's tales of adventure and, as I grew up, rejected his concept of communism because it seemed to prohibit individualism. When I challenged him on this point, he replied that it was alright to be an individual during the revolution but after the revolution one had to give away one's individualism for the greater good of the masses. I didn't like that concept.

I was also partly influenced by the great hysteria created by the media. After all it was the middle of the Cold War with the west, led by the United States of America rejecting and protecting the rest of the world against the Great Russian bear, Communist USSR. (The Union of Soviet Socialist Republics)

The one thing I hated in my childhood was being made to attend Sunday school and church. Every Sunday after church our father and mother would pick us up outside church and take us to our grandparents for 'brunch'. My grandmother, who was Dutch/German with some white Russian thrown in, normally made borsch soup, summer or winter. I liked the summer borsch best, because it had summer sausage added to the broth. Both were made with beet leaves.

My grandpa, Jacob Harder was born in 1888. He was an entrepreneur in business and a hard-living, heavy-drinking individual until the day he married my Salvation Army member grandmother, Margaret. On the Saturday morning of his wedding day my grandfather was so intoxicated that he walked past my grandmother in the main street and failed to recognise her! The morning after the wedding, grandpa poured himself a shot of whisky. Before he could pick it up my grandmother grabbed the shot glass and poured the 'demon drink' down the sink. Grandpa pleaded it was, 'Just an eye-opener, Honey'. To which my taller and broader grandmother replied, 'You've had your LAST eye-opener darling!'

After a few years of marriage my grandparents joined the congregation of the Apostolic Church. A fundamental, Old Testament-based religion, this influenced my grandfather's attitudes and later moralistic values which he tried desperately to instil in me. During the Depression, my grandpa's altruistic character saw him allowing local farming customers to run up bills in excess of $100,000 that he forgave when they couldn't pay. For example, not having the heart to say no, he used to purchase all the locally produced eggs from the farmers. They were infested with locusts and so he used to get my dad to break them all by throwing them at the fence out back.

The routine trek to my grandparents normally saw my twin Gregory, and younger brothers Paul, and later Brian go out to the garage and play with grandpa's key-cutting machine and the zillions of boxes of different key blanks. They would look at the various key cutting catalogues and the secret key cutting codes. My grandfather had blank keys for every motor vehicle ever manufactured in North America.

For me, my Sunday morning visits to our grandparents were different. Every time I visited, my grandfather would take me into a little sunroom at the front of their little house and sit me in a chair in the corner. Above the chair hung a picture of Jesus with the sun shining through the clouds above his head. Grandpa would tell me I was one of God's lost lambs but that if I gave myself to God I could do great things, even save the world! I believe I reminded him of himself as a boy!

I remember the time in 1958 when my father took my brother and me to a religious revival at the Vancouver Empire football stadium filled with people eager to hear the word of the Reverend Billy Graham and his view on God. On that occasion he called for anybody who wanted to give his or her heart to Jesus to come down and walk to the front of the stage.

For some reason, maybe the influence of my Sunday morning sessions with my grandfather, I stood up and turned toward the stairs, my father and my twin brother remained in their seats, and my father said, 'I'm proud of you son.' I walked down the stairs to the grass field that North American BC Lion football legend No. 15 Willie Fleming, would run winning touchdowns on, and walked up to the front of the stage. There I met Reverend Billy Graham, and he said to me, 'God welcomes you son!'

Irrespective of the frequent clashes I had with my dad, he provided well for us and we always had an annual camping holiday.

My younger brother Paul had a menagerie of animals over the years, including a fox, wolf, racoon, woolly monkey, a pony, chickens, ducks, pigeons, a magpie, an alligator, a skunk, hamster, cats and dogs. When I was ten, my favourite dog Klondie a beautiful Samoyed, was run over by a concrete truck driving past our house at 1515 Coleman Street in Lynn Valley, North Vancouver; it was the first real trauma of my young life.

I joined Cubs but was soon suspended for 'improper use of a hatchet'. Walking to Cubs early one summer evening, with my new hatchet my mother had bought me for my tenth birthday, someone driving a big old car down rain-sodden Coleman Street, drenched me in my uniform with muddy water. I became angry and quickly plotted my revenge.

The offending driver would have to return the same way in time, because the culvert further up the road had been washed out making our road a temporary dead end. I spent the next hour chopping down (with my new Cubs hatchet) an Alder tree about 30 feet high and 6 inches in diameter, so that it would fall across the road and block the path of the arrogant driver, who didn't even say sorry, and his vehicle.

I remember one occasion when I was eleven years old. I had stolen a number of chicken eggs from the chicken farm across the road. My friend Conrad Swanson joined me in my chicken raiding adventure. Once, we put the warm eggs on some straw in a box and we carried them outside. Next we caught a rooster that refused to stop crowing, thinking it would sit on the eggs and hatch them! We ran off into the bush to hide. Next we drafted my twin Gregory, who seldom did anything wrong, into the chicken stealing conspiracy but only after he swore not to tell if he didn't want to join us. On our second trip to the hatchery we almost got caught because of all the noise the laying hens were making as we ran by. A short time later the chicken farmer Smith and my father caught the three of us in a clearing in the bush. Soon the neighbours gathered round. My father was very angry. He intended to demonstrate to the neighbours that we would be punished for our actions. My father required my brother and me to drop our pants and bend over the log in front of everybody. As we lay waiting for the first whack my father stood up straight, undid his belt then raising his arm with belt in hand prepared to mete out the punishment. But before he could swing, his own pants fell down and nobody, including my father, could stop laughing. We would be punished when we got home.

Like most kids, I encountered the school bully. His name was Billy Pitman. It was after woodwork class one day, standing by the lockers, when Billy took a swing at me. I ducked and he hit his fist on the metal locker, yelping in agony. He disappeared holding his wrist. Next day he came to school wearing a cast and loudly blamed me. He threatened to wreak his revenge on me as soon as the cast came off in six week's time.

I lived in fear and trepidation all that time. Just two days after the removal of his cast, he invited me to the Lynn Valley playing field where half the school seemed to have gathered to cheer on the bully! We circled each other while the crowd continued to cheer. I stood with my hands by my side and then as he came menacingly closer, I sank to my knees pretending to plead with him not to hit me. As he raised his fists, I reached out my arms and grabbed him behind the knees, unbalancing him and making him fall to the ground.

Then I jumped on his stomach and straddled him with my long legs so he could not flip me off, then I started punching him in the face and didn't stop until he said 'Uncle' (I give up). The crowd of students went silent all of a sudden and started to disperse. It was the first and last time I ever had a physical fight at school.

The range of jobs I had growing up, would make an interesting CV. I sold Fuller brand brushes door to door when I was about 13 or 14. In winter when it snowed there would be drifts of two and three feet, so that shovelling snow became very lucrative, especially clearing snow from neighbours' roofs because the insurance companies would pay good rates for this before the weight of the wet snow crushed in the roof. One summer I hitchhiked through the British Columbia interior and was press-ganged by the forestry service into fighting a raging forest fire.

I even bottled water and put silver tops on them and tried to sell it over 40 years ago! Everyone thought I was mad, but I was clearly a bit ahead of my time in thinking bottled water could be sold. I think I also inherited my mother's canny Scot's personality with an eye for the opportunity to make money. Watching stump fires on Grouse Mountain for local property developers, sitting though the night with water hose at hand for hours mesmerised by the flame of the fire, was another of my career samplings.

I also tried out for English style rugby once at school and was rewarded with a straight-armed fist in my face that chipped my bottom teeth, so gave it up after one practice.

When I was 11 I started smoking and stealing my father's Kool menthol cigarettes. I ran away from home at age 14 and again at 15, hitchhiking across Canada. On reflection, I guess that was the earliest of my adventures that possibly gave me a taste for travel. I think I was also running away from emotional pain.

I was distraught when very good friends Diana and Donna Ring, also 14-year old twins but identical, were raped and murdered. They moved away from Lynn Valley to the British Columbia interior where their parents purchased a fishing resort in Enderby. Each day the twins had to walk a mile down an old country road to catch the country school bus.

The bus driver dropped them off at the junction every day at 4 pm. It would take the twins half an hour to walk the rest of the way home. One day they never made it home. When their parents and later the police went in search of them, both girls' bodies were found in the long grass not far from home. Both had been strangled.

Some of my anger abated when their killer Herman Hause, a man in his 20s was tried and convicted of their rape and murder and sentenced to life in prison. I felt that now at least some justice had been done and the nasty, nasty man, whom I dreamed of killing myself, would at least be locked up in prison for life.

The one thing I could do well in my youth was run (long distance) because of the length of my legs and my slim build back then. I entered a marathon race one 'Lynn Valley Day' celebration in which a semi-professional was competing and whom everyone assumed would win. He was, however, not familiar with the specified course and inadvertently cut off a large chunk of it. I thought he had taken the wrong turn but, still, like a fool, I followed him because he was recognised as the leader and I was not far behind.

He appeared to have won, but was immediately disqualified, as I was, when I came in a close second, and the lesson I learned from this experience? 'Never follow the leader, always follow your instinct and your own route to your destiny!'

At 16 I quit school because I was sitting in class, playing with the girl in front's pigtails when I got a whack on the head from behind. Without thinking or looking to see who had delivered the blow, I stood, swung round and hit the perpetrator, who happened to be the teacher. I was told I would receive twelve of the best (six on each hand) when I presented myself at vice-principal Tady's office.

Halfway through the punishment, I withdrew my hand, and said I was going to call my mother and leave school.

Vice-principal Tady said, 'You can't do that!' As a result of my conditioned response to reverse psychology, used by my father on me as a child when he knew I would always do the opposite of what I was told, I said, 'Watch me!'

My twin brother, who was perfect by comparison, constantly left me in the shade so I joined the Royal Canadian Air Force to try to impress my father because he had been an Air Force pilot during World War Two. I quickly learned that submitting to a military regime was not in my make up.

On one occasion while marching with my squadron on the parade field I put a pair of clip-on sunglasses over my ordinary glasses. The little Pommy drill sergeant who marched us back and forth in the hot sun suddenly called the squad to a halt then had me stand front and centre. He began to dress me down ordering me to take off the clip-on sunglasses. He was brutal and I was humiliated but I would get my revenge.

The next week we were all back on the parade ground marching to and fro. Then when the drill sergeant was not looking I took off my ordinary glasses and put on what looked like an ordinary pair of sunglasses. It did not take the sergeant long to spot the renegade in the squadron. Again I was ordered to stand front and centre. 'Take off those glasses!' he bellowed. 'No Sir!' I replied. 'Take off those glasses!' Now he was turning red in the face, then just before he exploded I thrust a piece of paper under his nose. He read it then went bright, bright red, ordered me to return to ranks without comment then dismissed the squadron. The drill sergeant then turned and walked straight to the bar on base. The piece of paper I had given him was a letter from the base doctor stating that I had permission to wear prescription sunglasses because I got head aches from the sun.

The Royal Canadian Air Force was obviously not my calling because I went AWOL (absent without leave) three times, and stole a blank ID card so that I could drink in the bars off base. In the end we parted company. My father never said anything but I knew he was ashamed of me for failing to fit in and make a go of a career in the military. He thought they would be able to break me, then control me. They were all wrong. Believing I was now a disappointment to my father I determined to spend the rest of my life trying to redeem myself in his eyes, as I saw it.

After I returned to Vancouver I found a job with a company called Lenkurt electric. I used my electronic skills learned in the air force to install microwave equipment across the Canadian provinces of Alberta, Saskatchewan, and Manitoba. One Saturday afternoon in the middle of winter I had to drive in a blizzard to a repeater site near a little town called Asquith outside Saskatoon, Saskatchewan. I became stuck in the snow and almost froze to death. After that I decided to give up the job and return to Vancouver and finish my interrupted education.

I desperately wanted to catch up with my twin bother and my best friend who were both about to enter Simon Fraser University. I tried to convince the Vancouver school board to let me in two thirds of the way through the school year in an attempt to catch up on three years of schooling in three months. I was laughed out of the office by an old battle-axe of an administrator. Not to be beaten, or at least not easily, I decided to go back and see Mr. Tady, the vice-principal of my old school. A fair man, he welcomed me back. Had he not done so, my chances of becoming a lawyer would have been about zero.

I enrolled for day school, night school, afternoon tutoring and correspondence school so that I could try to do the three years in four and a half months. Despite intricate timetable juggling I could not fit in twelfth grade English or Maths, but having made significant steps in catching up with my twin, I applied for admission to a local college.

However, the principal of West Vancouver College allowed me to enrol on the condition that I did my missing grade 12 courses. Considering what I had done in four and a half months at high school I thought this extra requirement was unfair and excessive. Refusing to give ground, I challenged the principal's authority and elected to take the matter to a higher forum. I booked a flight to Victoria, the seat of provincial government in British Columbia. I recall the secretary for the Minister of Education, Donald

Brothers, saying, 'I am sorry Mr. Harder, but you cannot see the Minister without an appointment. He is a busy man.' I decided to wait all day if necessary.

With timing just like you see in the movies, a man walked out of Mr. Brothers' office and asked the secretary for a file. Dressed in my grey pinstripe suit I turned to him, extended my hand and said, 'Sir, my name is Chris Harder, I am awfully sorry to have to bother you today, but I need your help with a serious problem and only you can help me solve it.' He looked at his secretary who was standing with her mouth open and said, 'Come in, Mr. Harder.'

He had a few minutes to spare before his next appointment and quickly got to the root of my problem. The minister picked up the phone and got the principal of my college on the line. 'Hello, this is Donald Brothers, the Minister of Education, I have one of your students in my office who says,...' and then he broke off in mid-sentence, obviously having been interrupted. 'Well, yes', said Brothers. 'How did you guess it was Mr. Harder?' Pause.

'Well, I am telling you he does not have to do those two courses, do you understand me?' From that day I realised that most obstacles in my path through life could either be removed or avoided. It was a matter of looking forever forward, never back. The main lesson I learned from this experience was, always go to the top!

As a student at the University of Calgary my prized possession was a convertible Volkswagen Karman Ghia car with stereo speakers, sheepskin seat covers from New Zealand and a good motor. I used to drive it down to the Bow River just below a big hydroelectric dam to do some fishing.

One day the gate was locked, blocking my access. Further up the road there was a spot where the only thing between the fish and me was a railway track and a three-foot embankment. Over summer I had developed a technique of jumping the tracks with my car so I could drive to the other end of the dam. I would lay two thick planks leading up to the side of the track and another pair across the two rails.

On one memorable occasion, having had a great day's fishing and finally bagging a large rainbow trout after a heroic battle, it was almost sunset as I packed up to leave.

By the time I got back to the railway track it was getting dark. The full moon was out as I got my jumping track gear ready for action. I floored the accelerator and drove like a wild man up the launch pad.

Bang! I was thrown onto the steering wheel by force at the sudden stop. The car had slid off the boards and now hung half over one of the tracks. No amount of revving or pushing would budge it. My prized Karman Ghia was firmly stranded on a well-used railway track and it was not insured. Then I heard the train and saw a long beam of light come searching round the corner. It was not until I heard the whistle that the extreme danger registered. I sat there frozen. It seemed like minutes until I snapped to and leapt out of the car leaving the headlights on and the stereo blaring. With chest heaving, I ran towards the train realising the likely awful consequences ......

Faster and faster I ran towards the diesel engine lumbering down the track. I yelled, screamed, waved my shirt and arms all to no avail. It did not slow down. Finally, out of breath and shaking with shock and fear, I turned towards the hill and kept running. With a last glance over my left shoulder, I saw the Canadian Pacific train bearing down on my precious car. Like a feather in the wind, the Karman Ghia flew into the air, somersaulting over and over.

My first appearance as an advocate came about as a result. I was my own client in the Calgary Magistrates Court, charged with driving without an existing driver's licence and crossing a railway track at an unauthorised crossing. It was important to win and not just because I didn't like losing.

While studying I worked part-time for Canadian Pacific Railways, steam cleaning train engines. If convicted I would lose my job and be liable to pay the $6000 worth of damage my car did to the train's cowcatcher. The first witness was a policeman. He had examined the initial contact points on the car and train and believed the train hit and demolished my car travelling at about 30 miles an hour. It was a full train pulling 46 cars and a caboose.

The engine driver told the court he had seen a person, presumably me, running towards the train about three hundred yards from the point of impact. I cross-examined the witnesses about the evidence. Photographs I had taken of the scene, the day after the accident showed the 'road' worn in the grass where I had been driving the car up to the track. I asked the Canadian Pacific policeman if he saw what looked like a road in the photograph, leading to where the accident was alleged to have occurred. Begrudgingly, he said yes. Did he see any official train post or fence blocking the path at the end of the grass 'road' to the tracks? 'No.' I showed him another photo of a wooden crossing on the inside of the track. This picture showed an area used by linesmen for turning around their push carts called jiggers, when they check the tracks for fallen rock.

The judge asked to see the photos again. After a moment, he said, 'Mr. Harder, you have successfully raised a doubt in my mind in relation to your state of mind at the time.' To this day, I don't know if he meant I was crazy or that the Crown had not proved the *mens rea,* the mental element of the offence, whether or not there was the required intent. I was acquitted on the accident charge.

On the charge of not having an Alberta driver's licence, I produced my British Columbia licence and asked the arresting officer if it recorded my details. He replied 'Correct.' I asked him had the licence expired and he said 'No.' I then put it to him that I did have an existing driver's licence, it was just that I did not have an Albertan driver's licence.

'That is right, that is exactly what you are being charged with!' said the police officer. I asked the clerk to hand the charge sheet to the officer to read. I then asked him if the wording of the charge was 'existing licence' rather than 'Albertan licence.' 'Yes.' Then I said, 'Do you accept that the British Columbia licence is presently existing?' 'Yes.'

Surprisingly the prosecutor declined to re-examine the witness. 'The defence rests, Your Honour,' I said in my most impressive legal tone and sat down with a smug look on my face knowing I had done well. The decision of not guilty on both counts made me grin from ear to ear.

In 1971, whilst still a student at the University at Calgary, I had joined the Provincial Liberal Party, became a student delegate, and then hitchhiked from Calgary, Alberta to Ottawa, Ontario for the Liberal Party National Convention at which Prime Minister Trudeau was to speak and later answer questions from the delegates.

When the question period started, I walked straight to the microphone. I said, 'Prime Minister, in 1964 a man by the name of Herman Hause who murdered and raped my two best friends, Diana and Donna Ring, was convicted of their rape and murder. He was sentenced to life imprisonment and has just been released from prison last month after serving only seven years in jail. How can you advocate the abolition of capital punishment?' I asked. The conference hall was filled with reporters and television cameras from across the country. With cameras whirring, the Prime Minister found himself in a difficult position and the crowd became hostile toward me. Shortly after, I left the conference.

One Saturday, I was watching the 5 o'clock news having had an afternoon of watching gridiron football, the Calgary Stampeders versus the British Columbian Lions. We had all been drinking Tequila with salt and lemon juice and the man to take the last swig of the bottle, got the worm. The news headline announced that the Conservative Party Cabinet Minister, whose electorate encompassed the University of Calgary, had died in an auto accident. No sooner had this disturbing news been broadcast, and less than halfway into the bulletin, the leader of the Provincial Liberal Party which had no elected members in the legislature, announced that he would be running in the by-election that was anticipated due to the Cabinet Minister's death.

When I heard this, I thought it was in the worst possible taste because the Minister's body was not even cold! In reaction to this ill-timed declaration, I told my friends that I would run against the leader of the PLP for the upcoming nomination.

Despite the fact on the night of the election I had more voting delegates than the leader, I was declared the loser when 75 of my voting delegates were disallowed because of a time restriction around enrolment. The Liberal leader was trounced in the election by 20,000 votes but when it was over, he and I became friends because he was impressed with my youthful exuberance.

In the course of our coffee cup conversations, he told me how his neighbour, who was the head of the Alberta Housing Corporation at the time, had corruptly conspired with another neighbour (a lawyer) when the lawyer bought up a green belt of land anonymously with a blank cheque book sanctioned by the Housing Corporation Director and gave the Director half of his 10% commission on each purchase by way of a secret commission.

Being a natural investigator, and more interested in the chase of corruption than finishing my BA, I moved to the capital, Edmonton. There I began a Citizen's Action Committee that investigated the corruption allegations previously passed on to me by the Leader of the Provincial Liberal Party, Bob Russell.

Having no legal training and being unable to find a lawyer prepared to help me, and using legal documents from a previous insurance company scandal, I duplicated notices of motion on the head of the Housing Corporation and the Attorney General, requiring them to answer a list of questions, and filed an interrogatory application. The day my court motions were first called, I stood up against half a dozen lawyers from the Attorney General's office and the Housing Corporation.

Each lawyer opposed my application for the court to grant my motion, because I had no legal vehicle (statement of claim) filed and that my application should be dismissed with costs. Instead, because of the serious nature of the allegations, the judge passed it up to the Alberta Supreme Court for final determination.

Two days prior to the Court of Appeal hearing, I prepared an affidavit and swore that I was informed and verily believed, that the lawyer I named and the Head of the Housing Corporation, had split the commissions earned on the secret purchase of land to be used as part of a green belt around the city. I also alleged that Government loan documents had been forged by the Head of the Housing Corporation and his lawyer neighbour.

They borrowed $2,200,000 and put two million dollars into the Provincial coffers and split the remaining

$200,000 between the various parties, each getting their share in a brown paper bag.

I filed my affidavit with the Registrar of the Appeal Court moments before the hearing began and it was stamped as having been received. In court the judge explained in the kindest of fashion that my application had to be dismissed because the proper papers had not been filed.

Never one to give up, I gave an interview on a local radio station, reading my affidavit on air, believing naively I had immunity as it had been stamped by the Registrar.

Soon after, I was served with a number of defamation writs to the tune of $500,000. The next day I received a phone call from a journalist friend who told me the Attorney General was making an announcement at 2.15pm that I was to be charged with criminal libel. I waited in trepidation. The time came and went and just before 4pm the Attorney General announced there was to be a Royal Commission of Inquiry into the allegations I had made. A QC was appointed to head the commission. He interviewed me in his office and took detailed notes of everything I said, telling me he would be investigating my allegations and we would talk again.

Months later I was called to another meeting with the QC. He told me after investigating my allegations, there was not a word of truth in what I had said and I would end up with egg all over my face. I left feeling very despondent. Some weeks later, the Royal Commission of Inquiry was about to start. I received a call from an old friend, Ed Leger who had been an Edmonton City Alderman for almost 25 years and had a reputation for exposing corruption. He told me that I should leave the jurisdiction because the Commission was intending to issue a summons requiring me to attend as the first witness. I flew to B.C. and the Commission began without me.

The QC heading the Inquiry called the then mayor of Drumheller, Ennis Tosack, to the witness stand. I had alleged that the mayor was the middle person in the scandal. The QC put my allegation to him and after a long pause the witness admitted he was involved.

Suddenly, the QC exploded, saying to the witness, 'I interviewed you two months ago and you denied everything, saying there was no truth to these allegations whatsoever!' There was a long silence then the mayor replied, 'But I wasn't under oath then, was I sir!'

My friend Ed Leger then telephoned me and gave me the good news that I could come home. With the admission from Tosack that he had been involved, the scandal unravelled and people were charged and tried. For all the alleged corruption, the person who got into the most trouble was the lawyer who lied under oath and was sent to jail. I never forgot that lesson!

The Bus Strike Injunction Case

At first I thought the bus must be running late. I had been waiting for over half an hour at the Mission Bay bus stop with my eight-month-old son Justin. The year was 1977. I was a first-year law student attending the University of Auckland.

Normally we would take the bus into University because we did not own a car. I would drop my son off at the University crèche then go to my law school lectures. My then wife Anita was working part-time as a pharmacist in Glendowie, Auckland while I attended university and looked after our son.

After waiting for over an hour with my baby son I turned around and walked back up Atkinson Avenue to the colonial style house we were then renting.

When I read the *New Zealand Herald* the next morning I learned that the bus drivers were holding a weekly stop-work meeting. The union secretary called it a weekly rolling strike. The next week there was a second stop-work meeting. I was better prepared for the second rolling strike, because I knew about it in advance, it having been reported in the paper, so I was able to arrange alternative transportation for my son and me. Forty-five minutes before my legal studies class at law school was due to start a taxi beeped its horn outside our house.

Law lecturer David Williams taught the class. That day he introduced us to a recent British legal precedent called Gouriet v The Post Office Worker's Union. He wanted us to read the case as homework and be prepared to discuss it at the next class.

A man named Gouriet applied to the High Court in London for an injunction against the Post Office Workers when the union refused to deliver mail or handle long distance calls from South Africa because of the then existing apartheid policy operating against blacks.

The uniqueness of this legal case was that Gouriet was acting as a private individual when he applied for his injunction. In a legal first he was given legal standing to sue the union because he had suffered special damages above and beyond the ordinary person. Gouriet was expecting a business contract in the mail from Pretoria. When it did not come he lost the job he had contracted for so he sued the Union and won his injunction!

As requested by the lecturer, I settled to read the case that night so as to be prepared to discuss it in class the next day. My wife was out. I remember sitting on the rug in the lounge with my back to the radio. As I studied the British judgement I read a line that stated that the strike in London was believed to be unlawful but that nobody did anything about it until Gouriet got up the gumption to sue the union.

As I continued to read the London judgement, the local news reporter on Radio 1ZB was making the very same point about the Auckland bus strike. Everybody accepted that it was illegal because the union had not given 14 days' notice of strike action, but still nobody seemed to be doing anything about it.

After listening to the local radio news I re-read the English judgement. Suddenly I got a bright idea. I didn't sleep much that night and I was up early the next morning. I was on a mission. After my first class of the day I had coffee with a law student colleague named Mary Anne Shanahan. We discussed Gouriet v The London Post Office workers Union. I pointed out the similarities between the unlawful bus strike in Auckland and the unlawful Post Workers strike in London. Snap!

It did not take the two of us long to decide that we would pool our bursary cheques, find a good industrial law lawyer then try and test the legal principle demonstrated in Gouriet in the New Zealand judicial system.

It took Mary Anne Shanahan and me less than a day before we approached then unknown barrister, Dr Rodney Harrison. Inquiries that the two of us made indicated that Harrison was a very good industrial law lawyer who had a reputation for thoroughness. Harrison was very interested in the principle of unions, strikes and court injunctions. He accepted our $1500 retainer and the case.

The rest of his fee was subsequently paid out from thousands of dollars members of the public sent to the *New Zealand Herald* for forwarding to Harrison. Once the injunction papers had been filed and the details printed in the press, all hell seemed to break loose. A union spokesman argued that it was wrong to apply to the Supreme Court for an injunction against a trade union. It should be dealt with in the Industrial Court.

Then industrial law lecturers Bill Hodge and Margaret Wilson (now New Zealand's Attorney General) were enthusiastic about the legal challenge we were mounting. Margaret Wilson was the most congenial, helpful and friendly law lecturer I ever met at University. She and Bill Hodge discussed the principles set out in Gouriet and compared them with the New Zealand situation. Wilson and Hodge both seemed to support my action as being an academic exercise. I had no political view whatsoever when I first applied to the Supreme Court for an injunction to stop the bus strike.

On the morning of the first hearing at the old Supreme Court in Waterloo Quadrant I walked across the courtyard towards the front door. A television camera and crew were standing nearby filming. Then I saw Margaret Wilson on the other side of the courtyard. She was heading in the same door as I. Because I perceived Ms. Wilson to be an ardent, behind the scenes supporter of the legal action Mary Anne Shanahan and I had commenced, I was keen to talk to her before the court started because I had no idea what was going to happen. When our paths met in the middle of the courtyard Margaret Wilson walked past me without saying a word. She acted as if she didn't know me.

I caught up to her and asked her why she was ignoring

me. She looked towards the TV camera then back at me. With her head down she told me she could no longer talk to me. She said something about the trade union movement but I didn't catch all of what she said. The brief conversation ended with Ms. Wilson referring to me as "Mr. Harder". Previously she would refer to me on a first name basis 'Christopher'. That was my first experience of being ostracised in New Zealand and it was not to be my last.

In the august, wood-panelled Number One Court at the Supreme Court, Justice Chilwell heard our application for an interim injunction. Rodney Harrison appeared for Shanahan and me. Her father was lawyer Mike Shanahan, recognized back then as one of New Zealand's better lawyers who brought a colourful character to the bar.

The union lawyer G. P. Curry submitted that the Supreme Court had no jurisdiction over the trade union movement, that it was the domain of the Industrial Relations Court and not the Supreme Court. I could see that Justice Chilwell was not impressed with the union submission that the Supreme Court had no jurisdiction.

Harrison argued that the union was obliged to give 14 days notice in writing of strike action before they could in fact strike. He further submitted that I as a private individual should be given the legal standing, like Gouriet, to bring my action because I had suffered special damages above and beyond that of the ordinary person because I had to come to town every day with my young son. If the bus was not running I had to pay for a taxi to take my son and me to the university. If I had not kept the taxi receipts my legal action would have failed.

Justice Chilwell declared the strike illegal and granted me the injunction I sought. The union was fined and the judge warned that each of the striking drivers could be subject to a fine of $150 a day if the strike continued.

Initially the Tramway Workers' Union and its national secretary Henry Stubbs ignored the court order. They refused to pay the fine or stop the rolling strikes. Immediately Harrison returned to the Supreme Court to enforce the injunction. He asked Justice Chilwell to rule the union in contempt of court. The union lawyer argued that

Henry Stubbs, the secretary of the Tramways union, had yet to be served with the injunction papers, there could be no contempt of court. The reason Stubbs had not been served was because he was hiding in the home of barrister, Russell Fairbrother who years later some would call a real 'lefty' for harbouring the union official.

After some very heated argument between the lawyers and Chilwell J, he ruled the union was in contempt of court and fined it a further sum. When the union continued to disobey the judge's order our lawyer applied to the court once again this time for an order of sequestration against the union. This meant the union would be subjected to court ordered supervision. All its bank accounts would be frozen until it obeyed the court orders and paid the fines.

I would have to recover my $412 costs awarded to me on the injunction application separately. By now I was caught up in the legal chase of the Tramways union. I applied to the Supreme Court to recover my costs from the union. When the bailiff went to freeze the union's bank and to seize my money he was told by bank staff that union officials had emptied the bank account of its $36,000 shortly before the third 48-hour rolling strike started.

Defeated by the left, but not for long I thought to myself. Now it was a straight-out contest. Using my lateral thinking ability I asked a friend at law school to send the Tramways union a $10 cheque towards its fighting fund. A week later he obtained his cancelled cheque from his bank and gave it to me. On the back of the cheque was the name and branch of the bank where they had set up a new account. Two days later the bailiff recovered my costs from the union.

The combined effect of being North American and a law student who had taken legal action against a New Zealand trade union and won, was to have an enormous and immediate effect on my private life. TV crews waited daily at my front doorstep. I received hundreds of letters. Most were in praise for my standing up to the union. Some were offensive, and then there were the abusive telephone calls. One man rang up at 4am and told me, 'When the revolution comes, you'll be the first bastard up against the wall.'

At the same time as the court action I was working at the Kiwi Tavern in Symonds Street near the University. That evening the television news announced the Supreme Court decision granting me my injunction against the bus drivers. I was at the top of the six o'clock news. The TV was on in the bar. The dozen or so people present watched the news. One of the customers turned and said, 'Isn't that you on the TV?' Like a fool I said, 'yes' with pride. Nobody said anything but a short time later the bar was empty of customers. I was working the bar by myself, as it was the manager's night off.

About an hour later the place suddenly filled up with about fifty people. One at a time they came up to the bar and I asked what they wanted to drink. Each time the potential customer pointed to the top shelf where the expensive liquor was displayed and ordered a gin, whisky, vodka or bourbon. I poured the drink then put it on the bar and asked for the money. Every one of them said, 'No, I don't want to be served by a scab' and walked away. Later I learned that the sudden swell of custom came from the SUP (Socialist Unity Party) then headed by trade union movement icon Bill Andersen.

This game of 'order a drink but refuse to pay for it or drink it as long as I was working behind the bar' went on for an hour before I was forced to call the manager at home and ask him to come back to work because there was a problem.

When the manager finally returned he was rushed off his feet. It did not take him long to find out what was happening and why. An hour later I was fired because the hotel owner could not afford to employ me as a bartender if customers refused to be served by me.

He was sorry but I would have to go, that was the way it was in New Zealand back in those days.

Every cloud has a silver lining and the one good thing to come out of the loss of my job was in the person of Len Simpson. Ex Royal Navy, he was the owner of a local paper, the *Courier* and had a colourful background including being an unarmed combat instructor and a citizen of the world with a passion for boxing. Clearly, he had been following the bus strike saga and when he learned I had lost my job, because of union interference, he came to my house one day and informed me he would be giving me $50 per week every week, tax free, until I finished my Law degree. I had never met him before that day.

Len was a true philanthropist and I have never forgotten his generosity. A charming and sincere gentleman, a devotee of youth sports, and vehemently opposed to union interference in his newspaper business. As I was completing this book my friend was dying and being cared for by his wife Sheena at home. A week before he died we moved him outside into the backyard and placed him under the apple tree in the sunshine. As he lay there and I talked to him, I said, 'You know Len, there are only two certainties in life, death and taxes!' No sooner had I uttered those words than my mobile phone rang. It was someone from the IRD calling to give me some good news for a change. Len died peacefully on February 8th 2002. I will miss him.

Next the Auckland University Students Association tried to discipline me for allegedly soliciting money on campus to help pay for Rodney Harrison's legal bill. After all the TV publicity and my picture in the papers I noticed that every time I took a bus now the driver would gave me the evil eye. I guess they recognized my face from the front page of the *New Zealand Herald* and the television news.

People who knew nothing about me formed perceptions about me. I was seen as a union basher, as anti communist and anti worker by the SUP. Some in the trade union movement said that I was a CIA agent sent from the United States despite the fact I came from Canada.

My subsequent actions involving the union movement after the bus injunction matter ended did little to dispel the common belief that I was anti-unionist. At the beginning of 1978 I met an Auckland baker named Tony Oric while I was dining at a little restaurant in upper Symond Street. Oric's business had been under siege from the Northern Drivers' Union. The union had banned all deliveries of flour, fuel and yeast to Oric's Pacific Continental bakery. He applied, just as I had, for an injunction in the Supreme Court to stop the ban on delivery of his goods. Oric, like me, was granted his injunction.

In the anti union days of Robert Muldoon (New Zealand's

Prime Minister) with political commercials alleging 'Reds under the bed,' Oric and I decided we should get together for lunch. After my successful injunction, the news media, mostly the *New Zealand Herald*, would continue to call me up and ask what I was going to do about the latest strike. The flattery went to my head for a time!

Following a long liquid lunch, with Tony Oric and me patting each other on the back about our successful injunctions against the trade union movement, the two of us decided we would try and make a difference. We realised that once we knew how to stop one strike there was no reason we could not do two or more. The media was hungry for a David and Goliath battle in the trade union movement.

In those days it made good copy to oppose a union so the two of us started a group called Strike Free. The purpose of the organization was to oppose strikes by taking legal action against the offending union. We had big dreams that our efforts would make a difference.

Tony Oric was a newcomer and an immigrant to New Zealand as I was. As an immigrant from the former Yugoslavia, he was fiercely anti-communist. The fact that the leader of the Northern Drivers' Union, Bill Andersen, was New Zealand's best-known communist, simply added fuel to Oric's sense of outrage.

Ironically, unbeknown either to Tony Oric, a co-director of Strike Free, or Union secretary Bill Andersen, the old man I had adopted in Lynn Valley, British Columbia many years before as my surrogate grandfather was a fanatical communist. Despite this, I considered Melvin Burritt who used the romantic nickname of Silas Huckleback, as my hero.

To me, regardless of his politics, Silas was a lovely man whom I was very fond of. A measure of his personal integrity was clearly demonstrated to me when despite his fanaticism for communism, he frankly admitted to me on his return to Canada (from the motherland) that the communism he had observed being practised in the USSR, had not lived up to his expectations.

I continue to miss his company and influence, but I still remember and am inspired by his revolutionary tales and sense of international adventure. Because of this background I was initially not afraid of the New Zealand Communist Party or its influence. However, I did learn to have a healthy regard for the people power of the SUP (Socialist Unity Party) when they caused me to lose my part-time job at the Kiwi Tavern.

Strike Free with Oric and me acting as media spokespersons began to take protest and legal action against striking trade unions. At the time the trade union movement had imposed a trade ban on Chile because of the alleged human rights abuses then being committed by military dictator Augustus Pinochet.

On one occasion Strike Free applied to the industrial relations court for a declaration that the New Zealand Union movement trade ban against Chile was unlawful.

In due course the industrial relations court declined Strike Free's application for a declaration that the trade union ban on trade with Chile was unlawful. Instead, the court ordered that Strike Free pay $700 costs to the Watersiders' union.

Barrister John Haigh, son of long time labour and union supporter, Frank Haigh, of Haigh Lyon and Co., Barristers and Solicitors, pursued me on behalf of the union for the costs Strike Free was ordered to pay. When the obligation of paying the costs ordered by the industrial court could no longer be put off, I obtained a bank cheque for the sum ordered made out to Haigh, Lyon and Co.

Then I cheekily lacquered the cheque securely (or so I thought) to a bottle of red Chile wine and personally delivered it to John Haigh's secretary in full and final settlement of Strike Free's obligation to the union. Several days later an unknown person without explanation dropped off the bottle of unopened wine minus the bank cheque, at my office. So much for my memento.

My biggest adrenalin rush during my involvement with Strike Free in the late 1970s came from the time I addressed 1200, mostly female, clerical workers union members in the Auckland Town Hall, and convinced them to vote overwhelmingly in favour of voluntary unionism. This was despite the contrary plea from an articulate and normally persuasive union secretary, Syd Jackson.

At this time the left wing of the New Zealand trade union movement accused then under-secretary of labour, Aussie Malcolm, of being in an unholy alliance with Strike Free. They called the voluntary unionism clause introduced by the National Government, the Harder clause. The hatred generated by segments of the labour movement following my successful injunction against the Tramways union only escalated after Strike Free was in full stride.

Strike Free was very much a product of its time, growing out of my bus strike injunction. Eventually it became superfluous in the face of a changing industrial environment.

Unfortunately for the Dean Jack Northey, then the head of the Auckland University Law School and the professor who taught Administrative law, he had to, each term thereafter, teach his students about Harder v The Auckland Tramways union. At the time I was unaware that Northey was a staunch labour supporter and by definition a union sympathizer.

Following my graduation from law school I went on to complete my professionals before I applied to the Law Society to be admitted to the bar. In making the application one has to submit the names of two character referees. I first asked prominent criminal lawyer Peter Williams if he would write a letter of reference. He agreed and did. Then I asked Professor Northey (now deceased from throat cancer) if he would be my second character referee to the Auckland District Law Society for my admission to the bar. I was elated when he agreed.

However when I first disclosed to the Auckland District Law Society that I had a conviction in Alberta for practising law without a licence for which I was fined $50 for putting my name on the bottom of an affidavit, my application was refused. Ted Thomas QC then president of the Auckland District Law Society, and another labour stalwart, personally told me that my conviction set off alarm bells in his head. However he did write to the Alberta Law Society who informed him that, 'it was unlikely such a conviction would bar Mr. Harder from admission to the Law Society in Alberta if he made an application.' The Auckland District Law Society still refused to give the necessary certificate of good character that was essential in order to be admitted to the bar.

Lawyer Des Piggin (now deceased), on my behalf, then asked for an opportunity for the two of us to appear before the full Law Society council. After some struggle I was eventually granted this request.

Piggin made submissions in relation to my conviction for practising law without a licence saying it was a one-off incident. He said, 'One swallow does not a summer make.' He explained that I had obtained the conviction inadvertently in the early '70s for helping an old lady prepare an affidavit to recover some of her dead husband's shares. I had put my name at the bottom of the affidavit as being the person who prepared it, when in fact that space was reserved for the name of the instructing solicitor and not a layperson, as I then was.

When Piggin had finished making my case he asked the Law Society council members if they had any questions for me.

There was a long silence in the room before one bold council member asked, 'Mr. Harder, do you really believe that New Zealand could be strike free?' Obviously when I replied, 'Yes' my response demonstrated to my inquisitor that I was out of touch with reality and not suitable for admission to the bar.

That I had bought a house for renovation off an old lady neighbour and resold it, prior to settlement at a much higher price, also left a concern with the council.

And unbeknown to me at the time was the fact that Professor Northey, who agreed to act as a referee for me, had written a character reference to the Law Society all right, but it was rather ambiguous to say the least.

"He can hardly be described as a normal student. You will know his association with Strike Free. I might be inclined to doubt his judgement on some matters including those that could be important professionally. What I am saying is, his sense of values differs from mine. I have no reason to doubt his honesty. I hope this is helpful."

Against that background the Council turned down my further request for a certificate of good character.

Despite this further refusal to give me the very necessary certificate of good character, Des Piggin still applied to the Supreme Court for my admission to the bar. Peter Williams, then Auckland's leading light at the criminal bar, had taken a day off from his holiday on Great Barrier Island and flown back to Auckland to move my admission in early January.

Unfortunately the judge ruled I could not be admitted to the Supreme Court roll without a certificate from the Law Society. It was a sad day for me but I knew I would come again. It was only a matter of time.

One day out of the blue solicitor Mark Vickerman contacted me and told me that Peter Hillyer QC had offered his services to me on my appeal to the Court of Appeal in relation to the Law Society refusing to issue me with a certificate of good character.

When I told the Queen's Counsel that I could not afford him he assured me I could. When I pushed the point that I had no money he replied, 'One day you will repay me by helping somebody else for free.' He was unsuccessful in the Court of Appeal but the court did make an obiter statement (not binding) that there was room for different kinds of personalities in the law. To this extent I felt beholden to Peter Hillyer QC for his help.

After I had been a member of Alcoholics Anonymous for over a year and a half the council agreed to reconsider my application. In the two years since I was first refused admission to the bar I worked part-time for criminal lawyer Peter Williams, and ran Harder's Document Service serving legal documents for Auckland lawyers. My motto was 'Nothing is impossible!' I also repossessed cars part-time for Sonny Reid of South Auckland.

Colin Nicholson QC, one of the few District Court judges elevated to the High Court bench, was on the Law Society council at the time my second application was considered. It was he who telephoned me with the good news that, by a majority, the council had voted to give me my certificate of good character. My first phone call was to my father in Canada to tell him of my success at last! 'They can't take it away from me now', I yelled down the phone! Little did I know how hard some would subsequently try!

3
A Heroin Import

I still remember the day I walked up to the receptionist sitting behind the front desk of the Auckland District Law Society. I was on a mission to pick up my hard-earned, long-awaited practising certificate. Here I was, the first law graduate ever admitted to the High Court rolls in New Zealand to go directly out to practice as a 'barrister sole' doing criminal court work only. In those days a newly admitted lawyer worked for a law firm as a 'barrister and solicitor' for at least five years, gaining general skills in relation to mostly civil and commercial law.

Such a junior lawyer working for a law firm was likely to appear in the Magistrate's court, as it was back then, only on rare occasions. Obtaining criminal experience in court as a young self-employed lawyer in the early 1980s would be as unlikely as finding rocking-horse shit. Unless you were assisting a senior partner on a criminal legal aid case, little experience was likely to come your way. Waiting for such brief occasions held little appeal to me. And the pay for a new law graduate was worse, starting at a meager $264 a week.

Two years before, I had boldly walked into the legal chambers of the high profile New Zealand criminal barrister Peter Aldridge Williams. I was determined to work for the star of the bar, and so I asked the legal legend, 'How much do I have to pay to work for you?' This caught the master so off guard he was flummoxed for a reply.

But my ploy worked. The job was mine. At the time Williams was the only barrister in New Zealand who employed a fellow barrister. Barry Wilson, of Civil Liberties and TVNZ freelance reporter fame, was Williams' 'man on the ground'.

Williams had convinced the Law Society to change the rules so that a barrister could employ another barrister. Now I was employed at no fee but keen for the opportunity to work with, learn from and observe the best.

On my first Monday, Williams pointed me to a small desk in Wilson's office. Star law student Karen Soich had previously occupied it. Unfortunately at the time, Soich had fallen for a criminal client of Williams. This charming villain had a warm heart and an ability to turn the head of a young and impressionable woman. Her admission to the bar was delayed for a time because as a result of this attraction she spent 14 months in prison and then was acquitted.

This was to my professional benefit because she worked part-time for me as an exceptional legal clerk who prepared legal submissions on my behalf in a fashion that over time, gave me the reputation of being the undisputed Section 347 Crimes Act 1961 (discharge without conviction due to insufficient evidence) king! She learned to think in the unusual and abstract manner that I did and she wrote my submissions accordingly. It helped build the reputation I gained for filing frank and appropriately pitched legal submissions.

After less than an hour on the job, Williams invited me into his chambers while he interviewed a new client charged with failing to stop and ascertain (hit and run), and possession of cannabis. He had been observed backing out of a car park on Quay Street on the Auckland waterfront, and hitting the car parked behind. The police followed the offender for several hundred yards before pulling him over for questioning. The police officer spoke to the driver and in the course of that discussion noticed a bag of cannabis lying on the road beneath the driver's door.

Besides the hit and run charge, he was now charged with the possession of cannabis. A drug conviction would mean an end to the tugboat pilot's $75,000 per annum job so the legal 'ace' was hired to save the client's career. I was immediately excited, butted in and said that I would do a survey of the wharf police to ascertain the frequency of bags of cannabis being found in and around the wharf area.

Wisely, Williams refrained from restraining me from my eagerness to try to help him find an answer or a legal explanation for this important, well-paying client, despite his skepticism. Almost two weeks passed and I had walked the length of the wharf, interviewed police officers and done my best to find a plausible explanation for the cannabis being found on the roadside next to our client's car.

On my second Monday, at work at my treasured desk, Barry Wilson was on the phone talking to the police prosecutor about Williams' tugboat client. As he explained that Williams just wanted the case remanded for two weeks without plea, I attempted to interrupt the conversation by whispering to Wilson, 'Tell him we'll plead guilty to hit and run if he drops the cannabis charge'. He ignored me, continuing to talk to the prosecutor about the remand. Again, this time with a slightly elevated tone I repeated, 'Tell him we'll plead guilty to the hit and run if he drops the 'cannabis charge!' Wilson flagged me away with his hand.

Then just as Wilson was about to terminate the conversation, I repeated my comment for a third time. Suddenly, as if he finally realised we had nothing to lose and everything to gain (saving the tugboat pilot's $75,000 per year job), Wilson said to the prosecutor, 'How about we plead guilty to the hit and run and you drop the cannabis charge?' His next response was, 'It's a done deal!' He then hung up the phone and begrudgingly shook my hand.

The two of us walked into Williams' office, pleased with ourselves and Wilson told the 'boss' that his client's Master Mariner's ticket had been saved because the critical drug charge had been dropped. Williams was very happy with our efforts and I had proved myself early in the piece. Williams' accountant was extremely happy with the outcome also.

Because Williams was not the flavour of the month with the Auckland District Law Society (due to his successful representation of drug boss Terry Clark), and his charging this grateful client a $100,000 fee (considered big at the time), and because I worked for Williams part-time as a legal clerk, I believe I was suspect as lawyer material. Little did they know how great Williams really was and how good his protégé would become. The society investigated Williams' actions for a number of years. No charges were ever laid and in the end the Law Society was forced to clear him. When they did, I hired a plane and had it pull a drogue (banner) across Auckland reading 'Blue skies for P A Williams'.

Williams and I grew apart but in the end, some years later, he was big enough to say, 'Harder, you have carved out a great piece of legal turf for yourself in New Zealand law'.

When I declared I intended to practise law as a 'barrister only' which was against the norm, and my continued association with the then suspected 'bad boy' of the law, it set off alarm bells with then Law Society president Ted Thomas, and former president Paul Temm QC, who warned me about practising law without an instructing solicitor.

As the Law Society's frumpy looking middle-aged receptionist handed me my prized practising certificate she also handed me a telephone message with the name Paul Temm QC scribbled on it. She told me that Mr. Temm wished to see me. She described to me the location of his office. 'Just walk up the hill, you will find his chambers next to the old Grand Hotel.'

With a spring in my step I walked briskly up the hill until I came to an imposing door bearing a brass plaque inscribed with the words Paul Temm QC. QC stands for Queen's Counsel. This is recognition by the Government, and ratified by the Queen, acknowledging the barrister's skills, experience and declared loyalty to the Crown. To become a QC you have to first request such recognition.

Paul Temm's elderly receptionist asked me to take a seat in the waiting room while she notified Mr. Temm that newly admitted barrister, Christopher Harder, was in his waiting room without an appointment. Impressive paintings hung on the wall. One was of an old Maori man with full moko on his face. Another was of a young and attractive wahine with a moko on her chin.

Paul Temm was a big man with a larger than life presence. He also lived next door to Peter Williams' mother, now deceased. In the two years I worked for Peter Williams, in between law school and waiting for my practising certificate, I heard great tales of Temm and his love of drink and women. He had a reputation for charging fees like a wounded bull. This Papal Knight of the Order of Saint Sylvester bid me enter his legal chambers with a gracious wave of his arm. Once inside I was pointed towards a large overstuffed brown leather chair. Temm QC sat behind the large oak desk opposite me, his elbows resting on the desk and his chin cupped in the palms of his hands.

For a moment the silence was unnerving. I looked past this daunting figure. The wall behind his desk was covered from floor to ceiling with shelves full of leather-bound law books. Next to his desk was a large cabinet full of the best liquor, wine and sherry.

Over twenty years have passed since that day and my memory no doubt fails me in some regards, but I recall how he told me the law was an honorable profession and how I had a duty to the court to be frank and honest at all times. I was never to mislead the court. As an aside, he noted that I intended to practise as a barrister only. This was unusual. He explained the role of an instructing solicitor to me. Then, as if he had suddenly developed a split personality, the leader of the bar pointed his wagging right hand index finger at me.

'If I ever catch you without an instructing solicitor I will see that you are struck off the rolls!' Then, with that colder than ice warning from the acknowledged master, I walked quickly out of the chambers of Paul Temm QC and into the street in search of some fresh air.

Next morning found me standing in the lobby of the old District Court in Kitchener Street in downtown Auckland, wearing my grey pinstriped suit and carrying my shiny, new black leather brief case. I was giving my new work environment a good look over. I watched the different people walking the corridors of the courthouse lobby. I had been standing in the middle of the court foyer for no more than five minutes, when suddenly I felt a tap on my left shoulder. The question came as a surprise.

'Sir, are you a lawyer?' I could hear the nervousness in the old man's trembling voice. Straightening my tie I cleared my throat and replied.'Yes sir, I'm a lawyer,' I proudly declared.

'Sir, I need your help,' he pleaded. I could see from looking into his eyes that he was a very worried man.

'Christopher Harder, barrister, at your service. What is your problem?' I asked.

'My daughter is down in the police cells. Can you help her get bail?'

'What is her name?'

It would have been open to me then, instead of saying what I did, to give the man the following advice:

'As a barrister I cannot appear for your daughter without first receiving instructions from a solicitor. You must therefore find a solicitor somewhere and pay some money into his trust account and tell him you want him to instruct Christopher Harder to appear for your daughter.

The solicitor will then write to me setting out my instructions, and some time next week I may be able to assist you.'

Despite the warning from Paul Temm QC, still ringing in my head, commonsense told me that if I followed the unfriendly advice he had given to me the day before, I would lose my first client before I even met her. I had no regrets about not saying those words. I would get an instructing solicitor as soon as was practicable. One of Peter Williams' close friends was a barrister and solicitor named Christopher Reid. I had met him while working for Williams. Reid was the local gun lawyer who practised criminal and traffic law out of a little office next door to the courthouse. I was confident he would instruct me.

Writing down my first client's name on a scrap of paper, I charged down the stairs to the holding cells three steps at a time sliding my hands down the side rail. I was flush with enthusiasm. I introduced myself to the sergeant in charge of the cells, and then asked if I could see a prisoner by the name of Miss T. He opened the cell door across the hall and called out my client's name. A moment later a very attractive but worried looking young woman was sitting across from me in the interview room.

'Your father has asked me to help get you bail. Um . . . What are you charged with?' I asked. First she was silent, then in a voice showing the weight of the words she was about to utter, my client said: 'Importing heroin and opium.'

I tried to hide my surprise. Nothing small-time here, I thought to myself.

'Well, let's see if we can get you bail first then we'll discuss your case.'

Back then, a prisoner facing a Class A drug charge, the most serious class of drug offence in New Zealand, has to apply to a Supreme Court judge, as they then were, for bail. 'How did you come to get arrested?' I probed.

'I flew in from Singapore to Auckland yesterday. Customs went through my luggage at the airport. During their search they found a straw full of white powder in my suitcase. They asked me what was in the straw. Like a fool I told them it was heroin.' I felt a certain pang in the pit of my stomach as my client continued to talk.

'They asked me if I had any more drugs with me and I said no. They didn't seem to believe me though. They just kept going through my belongings in my suitcase. The Customs officer rummaged around my clothes and picked up a matchbox. He opened it then asked "What's this?" This time I said "opium". Next I was asked "whose is it?" Again I replied, "it's mine. I bought it in Penang".'

'What happened then?'

'I gave the police officer a full written statement admitting I had bought the drugs and that they were mine.' To myself I said this lady has serious problems.

'I'll have to go talk to the prosecutor and see what the police attitude to bail is.'

As I left the interview room I told my client to relax. I'll be back. Quick as Jack Flash I was up the stairs and down the hall, into the number one courtroom and up to the prosecutor's file-littered table. I waited my turn in the lawyer's line. Once at the front of the line I introduced myself and asked the prosecuting sergeant for a copy of the summary of facts for my client.

I read the brief narrative of the police interpretation of the events. It seemed to record a similar story to the one my client down in the cells had just told me. On that basis coupled with the summary of facts I had just read, my first client seemed to be caught red-handed.

I asked the sergeant what the police attitude to bail was for my client. My hopes were not high. I knew that importing heroin was punishable under the Misuse of Drugs Act by a maximum term of 14 years imprisonment. The sergeant picked up the police file. He flicked through the documents a page at a time looking for the 'opposition to bail' form. The arresting officer for the police prosecutor normally prepares this. Then the sergeant replied slowly:

'No . . . we won't oppose her bail. She's a clean skin (meaning no criminal record), but the Crown prosecutor in the Supreme Court may want a surety.' (A promise by a person who knows the accused to pay the court a sum of money if the accused runs off or fails to appear for trial).

I was elated – punching the air I yelled out, 'Yes!'

My first victory!

To gain immediate freedom for my client I had to file a motion seeking an order from the Supreme Court granting bail. I also had to file a supporting affidavit from my client. I rushed down the road to a nearby secretarial service, where I dictated the bail motion and a 'draft affidavit' to a stenographer named Jo Nicholas who ran a little secretarial business in Durham Lane called Private Secretary.

Now I needed an instructing solicitor. Pretty soon I had the name Christopher Reid, instructing solicitor, typed at the bottom of my client's affidavit.

The next day I made my first appearance before a Supreme Court judge. The bail hearing went without a hitch when the Crown prosecutor consented to the police-approved terms of bail. I then waited patiently at the back of the court for the clerk to bring me the judge-endorsed bail motion.

Next I took the approved order down to the Criminal Registrar, where the 'Order to Release' would be prepared. Half an hour later the order was sealed and initialed. The original and a copy of the order were then placed in an envelope and addressed to the officer in charge of the receiving office at Mt Eden prison. With no time to spare

I climbed into my double-parked green Ford Escort and drove to the remand prison as fast as I could without getting a ticket. Once at the receiving office I handed the envelope from the Supreme Court Registrar to the prison officer behind the counter. He took a quick look at the papers.

'It'll take about fifteen minutes for us to process your client, sir,' he replied. 'If you wait out in the car park we'll send her out as quickly as we can.' I walked outside and waited. A short time later I heard a clang, then the front door of the prison opened. A very relieved young woman, obviously happy to be out of jail, skipped across the car park to the waiting arms of her very distressed parents. 'How much is your bill for the bail, Mr. Harder?' asked Mr. T.

I pondered the question for a moment. I had never charged a fee for bail before. I didn't even know the going rate. Suddenly, I uttered the words, 'Four hundred dollars.'

I wondered to myself for a moment if that was too high – after all, all I had done was talk to the police, prepare and file the unopposed bail papers, then make a brief appearance in the High Court with a white horsehair wig perched on my head and wearing a black courtroom gown, both borrowed from my former employer Peter Williams. Never mind that I didn't have to say too much. The fact was everybody in the family was extremely happy the moment the judge said, 'Bail granted in terms of draft order.'

'Will you do the trial for my daughter?' asked Mr. T. 'How much would your charge be for the case?'

Well, this was my first client, and it was her father who first raised the question of my fee. I had learned from Peter Williams that it was a very important question to resolve. What was the last agreed fee he had charged? I tried to recall. Was it $20,000? Then I divided that figure by four because I was a just very junior lawyer after all, and blurted out, 'Five thousand dollars.' Without a moment of hesitation my client's father replied, 'Fine. I'll organise that as soon as I can, hopefully this week.'

The next day the father called at my 'office' downstairs in the garage of my rented Remuera home. In his hand he held a bank cheque for $5,000, my first agreed fee. Now all I had to do was perform.

I was not optimistic about T's chances. Her father asked me what I thought.

'To be honest sir, it seems like at first blush the police have a fairly airtight case against your daughter. It might be more appropriate to see what the sentencing regime is for importing this amount of Class A drug. But that's just a comment. I have no idea which way this case is going to go, and I won't until I sit down and have a talk with your daughter and a good look at the police file.'

The next day, I invited my bailed client, the alleged drug importer, back to my 'office' in my garage.

'Listen, you couldn't be any deeper in the shit if you tried. So I want you to sit down and tell me the truth, the whole truth – and nothing but the truth. And I mean the *whole* truth.'

She stared back at me for a moment.

'Everything. Like I said, you can't be in any worse trouble than you are already in.'

As her story went, T had been living in Singapore with her Maori boyfriend from New Zealand. He had been working on the oilrigs off the coast. It paid extremely well. One weekend the two of them flew to Penang for a brief holiday. While there they had picked up the 'discovered' drugs for their own recreational use back in Singapore. T had smuggled these back into Singapore by hiding the drugs in her vagina. They had used some of the drugs, and then stashed the remainder.

One morning several weeks later, T and her boyfriend had a terrible early morning row. He stormed out the door and off to work, leaving his girlfriend crying and lying on their bed. A short time later she called her mother. They talked for a time before her mother suggested maybe she should come home for a break, if it wasn't going that well. Daughter agreed, then called Air New Zealand and made a reservation on the next flight out of Singapore. Next she called a taxi, which took her to Changi international airport. She then boarded her plane and flew to Auckland, where New Zealand customs officers found the drugs in her luggage.

'So how did the drugs get in the suitcase?' I asked. For some reason the customs officer and the interviewing police officer both failed to ask this critical question of my client.

'Well, after I got off the phone to my mother I put my open suitcase on the bed. Then I pulled out my drawers one at a time and just dumped my stuff into the suitcase. At the time, drugs were the last things on my mind. It's like, you use them, you put them away, and you forget where you put them. That's what happened.'

The beginnings of a strategy were beginning to form in my mind. There are two elements in any criminal charge. Both must be established then proved beyond a reasonable doubt before the prosecution can gain a conviction. That's the theory. The two parts of an offence are the *actus reus* and the *mens rea*. The *actus reus* is the physical act of doing the offence – for criminal assault, that might be the physical hitting of someone. The *mens rea* is the mental element of the offence (the intent) e.g.: – 'I'm going to knock your block off.' Then I hit you in the head with my fist. This would be evidence of intent to do the crime charged. For a conviction to be entered, the accused must have formed the necessary intent to do the unlawful act complained of.

It was becoming clear to me that T had not intended to import Class A drugs into New Zealand. If my interpretation of the facts was correct, my client ought to be found not guilty and set free. Only time would tell if a jury believed my client's explanation was credible.

I called T's ex-boyfriend in Singapore and tape-recorded a statement from him over the phone. His version corroborated what I had been told by my client. It set out how the couple had fought, and how the boyfriend had stormed off to work. He stated that he returned home that evening only to find that his Kiwi girlfriend had left the flat taking many of her belongings. He added that it was obvious she had left in a rush because certain valuable items were left behind, something she would not normally do.

Next I used the international telephone operator to track down the Singapore taxi company, and taxi driver, who took T to the airport on her fateful journey home. The private investigator I hired in Singapore took the man's statement. The driver said he had been called on short notice to my client's pick up address. When he arrived at the address he had to wait only a moment before his passenger came running down the driveway dragging her suitcase behind her. She was in a rush to get to the airport.

I called and spoke to the head of Air New Zealand's Singapore reservations service. I had an affidavit prepared and signed confirming that my client's flight reservation had been made on short notice. With this additional information in hand I then re-interviewed my client. This time I took a fuller statement from T. It set out how the drugs she possessed in Singapore had innocently found their way into her suitcase, and New Zealand, without her knowledge or intent.

I was enjoying the challenge of trying to save my first client from a drug conviction or a jail sentence. While working for Peter Williams I had learned that if you investigate a police case thoroughly before 'the concrete sets' so to speak, and before all the police paperwork is completed, amazing results could often be achieved. All this investigation might not fit within the classic job description of a criminal barrister, but because I seem to have special skills when it comes to investigation, I continue to act as I do.

Two weeks after I had first been tapped on the shoulder, I walked into the headquarters of the Auckland Police drug squad, wearing my pin striped suit and carrying my black briefcase containing the various statements and affidavits I had obtained in relation to my client's case. I was full of confidence. I asked to speak to the officer in charge: I had an appointment to discuss the T matter. A sergeant, three stripes on the shoulder, stepped forward. Wally Hayes and I introduced ourselves. I was the new boy on the block with the defunct Strike Free background and exposure. We stood in the middle of the large room. There were a number of plain-clothed detectives sitting or standing nearby. One detective appeared to be leafing through a police report. Another was on the phone. Everyone looked to be busy, but I could see that some had an ear toward the sergeant and me.

'What can we do for you Mr. Harder?' asked sergeant Hayes.

'I was hoping we could discuss the charges in relation to T.'

'Well, I think we have really done all that we can do for your client on that one. She did get unopposed bail.'

The summary of facts was short; it disclosed that the amount of drugs involved was small. He also pointed out that the police summary revealed that my client had no previous convictions.

'What were you thinking of, Mr. Harder?'

'Uh ... well I sort of thought maybe you would consider dropping the charges.'

'I beg your pardon?'

'I thought you might consider dropping the charges.'

The expression on the sergeant's face changed from one of incredulity to one of out-and-out hilarity. He turned to the detectives in the room.

'Hey, the new boy on the block, Mr. Harder here, would like us to drop the importing charges against his client. You know, the one caught red-handed by Customs? She has made a full and frank statement admitting she bought the drugs. She has signed it as being true and correct. Anything else, Mr. Harder?'

'Well, listen,' I said, 'I know I'm the new boy on the block but I also learned certain principles of law at law school. There are two parts to a crime, as you well know. The *mens rea* and the *actus reus*. For example sergeant, if you were lying in bed, and in the middle of the night you rolled over and bopped your wife on the nose and made it bleed while you were asleep, you would have done the physical act of assault, the *actus reus*, but because you didn't intend to assault her you didn't have the necessary mens rea. 'No guilty mind.'

I pulled the various statements out of my briefcase and handed them to the sergeant. These statements showed that T left Singapore in a rush, that the importation was not premeditated or pre-planned. The Customs officer and your police officer didn't cover this critical point. I have. I would be obliged if you would re-consider then drop the charges.'

The smirk on the sergeant's face disappeared; the tittering of the detectives in the background ceased. He looked briefly at the documents then asked me if I would give him ten minutes to have a look at the papers with the officer in charge. He even added the word 'please.'

I stood by myself staring at the police bulletin board as the sergeant withdrew from the room to discuss the statements and affidavits I had supplied, with the young detective involved in this 'caught cold' case as they called it. As I waited, the minutes ticked by ever so slowly. Every couple of minutes one of the detectives still in the room would look over at me, then back at the papers on his desk. Nobody said a word. It felt like some of them were trying to size me up. Ten minutes later sergeant Hayes came back into the room with a smile on his face.

'Tell you what, Mr. Harder; this is your client's lucky day. We're prepared to drop the importing charges – that's fourteen years imprisonment, to simple possession – that's three months, or a fine.' The policeman looked at me waiting for a response.

'Thank you very much, Sergeant I said...but no thank you. If you accept she didn't have a guilty mind for importing into New Zealand, then she doesn't have a guilty mind for simple possession in New Zealand. She may have committed offences in Penang and Singapore, and if she goes back there she might be in big trouble, but right now she is in New Zealand. I have advised her not to go back to Singapore.'

Again I repeated my bottom line. Dismiss the charges. Offer no evidence.

Silence.

I quickly added that if all charges were dropped now I would not apply for costs in court.

T was in court the next day. I appeared as her lawyer in my first appearance before a magistrate in the Auckland Magistrates Court. I had butterflies in my stomach. Previously lawyer Josephine Budge had acted for me in my own custody and access case in relation to my first-born son Justin after his mother and I had separated. I asked Josephine if she always had the feeling of butterflies in her stomach when she stood up and spoke in court. She said it came and went from time to time.

I stood and introduced myself to judge Denny McLean.

'May it please Your Honour my name is Christopher Harder. I appear for the defendant T. I believe the police have an application to make in relation to the charges against my client.'

From the first moment, I took charge in court. The prosecuting sergeant stood up.

'We seek leave to withdraw the charges, Your Honour.'

As the judge started to say 'granted', I bounced to my feet. Withdrawal of the charges would mean the police could come again with the charge if fresh evidence surfaced. That wasn't what we agreed! I addressed the prosecutor.

'No sir, not 'withdrawn' – you offer no evidence. Your situation is never going to change, it's not like it's going to get any better, and you're not going to find any more evidence. It was agreed by sergeant Wally Hayes that you would offer no evidence. There will be no application for costs.'

I guess that may have been the first time I almost lost my temper in court. At least the police would know I was not a pushover. It was a minor outburst compared to some of the storms that were to follow later in my legal career.

In reply I received a, 'Who the hell do you think you are?' look from the police sergeant, followed by the magic words: 'The police offer no evidence, sir.' With that, judge McLean said: 'No evidence being offered the case is dismissed. You are free to go, Miss T.' My head was in the clouds as I walked out of the courtroom with my client and her family in tow. T was elated. Her mother was crying. Her father walked straight up to me and shook my hand profusely.

'Well done! Well done!' said Mr. T. Nothing like a little bit of praise to make the day. 'By the way,' he said, 'you can keep your fee, you have earned it.' From that moment on I thought that I could walk on legal water.

4
Cannabis vs Japanese Maple

John S had a cannabis plant growing on his back porch. His neighbour noticed it, and 'potted' him to the police. The police came around, searched the residence and found the single plant. Back then, cultivation was a serious charge with a seven-year maximum penalty.

S was arrested and charged with cultivation. He appeared in the Magistrates Court the next day where he was granted bail. Then he called me. The client explained his predicament. The police had found the plant on his back porch. I asked if the plant belonged to him. Initially, he suggested that it may not have been his, but when I asked him if the police would find his fingerprints on the pot, he demurred. Things did not look good.

I visited the man's house, and saw that S obviously had a green thumb when it came to growing ordinary houseplants. The house was cluttered with all manner of them. It was like a jungle.

'You've got a lot of lovely houseplants.'

Based on what I had been told under lawyer-client privilege, I knew my client was guilty. I therefore could not let him testify, so his defence would have to revolve around me introducing a reasonable doubt to the prosecution case. The way to do this would be to show that it was, indeed, possible S had not known the plant was cannabis. The matter was set down for a defended, judge-alone hearing.

On the morning of the case I was unsure of how I would

deal with the case. My mind was racing searching for an answer. Then as I was walking out the front door of our house in Remuera and up the driveway I passed by a Canadian Japanese Maple tree my wife Philippa had planted two years before. The leaves of this plant turn red in the autumn, but while green, as they were now, they look almost identical to cannabis leaf. Then I got an idea. I went back into the house got a brown paper bag, walked back outside to the sinister looking growth, grabbed a handful of leaves, shoved them in the bag, then drove off to court with a grin on my face. Now I knew what I would do!

The police officer in the witness box gave his evidence of receiving a complaint about someone growing cannabis at my client's address. He told how he obtained a search warrant acting on information received, and then went to the address. He described how he had executed the warrant and searched the property, and located a solitary cannabis plant sitting on the back porch amidst many other plants in view of the neighbour. My client suspected he was the anonymous source.

In cross-examination I asked, 'Officer would you have a look at this?' Then I removed my Canadian Japanese Maple leaves from the brown paper bag.

'What does this look like to you?' He stared at it for a moment.

'Well, I'm not a forensic scientist and no tests have been done, but it looks like cannabis to me.'

'Thank you.'

The next witness was the Department of Scientific and Industrial Research scientist. She testified that the plant found and brought to her by the police, exhibit one in the plastic bag, was cannabis. Next I showed this witness the plant material in my brown paper bag.

'What does this look like to you?'

'It looks like cannabis.' She replied.

I then told the judge that I had no more questions for the witness.

The sergeant then advised the judge 'That is the case for the police sir.'

I then stood up and spoke to the judge.

'Your Honour, I would be obliged if you would dismiss

the charge against my client. No case to answer. The police have not proved on the balance of probability that my client knew the plant was cannabis. There is no interview of admission. The material I showed the police officer and the scientist looks like Cannabis but is actually green Canadian Japanese Maple, sir, and both the witnesses identified it incorrectly.' The judge objected to my approach. I was giving evidence from the bar and this was not to be condoned. However I explained that since my client had a house full of potted plants it was possible he thought he was growing a Japanese Maple. The judge blinked hard.

Although I had technically erred nobody was disputing that my green material was Canadian Japanese Maple. The prosecuting sergeant rolled his eyes, and then the judge spoke.

'A little bit irregular, Mr. Harder, but yes I accept your point, the case is accordingly dismissed. 'Saved by a Canadian Japanese Maple Mr. Harder,' grinned the judge. Another win. I was feeling good, like I was invincible. Winning my second case just made me stronger and more confident, as if I needed any more confidence at this point.

A Hot Gun
& Drugs On The Fire

This case involved the police stopping Joe S one evening on suspicion of drunk driving along Karangahape Road, Auckland's local red light district. He denied having been drinking. He was breathalyzed and passed the test. However during the initial stop the police also searched the car he was driving and found a small quantity of cannabis. Joe denied it was his, and told the officers that the vehicle wasn't his. The police checked the registration. It was confirmed that the car was registered to his daughter.

The police travelled to the address then knocked on the door. There was no response. The knock was followed by a loud police voice instructing the occupant to open the door. Scuffling noises emanated from within. The police banged on the door again, this time harder and louder. The police officer was shouting – open the door now! More scurrying and scuffling noises could be heard. Finally, after a third ignored pounding on the door the officers broke it down.

Inside they found a woman standing nonchalantly in front of a blazing fireplace. Despite Joe's daughter's efforts to divert attention elsewhere, the officers immediately looked behind her to see what was burning in the fire. On it they found a brick of cannabis burning. On top of this lay an old Colt 45 pistol. Now Joe's daughter had a problem. She refused to say anything. She made no admissions. She was then charged with possessing cannabis for supply based on the amount of the drug (one kilo), which was way over 28 grams, the presumption for supply. She was also charged with unlawful possession of the pistol.

Joe was a friend of lawyer Peter Williams, and had crewed on his various yachts over the years. I took the case as a favour to Williams. My mentor asked me to help his mate's daughter out.

I pointed out to my client and her father that the weight of evidence against her appeared overwhelming. Had she considered pleading guilty?

'No!' came a quick reply from her father. 'My daughter will plead not guilty. Our family never pleads guilty, do you understand?'

At the judge-alone trial, the police officer gave his evidence accurately recounting the events of the evening in question. He produced the partially burned block of cannabis. It was wrapped in a brown paper bag, securely sealed with tape and signed for by the officer who had collected it from my client's house. My client who was sitting beside me pulled on the sleeve of my jacket trying to get my attention. I was trying to concentrate on my questioning. She said something to me but I didn't fully listen or what she had said did not fully register with me, but it would, just in the nick of time.

Next the prosecutor had the police witness produce the pistol as an exhibit. Earlier he had asked me if the brief of evidence of the gunsmith could be read to the court instead of calling him as the witness. At first I agreed to this procedure. It is not an uncommon practice. However over the morning coffee break (11:30 – 11:45 am) I changed my mind.

Why, I wondered, did the police specifically want this brief read and the witness not called? I have a suspicious nature and a lateral thinking mind. Something was up, I just didn't know what yet!

As the prosecution had not been expecting to call this witness at the hearing, the court case was delayed for a day – an inconvenience unappreciated by the judge, especially as a young lawyer he no doubt thought was still damp behind the ears, had caused it.

When the gunsmith had finished giving his evidence-in-chief (evidence he first gives through the prosecutor) my turn came to cross-examine the witness.

'Do you have your file with you sir?' I began.

'Yes I do,' he replied.

'Did you complete a report on this weapon for the police?'

'Yes sir.'

'Is this your brief of evidence prepared for you by the police?'

'Yes.'

'Is that your signature?'

'Yes.'

'You signed your brief as being true and correct?'

'Yes'.

'Could I see your original draft report, the one you completed and forwarded to the police that was no doubt used to prepare your brief of evidence?'

The witness retrieved the document from his file and it was passed to the court clerk. In the early days it was absolutely taboo for a lawyer to go anywhere near the witness. Over the years times have changed. Sometimes now a judge will let the lawyer approach the witness, and police are now required to make full disclosure of all documents and reports to the defence.

I held the two documents, the brief and the report one in each hand - side by side - and compared them. The gunsmith had prepared the original report and passed it on to the police. The police had then prepared the brief of evidence and had him sign it. I looked for differences in the substance of the two documents, and then I looked at the witness with a cold eye.

'Tell me, is there any difference between the two documents?' He looked at the two documents for a moment.

'Um . . . just two lines sir.'

'Is that right?' I replied sarcastically. 'In your report to the police you refer to the alterations that would need to be made to the fifty-year old pistol before it could be fired, because it fired 'rim fire' rounds and only 'centre fire' ammunition was now manufactured. Is that correct? But that bit of information is not in your signed brief prepared by the police and signed by you, is it?'

'No sir it is not,' he replied.

'In the report it also says that *no such alterations have been made*, doesn't it? Is that right?'
'Correct.'
'But that doesn't appear in your brief either?'
'Correct.'
'But you signed this brief as being true and correct?'
'Yes,' he again replied.

Next came the police officer in charge of the case. During his cross-examination I put it to him that he had altered the gunsmith's brief to mislead the defence and the court. The policeman denied doing so, trying to obfuscate his way out of the matter without success. I put it to him that he had made the changes deliberately to hide the fact that the gun was fifty-years old and therefore classified as an antique and not a pistol because of its age and because ammunition was no longer manufactured for it. This hidden fact brought the pistol under different legislation. *Owning such a weapon did not constitute unlawful possession of a pistol.* The witness did not reply.

I then turned to the judge.

'Your Honour, I would be obliged if you would throw both these charges out. This is an unsatisfactory prosecution and it should go no further,' I insisted with force.

'I can see your concern in relation to the gunsmith's evidence Mr. Harder but what about the cannabis? That was found at your client's address in her constructive possession. It had just been put on the fire and she was standing in front of the fire when the police came into the room. You might say that she was caught 'red-handed' with the drugs Mr. Harder,' replied the judge.

'But sir, the police witness who testified about the cannabis was not the officer who found it.'

'What do you mean?' asked the judge. 'Well sir, you will recall that when I was questioning the police officer who presented the cannabis exhibit to the court my client was pulling on my jacket sleeve trying to get my attention. I sort of heard what she said but the significance of what she told me has only just dawned on me. Sir, she told me this was not the police officer who found the drugs.'

Still on my feet, I turned to the police officer still sitting at the back of the court.

'He's still present in court, sir. He can be recalled.'
Informally I asked the ex-witness,
'Is that your signature on the brown paper bag?'
'Did you pick up the cannabis and put it into this bag?'
'No,' came the reply.
'Where is the man whose signature is on the exhibit?' asked the judge.
'He's on leave in the South Island and not available sir,' answered the officer. The detective then repeated this evidence from the witness box.

When the police officer had left the witness box the judge spoke. 'I agree with counsel, the state of the evidence in this case is totally unsatisfactory. Accordingly all charges are dismissed and your client is free to go Mr. Harder.' The judge gave a stern look to the prosecutor before he retired from the bench.

It was one of those 'you couldn't have stuffed up the prosecution more if you had tried' looks. I walked from the courtroom elated once more – the rush of adrenalin that went with winning had become like an addictive drug to me. I was hooked. I loved hearing those words. 'Not guilty' and 'Your client is free to go Mr. Harder.'

Having discovered that even one line in an armourer's report can be critical to winning a case I had learned a very valuable lesson. In future I would be vigilant over full disclosure. My very next case was just such an example. I received a telephone call from a Fijian Indian businessman who had applied for permanent residence in New Zealand under the business skills regime. To qualify, the applicant was required to invest $650,000 in a business in this country. The client was pleading for help – he told me his application had been turned down by New Zealand Immigration because he had made a false disclosure.

He had left blank the question in relation to convictions. He had not declared an old conviction entered some 20 years previously in Fiji for the arson of a truck.

I asked him why he hadn't declared the conviction. He explained that when he had filled out the form he was in the office of the New Zealand Trade Commissioner in Fiji. The client told me that he had asked the Commissioner if he had to disclose his old offence.

He said they discussed the details of this decades-old indiscretion, and how the Trade Commissioner had told him he did not know if he had to disclose such an old conviction but that he would check.

Nothing happened. The application was submitted with the troublesome section left blank. In due course the client's Fiji police report revealed that he had a conviction. The client's immigration application was declined on that basis. Flying from Suva to Auckland the businessman approached me and asked me to handle his appeal against the refusal.

'I can't make any promises, but I'll see what I can do.'

An upfront fee was agreed and paid on the basis of 'no promises or guarantees except best efforts and a bonus if I succeeded!'

The first thing I did was to make an Official Information request to the New Zealand Immigration Service for my client's full file. The next day my ageing fax machine started grinding out page after page of information from the New Zealand Immigration Service in Wellington - more than 100 pages in total. My secretary Debbie carefully ordered, punched, and then placed each page in a file folder.

As soon as I had finished reading the 100 disclosed pages I decided to make sure that I had full disclosure from the Immigration Service. Suddenly I announced I was off to Wellington. I drove to the Auckland airport, caught the first flight to Wellington, and then took a taxi to Bowen Street and the New Zealand Immigration Service office.

I walked up to the counter and introduced myself. I explained that I was there in relation to my client's case and I asked to see his complete file.

'Mr. Harder, we faxed you the complete file yesterday!' replied the woman working behind the counter.

'Yes, I have it right here. I just wanted to make sure I had received everything on your file.' I explained. The original immigration file was retrieved for me, and then I began comparing the file faxed to me with the original immigration file. Every page matched except for one half-page that had been covered up, and on which was written:

'Before refusing this application for PR (Permanent Resi-

dence), check with the former New Zealand Trade Commissioner to Fiji.'

Nobody had.

The next day I flew to Melbourne to find the former Ministry of Foreign Affairs and Trade official, who was now employed in another Government position. A brief conversation with him revealed that he clearly recalled the conversation about my client's arson conviction. He said he regretted that he had never followed the matter up. Quickly I had his statement typed up as an affidavit and had him swear it. On my return to New Zealand I faxed the affidavit to the New Zealand Immigration Service in Wellington.

On receipt of the sworn affidavit the Wellington manager telephoned me and promptly asked: 'Mr. Harder, how long would it take your client to get from Fiji to Auckland so we can stamp 'PR' on his passport?'

'He'll be here within 48 hours,' I assured the very senior immigration official.

6

Mr Justice Speight

Justice Graham Speight is the most brilliant, sharp-as-a-tack, High Court judge I have ever appeared in front of. He is an ex-crown solicitor, formerly of Meredith Connell, with a razor-sharp intellect and a great sense of humor and not above admitting he can make a mistake.

Today he is old, and retired from the High Court bench, but still travels the world acting as an arbitrator in some of the world's biggest commercial disputes. He is treated like royalty and is handsomely paid for his decisions that are binding on the parties.

In one case over which he presided, I represented one of two accused concerning the robbery of a doctor. The two suspects were accused of having stolen a drug bag from the doctor's surgery. Both perpetrators had been wearing balaclavas, so the major issue to be argued was identification. Evidence was given that a man looking like my client was seen getting into a car down the road but that was not sufficient.

I didn't think much of the Crown case. However to make my point, I forced the prosecutor to call their fingerprint expert.

'Did you find my client's fingerprints anywhere on the premises of the robbery?' I asked.

'No.' replied the witness.

That was all I wanted from the witness, just to demonstrate to the jury that despite the best efforts of the police, there was insufficient evidence to establish that my client had been at the scene of the robbery.

Justice Speight however remained a prosecutor at heart. He thought for a moment, and then turned to the witness. 'I want to ask you a question, it is a judge's prerogative to do this, if they wish,' he said.

He then turned to the court stenographer. 'Don't take this down.'

Turning back to the witness he began to ask his question:

'If all the jurors got out of the jury box, and you examined it for fingerprints . . .'

He was just about to ask the expert what the chances of his finding any prints were, so that the witness would have the opportunity to explain that fingerprinting was not an exact science, and sometimes no prints can be found. This was all true, of course, but it effectively undermined the point I had just made, and I was not happy about it, and I was not happy that this evidence was not being taken down.

'Excuse me, sir,' I interrupted.

'Sit down' the judge snapped, and continued with his question.

'If you were looking for fingerprints . . .'

'Excuse me, sir . . .'

'Sit down, Mr. Harder.'

He started to ask his question again, so I stood up and interrupted again. And again. And again. And again.

'*I said sit down, Mr. Harder, or I'll find you in contempt.*'

The judge was angry now.

'Excuse me, sir . . .'

'*Mr. Harder, if you do not sit down I will have you taken into custody!*'

Finally I got my full sentence out. 'Sir, so long as I am a barrister in this court everything said in the witness box will be taken down and recorded!'

Justice Speight looked at me quivering with barely concealed rage, unsure of what to do next. Then suddenly he stood up, turned and stormed out of the courtroom without saying another word. This in itself was somewhat strange – a judge's entrance and exit is usually accompanied by the formal rising to their feet of all those present in the room, as a mark of respect. On this occasion it was all a bit jumbled, with people hurrying to stand while others never got off their seats, being a bit slow to work out what was going on.

We all sat around the courtroom as the minutes passed ever so slowly. This was not a scheduled adjournment, and the judge had given no indication of when he would be back, so we all had no choice but to wait. Personally, I thought there was a good chance he was devising some unique contempt of court fate for me – a judge's discretion in dealing with contempt is broad. From censure to large fine, even imprisonment.

Ten minutes after His Honour first rushed from the court he returned, sitting down in his judge's chair. We all waited with bated breath to hear what he would say. Then his Honour turned to the jury and said,

'Ladies and gentlemen of the jury, of course Mr. Harder was absolutely correct. *Everything* said in the witness box by the witness should be taken down and recorded and I now so order. The trial will now proceed.'

He abandoned his questioning of the fingerprint expert. My client was found not guilty of the robbery and set free. The rush of winning continued.

After the trial, I gathered up my law books. Outside the court I walked along the pavement, my hands full with a box of legal books and papers. As I approached the entrance to the judge's underground parking Justice Speight drove out. He looked towards me then opened his window.

'Do you need a ride Christopher?' he asked in a very pleasant voice.

'No sir, my car's not far away'. He then congratulated me on my win. I thanked him then asked, 'Tell me sir, would you really have put me in custody today for contempt if I had continued?'

There was a sparkle in his eye and with a grin he replied, 'Absolutely Christopher, absolutely!'

A Pocket Knife & A Severed Ear

Two young Maori men, Geoffrey and John Rakete, lived near Kaikohe, a rural town with two pubs – the 'top pub' and the 'bottom pub' at either end of town. On the evening of 2 November 1984, the Rakete brothers were drinking with their friend, Robert Tahere, in the top pub. During the evening a group of Black Power gang members from outside the district entered the pub. They were drunk, loud and threatening. Dunn Tahere, a friend of the group, became the focus of the gang's attention. He was hounded, and eventually took a minor beating.

The Rakete brothers and Tahere left the pub and went to the house of a friend, Willy Pou, where they armed themselves with a wide selection of the knives and belts they found in the house. Possibly they intended to avenge the attack on their friend; perhaps their intentions were not so specific. In any event, they returned to Kaikohe, to the bottom pub, armed to the teeth. By the side of the pub was a narrow alley, and it was here that Geoffrey and John Rakete, and Robert Tahere, came across a small Austin Mini car full of Black Power gang members. What happened in the alley was unclear, but certainly the two groups clashed. There was a lot of shouting and swearing as the gang members climbed out of their car, and then the groups began circling each other and, eventually, exchanged blows.

Within minutes one of the Black Power men, Mark Kapea, had been stabbed to death. He lay on the ground bleeding with knife wounds to his liver and heart. Indicative of the chaos of that evening was the fact that at about the same time all this was going on, Dunn Tahere, victim of the gang's assault earlier in the evening, was fighting with another Black Power member, named Shelford, on the other side of the main road. In that scuffle, Shelford's ear was cut off with a pocketknife.

The police thought Robert Tahere had killed Kapea, but he disappeared immediately after the killing. They immediately arrested the Rakete brothers, but it was not until two months later, on New Year's Day 1985, that Robert Tahere was arrested at gunpoint at a property near Kaikohe. Taken back to the Kaikohe police station, he provided a full confession to the crime.

At trial, Peter Williams defended Robert Tahere, with me acting as junior counsel. The trial was nearing completion when one of the court clerks informed me that the police constable looking after the jury had been sitting in the jury room with the jury. This information was passed on to the judge, who received conflicting accounts of the time spent in the room from the jury foreman and the policeman in question.

A mistrial was declared and a re-trial ordered. The judge was so furious at the misconduct of the police that he bailed the three accused on their own recognizance of $1,000 each, an almost unheard of event when a capital case carrying a life sentence was involved.

At the second trial, one matter of particular importance to the defence was the size of the knife wound found in the dead man's chest. The liver wound was not a problem – it simply did not match the dimensions of any of the three alleged murder weapons. It appeared likely, though, that the blade that penetrated the chest cavity matched that being wielded by our client on the night in question. Williams put it to the pathologist that Tahere's knife was wider than the chest wound, and suggested that the weapon had therefore not caused the cut. We expected the witness to explain that some tissue shrinks post mortem. Instead, perhaps because of inexperience, he agreed that the Bowie knife exhibit before him could not have caused the fatal wound in question.

While the trial continued with Peter Williams, I travelled through most of the hardware stores in Northland. I was looking for a pocketknife with a blade that matched the dimensions of the liver wound, because it was acknowledged a pocketknife had been used in the fatal fracas. Eventually I found such a knife. It was branded a 'Saturday Night Special' - brilliant. Given that Shelford's ear had been cut off at close proximity coincidentally on a Saturday night, we suggested there was a chance one knife had caused both wounds, and that it had not been Robert Tahere's knife.

Next, a voir dire was held (a trial within a trial, before the judge alone, to determine whether certain evidence is admissible). Robert Tahere claimed that he had confessed to the murder falsely because he knew that his two cousins, the Raketes, were both married with families. He said he had lied to the police taking full responsibility so that his cousins would get bail. It was the Maori way. They had families to look after, and he didn't. By itself, this claim would strain the credulity of the judge, so we needed something to back it up.

By sheer good luck I located a local policeman who, if he were prepared to come to court, would help our case. He had spent more than twenty years working as a police officer in Northland and he knew the local population well. After some argument the judge allowed the very experienced officer to qualify himself as an expert on Maori culture and behaviour. This policeman broke out of the mould by testifying for the defence in the Tahere murder trial. He stated before the court that in his experience it was not uncommon for one Maori to lie for another, falsely taking blame for a crime to protect the other's family from having their breadwinner put in jail.

The judge excluded the confession from the trial, and the policeman who gave evidence for the defence – a fair and principled man - later left the police under pressure for his betrayal. His colleagues 'sent him to Coventry' after his testimony, refusing to speak to him, shutting him out of their activities, and making his continued employment impossible.

The Rakete brothers and Tahere were each acquitted. Immediately after the not guilty verdicts were released, the Black Power gang to whom the deceased had belonged, broke into the prisoner's aid house next to the old Whangarei Supreme court, and trashed the inside of the place while they looked with rage for our acquitted clients. Fortunately our clients had already left the building.

The Prostitute/Secretary Rape

A number of years ago, when many in the New Zealand Police still considered me Public Enemy Number One, the department complained to the Law Society that I had sex with a police witness. It wasn't quite as simple as that. Nothing ever is.

I had been assigned the case on legal aid. My client was a Samoan man in his mid-20s. He'd been accused of abducting a young woman walking home after work on Auckland's Karangahape Road. He was alleged to have forced her to walk up a flight of 20 steps, down a long hallway and into a little room, where he raped her. My client said some of that story was true, but not all of it. He explained that he had met the woman on the sidewalk on Karangahape Road, that she was a prostitute and that he had walked up the stairs and down the hall with her. He said she came willingly. He didn't force her.

'She agreed to have sex with me for $50.' He said.

He demonstrated how he showed her the money. The street girls always ask to see the money first. Apparently my client showed her what looked like a folded up $50 bill.

Then he described how the two of them had consenting sex in the little day room, bent over a table. He explained that when they had finished, the prostitute asked for her money. My client then gave her the folded up note he had shown her earlier. Unfortunately for everyone concerned, it was not a $50 bill, but a $5 bill. Both were similar in colour. She was not amused. She threatened my client that she would get the gangs on him if he didn't pay up, or she would scream rape to the police. In due course this is exactly what she did. He promised to pay her out of his next week's wages but that was not good enough. She called the police.

First I went to the police station with my new information. I spoke to detective Tony Bouchier who was in charge of the case. I pointed out the different stories and how, if the complainant really was a prostitute as my client claimed, the police should be reconsidering the appropriateness of the charges. He was not interested. Bouchier was satisfied the complainant was not a prostitute. She worked as a secretary for the gas company he told me. Later that day I personally checked with the gas company only to find that the complainant did in fact work there, as a secretary.

I went back to my client and told him what I had learned. I said, 'Don't bullshit me, because it just makes my job that much harder if you do. Better you tell me nothing than lie to me!'

My client was adamant that he was telling me the truth. He said the woman was a prostitute. I said, 'I want to believe you, but we will have to prove it if you are to have any kind of a chance in court.'

The next step was obvious. Find the woman. Prove she is a prostitute then demonstrate that the complainant had lied to the police about her obviously relevant occupation. Perhaps she had lied about other matters as well. This would mean there would be a good chance the police would have to rethink the charges.

The client then told me that he had previously seen the girl working at the Tenderloin Massage parlour in Great North Road. A couple of nights later I went to Tenderloins to try to find the complainant. The receptionist played dumb not knowing anything about the girl. I told her I was not a policeman rather I was a lawyer but it seemed to make no difference. Then as I was about to leave a long-legged blonde walked into the reception area and asked if she could help me. I introduced myself again giving her my lawyer's card, explaining I would like to talk to her in private for a moment. She led me into one of the side rooms. When she had shut the door I began to explain my client's predicament. I was hoping she would at least hear me out.

Very quickly it became clear that not only was this woman acquainted with the complainant, she was the 'recent complaint witness' in the very same rape case. Neither woman's statement revealed to the police that both worked as prostitutes in the evening to supplement their day job income.

Apparently the complainant, her girlfriend, had complained to the woman I was now interviewing about the alleged rape by my client. This woman was a goldmine of information, but she was also a police witness.

A problem was emerging: she wasn't interested in talking to me, and as time passed and my questioning continued I could see that she was becoming very irritable.

Finally I twigged to what the problem was. This girl worked for money and I was wasting her time. Once I realized this, I quickly offered to pay her $100 for her time just to listen to me. She thought about it for a moment then replied OK. She wasn't terribly keen on taking a personal cheque from me for $100, but in the end she agreed.

Her working name was Kay. She didn't seem too bothered by the fact that she was selling her friend out. I was pleased. Her version of events substantially confirmed my client's story. The complainant was working as a prostitute the night of her alleged abduction. As a parting gift, Kay gave me the phone number of the massage parlour where the complainant now worked and her working name, Mandy.

The thrill of investigation is addictive. It surely was for me. Now I had to tie down Mandy, figuratively speaking. I decided to go undercover. With a degree of anticipation I booked a room at a motel in Parnell. Next, I called the phone number Kay had given me. I asked if Mandy was available for outside escort service. Mandy was available and in less than half an hour, the gas works secretary was at my motel room door.

It didn't take long the next day to convince the officer in charge of the case, Tony Bouchier, that his complainant had been less than truthful with him. The charges were soon withdrawn, but the matter was far from forgotten.

The police would try to have their revenge.

Two weeks later the New Zealand Police, in particular detective Lester Payne complained to the Law Society about my alleged conduct. He had seen my green MGB parked out front of the parlour. As I left he went in and interviewed the woman I had just interviewed as well as uplifting my $100 cheque. With this evidence a complaint was made alleging I had sex with a police witness (the recent complaint witness I had just interviewed). I was being accused of conduct unbecoming a barrister. I denied the allegation. The Law Society investigated. No complaint was made in relation to the complainant.

It is strange how these things work out, though. At the same time as I was being investigated over this incident by the Law Society, a senior practitioner was also under similar investigation. The lawyer's client had been charged with employing underage girls to work in his parlour. To be legal you had to be 18. The police intended to call 16-year-old under-age twin girls, who had worked in the parlour and as escorts, as witnesses.

It was alleged that the lawyer had sex with the same two girls when the parlour owner sent them to the lawyers' office as a Christmas present. Because he was part of the old boy network nobody wanted to do him any harm. Then there was me, the old boy network's worst nightmare.

Since my head was not the only one on the Law Society chopping block over sex allegations the Law Society was forced to do something they never thought they would; namely send me a letter stating that after full investigation it had concluded that having sex with a police witness did not amount to conduct unbecoming a barrister.

The Parnell Panther Rape Case

Shortly after my admission to the bar I was engaged to help lawyer Barry Wilson defend an indecent assault charge against an elderly Maori man. The matter concerned a young Maori boy and his uncle. The boy had recanted his story to his auntie after being interviewed by the police. The auntie had contacted her husband's lawyer. As a result I was hired to travel to Kaitaia, a small town near the top of the North Island one weekend in June 1983 to try and obtain a statement from the boy confirming that he had told his auntie that he had lied to the police about his uncle interfering with him so as to get him into trouble and out of the house. This was because uncle would not let him bring over his first girlfriend to visit except when he supervised.

I was sent to obtain a statement from the complainant. I took with me an off duty stenographer from the Auckland Magistrates Court. She was there to record the statement given in shorthand and then type it up so the boy could swear it before a Justice of the Peace before I returned to Auckland.

During the course of the weekend the stenographer and I had plenty of opportunities to talk and we did. Over a bottle of wine and dinner she gradually told me a story about a man called Stephens, who the police believed was a serial rapist. She told me that this person was going to be 'fitted' by the police. She didn't explain how.

At this early stage of my career I liked to think that

the New Zealand Police did not routinely act in such fashion. However on rare occasions it was not unheard of within the police for 'the bad ass individuals' the police 'knew' (i.e.: believed) were guilty of serious criminal offending to be verballed by a police officer. This is where the officer claims a suspect said something incriminating in the interview room when in fact he did not, but because it is written in the policeman's notebook it becomes evidence against the accused. The police suspected Stephens of a string of rapes committed up and down the country.

The press tagged the unidentified attacker as the 'Parnell Panther' – because two rapes had recently occurred in the area.

The way the 'fitting story' came to me was because the after hours stenographer worked for the Justice Department. Court staff mixed with the police officers that worked in the court, during coffee breaks, over lunch and at the Friday drinks after work. Because of this, information was passed back and forth.

This 'fitting rumour' made me angry. If it was true, and it sounded genuine to me, then the police actions were brutally unfair. If the police really were fabricating evidence in the Parnell Panther case then I was offended to the core. Back in my early days I found I could get pretty passionate about such misconduct. Invariably I challenged the fairness of the system, more often than not taking my anger out on the judge. At the beginning of this case I was a professional non-entity. Despite the fact that I had only recently been admitted to the bar, this perception was about to change.

I returned to Auckland from Kaitaia with a signed and witnessed affidavit from the boy complainant. Having completed my task I handed the affidavit to the uncle's lawyer, gave him my bill for $400, then focused on my next challenge.

The Parnell Panther rape suspect Mark Stephens was at the time being held at Auckland maximum-security prison, which is located at Paremoremo, north of Auckland, just past Albany. I decided to drive to the prison the following Saturday morning. I showed the prison staff my ID and my bag was searched.

Next I was escorted through three sets of prison doors before I was placed in a small interview room. A short time later the door opened and 24-year-old Mark William Stephens, a Maori, with a shocking list of previous convictions for dishonesty, burglary and minor assaults on police was ushered into the room.

Stephens was a tall man – he stood about six foot – and had big brown eyes. His cheekbones were pronounced. He had big lips and a noticeable gap between his two front teeth. His ears were pierced and he normally wore two gold studs in his left lobe. He had long plaited hair and he looked mean.

I told him about my trip up north and how this court stenographer had told me the police were talking off the record of 'fitting' him for a series of alleged rapes. I told Stephens I thought he needed a really good lawyer. With a grin on his face he asked me if I knew any good lawyers. In a matter of minutes he agreed to engage me if legal aid could be approved for his various cases.

My initial interview with Stephens led me to believe that he probably was being 'fitted up' but I couldn't be sure until I had looked at all the evidence. He may have been guilty of something, but some aspects of the prosecution case had an odour about it. Much of the evidence produced against Stephens had come from police 'verbals'.

'Verballing' a prisoner was where a policeman made up, and then wrote down, an alleged admission knowing it to be false. This was common practice by some police until the electronic recording of interviews became standard procedure.

In this case Mark Stephens faced a series of police verbals. He was not a stupid person – he had a good recall of events and conversations, and he was able to point out to me very precisely when something had been added, changed or left out by the police.

Stephens was very frank in indicating what he had really said in the police interview. It was clear that the police were absolutely convinced he was the Parnell Panther rapist, and that some police officers then in Auckland, would go to whatever lengths were necessary to ensure appropriate and prejudicial evidence was available to ensure Stephens convictions.

He had been charged with nine counts of rape relating

to different incidents up and down the country. Identification of the suspect was critical. There were 9 complainants in the police case against Mark Stephens. My instructing solicitor was Josephine Budge (now District Court judge Josephine Bouchier), who married Tony Bouchier, ex-Police officer, now a lawyer.

At the old Magistrates Court in Kitchener Street there was no separate entrance for the accused to be brought before the court. Instead, the police had Stephens brought up from the cells then walked down the corridor past the various witnesses waiting to give their evidence. I thought this was grossly unfair. Instead of biting my tongue I raced down to the criminal counter where I yelled and screamed demanding the Court Registrar front at the counter and explain this inequity.

In front of all the counter staff I verbally abused the then Magistrates Court Registrar McGuffog. For several minutes I carried on my tirade against him explaining what I perceived to be the gross unfairness of police walking an accused person hand-cuffed and in obvious police custody, down the hallway past all the potential eye witnesses.

McGuffog was lost for words but he would never forget his embarrassing confrontation with barrister Christopher Harder. One day he would seek his revenge. By the end of the depositions hearings, seven of the nine charges against Stephens had been dismissed, due to a lack of evidence, but that left two serious charges to answer.

Stephens was first tried for a vicious assault causing grievous bodily harm to Robin Scholes, a prominent television producer. This victim had been attacked from behind by a man who climbed through a window wearing a nylon stocking over his head as a disguise. The assault had been brutal. Neighbours heard Scholes screaming, but did nothing to help – a key event in the subsequent formation of the Neighbourhood Watch program in New Zealand.

The key piece of evidence at Stephens' trial for the Scholes assault was a footprint that was left at the scene of the crime by the attacker after he stood in his victim's blood. A scientist from the then Department of Scientific and Industrial Research analyzed that footprint. His name was Phillip Stanley Groom.

Groom matched the print to a pair of New Balance running shoes owned by Stephens. Working carefully through the evidence in defence of Stephens, it became clear to me over time that something was wrong with Groom's analysis. To put it simply, the shoes were shorter than the footprint. How could a scientist possibly have been able to match a shorter shoe to a longer blood print?

After a number of experiments I discovered it was possible to manufacture a match by bending the shoe into a sharp curve, pulling its toe up so it met the back of the heel then roll the ink covered sole on a piece of paper. When the running shoe was held in this position the sole stretched out unnaturally. Only in this way was it possible to generate a print that matched the length of the one found at the crime scene. It was, however, impossible to make such a print while there was a foot in the shoe.

Discovering this fact led me to conduct the most savage cross-examination of my career. Although this case was early in my career, that was not the reason for my growing anger. Here, I believed I had found a government witness misusing his position to adversely influence the case against my client.

At the trial, government scientist Phillip Groom gave what I believed was false and misleading evidence against my client, so I homed in on the key "fact", the 'matching' foot and blood print found at the scene. One thing I knew for certain, you could not make a matching print with the shoe worn on a foot. Mr. Groom swore under oath that you could. When I pushed the Crown scientist into a corner in the witness box requesting him to give me a demonstration he couldn't. Next I asked to look at all the test footprints he had attempted. He refused to reveal the test samples. When I refused to let up in my cross-examination he suddenly called out in open court to senior crown prosecutor Peter Kaye:

'Hey, help me Mister, what's he up to?'

Immediately Kaye stood up and asked the judge for a brief adjournment so that counsel could see the judge in chambers. His Honour agreed and the court adjourned. In chambers Justice Pritchard advised the prosecutor that if the scientist did not hand over his samples to defence counsel he would make an order that he must. With that advice taken on board Kaye left the judge's chambers ahead of me returning to the now empty courtroom. Then without a word he disappeared with the Crown witness who was still under my cross-examination into a little room next to the Crown room.

I was concerned at the length of time the two were spending together so I asked the court registrar to knock on the door and make them come out. It didn't take 25 minutes for the Crown Prosecutor to tell the witness that the judge said, 'Tell your witness to cough up the foot prints voluntarily Mr. Kaye or I will order him to do so in front of the jury.' Despite my lack of experience I knew that one of the fundamental rules of criminal procedure was being totally ignored.

No one, not defence lawyer or prosecutor is permitted to talk to a witness while he or she is under cross-examination. Here the judge said, tell the witness to comply or else. That message did not take 25 minutes to convey to this very experienced and senior DSIR scientist.

After the morning coffee break I continued my attack on the witness. 'Mr. Groom, what did you and the prosecutor talk about for 25 minutes in that little room outside the courtroom while the court registrar and I knocked on the door trying to get you to open it and come out?'

There was a long pause from the witness before he replied, 'Mr. Kaye was just holding my hand and consoling me'. I felt confident that I was making headway in my cross-examination and an impression on the jury. Then all of a sudden before I had completed my questioning of this obviously lying witness, the judge asked to see counsel in his chambers. Still wearing his judges gown but without his wig on the judge spoke directly to me.

'Mr. Harder, I think you've machine-gunned this witness off at the knees, and you should stop,' he said.

To my surprise, the judge then proceeded to cut *me* off at the knees. He constantly obstructed my efforts to make the scientist's perfidy clear to the jury, he refused to let me drive my points home and he prevented me from recalling the police officer who had helped the scientist stretch the running shoe to match the blood print. This made me very angry but to no avail. The jury found Stephens guilty of the savage assault for which he was later sentenced to ten years jail.

After the trial my complaints about the judge and the prosecutor and the scientist could be heard the length and breadth of New Zealand's legal community. At the same time I was making waves about the judge's trial conduct, I had invested huge amounts of time and a lot of my own money into investigating the questionable footprint evidence. I would not give an inch on the matter.

From that moment on I attacked every prosecutor, policeman and judge I came across like a fox terrier chasing large rats. I challenged every aspect of the evidence and corrected every judge who made a blunder. I invested three and a half years of my life in the Stephens' appeal; much of it spent peering at evidence through a magnifying glass.

Finally with the help of the news media, in particular Phillip English of the *New Zealand Herald*, I won a Government Ministerial Inquiry that was headed by Christchurch QC Brian McClelland (now deceased). His inquiry produced a report that contained damning findings against the scientist, the prosecutor and the trial judge involved in the Stephens/Scholes trial. In part the report read:

'Mr. Groom had a responsibility to report all relevant findings, and to ignore this highly significant dissimilarity or discrepancy between the shoes and shoeprints, was a gross deficiency, which can be interpreted as misleading to the court. Mr. Groom made an unjustified assumption regarding the tread pattern of a shoeprint, and failed to present a full and honest account of his examinations in comparing the shoeprint at the scene to the shoes of the accused. He thus demonstrated an unacceptable bias towards the prosecution case, seriously jeopardizing the impartial role of a DSIR forensic scientist. Mr. Groom contradicted himself in cross-examination, inviting an allegation of dishonesty, although a less serious alternative explanation is also possible.'

Finally I felt vindicated, but in the meantime the New Zealand Police were trying to discredit me in various ways.

I had challenged their integrity, and would reap the consequences. They wanted me charged for various wrongdoings including touting (soliciting for business) and making adverse comments to the press about an Australian police officer who had come to New Zealand to take an extradition client of mine back to Australia. This client had been held in police cells in isolation for over 66 days. This caused uproar in the media so the government quickly amended the law to allow prisoners to be kept in custody in police cells when the remand prison was full.

I also made other complaints about the second Stephens' trial, this time for the rape of a model in her Parnell flat. Justice Sinclair was the trial judge. This case was often referred to as the 'telephone cord rape case'. This was because during the trial the prosecution had produced a telephone handset and attached cord, allegedly cut from the main body of the phone by the accused.

The Crown attempted to prove this critical point by matching Stephens' serrated knife to the cuts on the cord. But there was a problem with this evidence: Photographs of the crime scene showed the handset and cord in the position it was found. When I had the picture blown up you could see the cord had five and one half coils on it. The exhibit produced in court had seven and one half coils. Not only that – the hand piece was a different colour to the one in the police scene photograph!

Despite this, the prosecution claimed at trial that Stephens' knife tied him to the crime scene. I felt this was fairly convincing proof that my client was being fitted up by someone in charge. This was especially so when one considered the Inquiry report criticizing the various players in the case. Again, this is not to say I believed Stephens was innocent – assessing guilt or innocence is not my role, that is for the jury - but I believed and I suggested that the telephone exhibit had been fabricated or somehow switched with another hand piece found at another crime scene.

I was adamant the exhibit had been planted. I was very insistent. Ultimately Justice Sinclair became very cross and angry with me. After the trial the judge complained to the Auckland District Law Society, alleging I had improperly questioned two Crown witnesses. Fortunately for me neither of those complaints went anywhere.

After the Groom forensic inquiry report was produced, I decided to take the Stephens case to the Court of Appeal. Before doing so, I obtained the permission of the Solicitor-General to present the report as part of the appeal. I regarded it as heavy artillery, condemnatory as it was of the DSIR scientist, the prosecutor and the trial judge.

Early in my submissions I told the Court that their Honours should read the report as I handed a copy of it to the Registrar.

'What's that, Mr. Harder?' asked the President of the Court Mr. Justice Cooke.

'It is a copy of a report of a Ministerial Inquiry into certain aspects of the Stephens case. It outlines and comments on the scientist's claims as to how he made the matching footprints sir!'

'We're not going to read the report, Mr. Harder. We haven't called for that report, it hasn't been tested under cross-examination and we don't know in what circumstances it was made. It has no weight in this court. We will not read the report!' His Honour was adamant.

'Sir, you must read the report.' I pleaded.

'We will not read the report, Mr. Harder. Carry on.'

'Sir, . . .'

'We will not read the report, Mr. Harder.'

For the next hour, I struggled to put my case using other material, but without the report I didn't have much of a chance. It was the foundation that held my allegations of misconduct by the authorities together. I felt battered (figuratively) by the President. In frustration I picked up the papers and files on the table in front of me. I was incensed by the judge's attitude, and I felt a rage building up within me. I said nothing for a moment (it was an effort). I stood there in silence as if I was about to turn and walk out of court.

Then I spun around on my heels and slammed my papers down on the desk in an effort to get the full attention of the five judges sitting on the appeal. Next I began to address the court with a tone and volume that probably bordered on unacceptable in proceedings such as these. I said,

'You can be assured of one thing, gentlemen: if the report I hold in my hand had been adverse to this defence counsel, and not to judge, prosecutor and scientist, you all would have wanted to read it!'

Justice Cooke had a habit of chewing on the corner of his handkerchief during appeal hearings. As my outburst climaxed, I noticed that his handkerchief had disappeared entirely into his mouth. For a second I thought he had swallowed it.

The judges quickly pushed their chairs together so that they could confer briefly in hushed tones. Then came a surprise reply from the President.

'Mr. Harder, we will retire now and read the report.'

From that point onwards, my relationship with the President was strained at best. I took a lot of satisfaction from that incident, although the next day the judges came back into court to say they had read the report and noted its comments, but would still have to exclude it from the appeal because of the rules of evidence.

Let me make one thing clear before moving on from Mark William Stephens. In my assessment he may not have always been a good person. But I also believe that Stephens was 'fitted' by at least one, possibly two police officers that used the DSIR scientist to help bolster a weak case against a publicly tagged serial rapist the police called the Parnell Panther. In reality Stephens was convicted of one count of rape on one victim and a second count of GBH (grievous bodily harm) on TV producer Robin Scholes. The Stephens' appeal finished on a Friday. I had spent two and a half years working on the case.

After the hearing was finally over and the decision reserved, the judges were standing around in the grand foyer at the Appeal Court chatting, when I walked past. Justice John Henry broke away from his colleagues, crossed the foyer and asked me if I was all right before shaking my hand and wishing me well. I got the impression that he understood how I was feeling. Henry J asked after my wife, Philippa who had previously worked in his firm, Wilson, Henry, Sinclair and Martin, even babysitting his children on one occasion.

Afterwards I wondered if he had not been thinking of

his own experience as an advocate, and how hard it can sometimes be to present a fair case.

Back in 1981 as a QC John Henry had been involved in a Commission of Inquiry looking into the circumstances of the conviction of Arthur Allan Thomas for the murder of Harvey and Jeanette Crewe of Pukekawa. Following a lengthy forensic inquiry by Dr James Sprott it was established that the cartridge case that had been 'found' by the police and used as the critical evidence to convict Thomas, was not manufactured until a date after the killing. The suggestion was that the bullet cartridge had been planted. Henry, who was acting for the New Zealand Police Association, felt his clients were not receiving a fair hearing and he said so.

HENRY: May it please the Commission, Mr. Fisher and I have conferred over the adjournment, and I wish to advise the Commission that we are not prepared to be treated as we feel we have been, or to remain involved in this inquiry in the way in which it is being conducted. We feel it is obvious that we as counsel can achieve nothing to ensure that the police are fairly heard, and accordingly we now withdraw.

CHAIRMAN: Are you suggesting they have not been fairly heard?

HENRY: I am suggesting, Sir, that we feel we can do nothing to ensure....

CHAIRMAN: Are you suggesting they have not been fairly heard?

HENRY: I am saying nothing more than I have.

Now I was looking for a new challenge. I read the Saturday *New Zealand Herald* next morning over breakfast of crispy bacon, eggs sunny side up and fried hash browns washed down with a cup of freshly brewed coffee.

On the front page of the paper there was a story about 6 Rotuman chiefs who lived on the island of Rotuma, just off the Fiji mainland who had been arrested for sedition because they ran up the Union Jack flag after military strongman Sitiveni Rabuka carried out his second military coup in as many years. This seemed unfair to me so I decided to try to do something about it.

10
Jail & An Arms Amnesty, Fiji

Seven chiefs from the Island of Rotuma were to be charged with sedition. Why? Because the populace of their island had been very unhappy about Sitiveni Rabuka's move to declare Fiji a republic and cut ties with the Commonwealth. The chiefs had encouraged a ragtag, South Pacific-style rebellion, the culmination of which was their declaration of allegiance to the Queen and the defiant raising of a Union Jack on a public flagpole.

The military regime had grossly overreacted, sending troops to Rotuma to arrest eight chiefs. Seven had been caught but the eighth - an eccentric man called Gagaj Sau Lagfatmaro, also known as Henry Gibson – who was the leader of the bunch, had escaped to his family home at Whenuapai in New Zealand.

That Saturday morning after I read the article in the *Herald* I went jogging. Running down the steep slope of Ayr Street in Parnell, past the Auckland Grammar Old Boys Rugby Club, I formulated a plan to get to Fiji. I would contact Gagaj Sau Lagfatmaro, who lived near the Whenuapai air base just north of Auckland, and attempt to obtain his approval for me to go to Fiji to defend the Rotuman chiefs.

By mid-Saturday afternoon I was drinking kava with 'His Royal Highness' Gagaj Sau Lagfatmaro (the title adopted when he was made leader of his clan six years previously) at his suburban headquarters. My offer of free legal services (but for my expenses) was accepted.

On Sunday evening I was on a plane to Fiji and then Rotuma to deal with what looked like an injustice to me, and my first overseas adventure in the law. I flew to Fiji with a clear plan in mind. I had previously read Brigadier Rabuka's book, *No Other Way*, and knew that in that text he had repeatedly referred to the ties with Queen and Commonwealth – there were no less than 27 references, a fair reflection of the traditional significance of these institutions to the Fijian people. All going according to plan, I would appear for the defence, Rabuka would be called as a witness, and I would have the opportunity to cross-examine him. Based on the statements made in his book, I saw a good chance to hoist him with his own petard.

My trip to Fiji had two purposes. Firstly, I wanted to meet with as many of the sedition accused as possible, obtain their approval for me to act as counsel, and see how I could help meet their immediate needs. Secondly, I needed to make my application for admission to the bar in Fiji so I would be able to act on behalf of the accused men in court in Fiji.

In short, this visit was a success. Nothing is ever easy or entirely smooth in a country run by the military, but my dealings were relatively trouble free (certainly compared to later experiences).

In Suva I met Tevita Fa, a Tongan-Fijian lawyer who would be the lead counsel on the bail hearing. I would assist until I was admitted to the bar. We took a terrifying flight to the island of Rotuma when our twin-engine plane nearly fell out of the sky when it hit a down draught. Then the pilot 'momentarily' lost the island we were supposed to be heading for. Some considerable time and many gallons of fuel later, we found it.

Once we had landed on the island we were driven to the local school where we met the accused men then under military guard. We interviewed our clients in the school kitchen, and I obtained their approval to represent them along with Tevita Fa once I had been officially admitted to the Fiji bar. In the meantime, Tevita Fa would appear alone.

The first priority was obtaining bail for the clients if

possible. The schoolhouse was used as a makeshift court, and the Fiji Chief Magistrate, Apaitia Seru, sat to hear the charges read. The Director of Public Prosecutions Isikeli Mataitoga opposed the bail application. Tevita Fa made a sound constitutional argument that as a consequence of the coups Rotuma was no longer under Fijian jurisdiction – it was historically not part of Fiji, but a colony of Great Britain administered by Fiji. With locals crowding the room, this issue was referred to the High Court of Fiji, while the bail application was rejected. The seven were taken to Suva in a gunboat.

Before we left the island the families of the accused men held a feast for Fa and me. The people were gracious and generous. It was a moving afternoon.

The rest of my time in Fiji was spent filing the appropriate papers for my admission to the bar. I had requested a certificate of good character from the Auckland District Law Society before leaving Auckland, and to my surprise (given the problems I had experienced in gaining admission to the bar in New Zealand) this was sent to me by facsimile in Suva.

I filed the appropriate documents with the Chief Justice Timoci Tuivaga and it was agreed that subject to the receipt of further documents from the Auckland District Law Society, and approval by the Fiji Law Society, I would be admitted on the morning of the case. This arranged I flew back to Auckland.

The following letter was written by J B Bowring (Miss), for the Executive Director to assist with my admission to the Fiji High Court rolls.

May 16 1988

To Whom it May Concern,
I hereby certify that Christopher Lloyd Harder was admitted as a barrister and solicitor of the High Court of New Zealand at Auckland on May 20th 1983, and has practised as a barrister sole since May 31st 1983, his current certificate being issued on February 19th 1988, and expiring on January 31st 1989.
I am not aware of any reason why Christopher Lloyd

Harder should not be admitted in the Supreme Court in Fiji.

For most of the next month I was occupied with other matters back in New Zealand, but I continued to devote significant time to the Rotuma seven. Communication with Fiji was expensive and unreliable, and it was difficult to discuss strategy with Fa because he knew our conversations and facsimiles were likely to be monitored.

Complicating matters further, regardless of the assurances I had obtained, it appeared that my application for admission to the bar had stalled: no action had been taken. This may have been due only to the inefficiencies of the system, but it seemed more likely that there were political reasons for the delay.

On Tuesday 14 June 1988 I flew back to Fiji. I did not have a work permit, having been told by the Fiji Law Society that I would not require one so long as I planned to work for no more than fourteen days, however I filled in my immigration card with the words 'barrister on visit'.

With me I had a tabua – a whale's tooth given to me by Gagaj Sau Lagfatmaro. He told me that offering a tabua and two bundles of kava root was a strong gesture asking for peace and forgiveness. It was my intention to make such an offer to Rabuka if I got the chance. I had a few minutes of difficulties in clearing Fiji Customs because a tabua is a prohibited export, but when I explained that I was *importing* the gift not taking it out of Fiji, it was eventually allowed in.

I spent the first day trying to make an appointment to see Rabuka without success. I also received a telephone call from Anand Singh, a lawyer I had met in Auckland back in May, and arranged to meet him the following day to discuss another interesting local case, which was quickly to drag my efforts away from the Rotuma seven entirely.

On June 6 the Fiji police and military had detained 21 people in connection with a significant cache of Soviet-made rifles, machine guns, hand grenades and ammunition. The weapons were found on cane farms near Nadi. The initial haul included 110 rocket launchers, five rocket propelled grenades, 93 AK47 assault rifles, 10 light machine guns, four heavy machine guns, 72 bayonets, 105 steel helmets, 300 hand grenades and two drums of ammunition.

Australian police had tipped off the Fijian authorities the previous week. A container load of similar weapons, originating from South Yemen, had been found in Sydney ready for transshipment to Fiji.

This provided just the excuse needed by Rabuka's regime to institute a brutal clampdown. The authorities spent a solid week on their investigation before arresting 21 people in relation to gun running. Anand Singh wanted me to become involved because being an outsider gave me a crucial advantage over local lawyers: any harassment of me by the Security Police could develop into an embarrassment for the government. I was not as vulnerable as Fijian nationals.

The next day, before I had spoken with Singh, I received a telephone call from my wife Philippa. She was very concerned for my safety, and read out an article from the *New Zealand Herald.*

'Fiji has declared draconian new laws understood to include the death penalty for possession of firearms, and detention without charge for up to two years. The laws are retrospective to March 1 this year, a move which will ensure that they apply to more than 20 people arrested in connection with large arms caches uncovered on June 6.'

I met Singh that afternoon, taking care to maintain a low profile and stay away from the military on my journey to his offices. We discussed the case and agreed that if the accused were agreeable, I would appear for six of them. We then travelled to Natabua prison to meet the men.

Eight prisoners were brought to a prison interview shack. Two of the prisoners already had counsel. The other prisoners I offered to represent saw the advantages of having an outside lawyer without political or emotional ties to the situation – we shook hands and I left.

Later that day I again pressed my case for admission to the bar with the Fiji Law Society. Though there were few further steps I could take, the fact that I was now involved with the gun running case influenced the local Law Society to look more favourably on my application. I have no doubt that my situation was advanced with the Fiji Law Society when I handed over my letter of reference from New Zealand Supreme Court Justice Graham Speight. He referred to me as a 'bonny fighter' and a 'man for difficult times.' The Rotuma matter was a thorny constitutional affair, however the legal profession was united in its belief that the accused gunrunners required a foreign advocate who was fearless in defence.

I spent Friday through Monday treading water. I lost contact with Anand Singh: he had said he would call me, but there was no communication and I could not contact him. I continued with my efforts to see Rabuka, but had no success on that front. I even attended his church on Sunday, but he was not present, I suspect because he had no desire to be accosted by me.

Finally, on the Tuesday, I appeared in front of the Chief Justice in relation to my application for temporary admission to the Fijian bar. His Honour looked at my papers including a letter of support from the Fiji Law Society. He then said, 'Mr. Harder, your papers look to be in order and I thereby admit you to the Fiji roll of Barristers and Solicitors in relation to the Rotuma sedition case'.

Then there was silence. Suddenly, I was compelled to speak and ask about the gun case. The Chief Justice said he did not understand. I explained how I had filed in relation to the Rotuma case **and** the gun running case. It was obvious that the gun smuggling case was far more politically sensitive than the sedition case. His Honour looked to the Registrar, Ruciati standing at the back of the judge's chambers for help and Ruciati indicated that the affidavit and motion in support of my application in relation to the gun case was at the bottom of the pile.

Fortunately for me, fate had stepped in again and my two applications were physically separated. Because of this, the Chief Justice thought he was only dealing with the Rotuma Chiefs sedition case and not the more sensitive gun smuggling case. Because His Honour had already admitted me to the rolls on the sedition case he now had no choice but to also admit me on the gun case. Progress at last!

Flush with this necessary success, I met that afternoon with a photographer from the *Fiji Times*. Over the weekend I had prepared a letter to the Fiji Solicitor-General and cabinet, protesting about the gunrunner prosecution, particularly the potential that my clients might face retrospective charges under the new Security Decree. The gun running charges carried a maximum penalty of two years' imprisonment, while under the new legislation they might be sentenced to life imprisonment with no chance of parole for a minimum of 25 years.

As a solution I proposed that an amnesty be declared for a time, providing an opportunity for any further arms to be turned in without fear of prosecution, and that the gun runners I was defending face the original maximum penalty of two years in gaol. I thought this was a common sense approach to the problem, but was extremely nervous about sending the letter – was it really wise to propose an alternative course of action to a military dictatorship?

So when I met with the photographer I wanted to make the best use of the media to mitigate the problems I faced. I explained that the letter I was sending might aggravate Rabuka, and detailed the problems I had encountered in arranging a meeting with the leader. After talking it over for a while, I agreed to be photographed with the tabua and kava bunches I wanted to give to the military strongman. I tidied myself up, dressed up in my suit and adopted a suitably serious expression.

Later that day I arranged for copies of my letter to be delivered to the Solicitor-General and cabinet. On Tuesday my picture was published in the *Fiji Times*. Maybe I'm slow on the uptake, but at the time it did not even cross my mind that my picture and the description of the difficulties I was having meeting Rabuka would be offensive. Looking back, I can see that if the presentation of a tabua and bundles of kava root had such cultural significance, then perhaps it could be embarrassing to have your refusal to receive a gift publicly aired. The Brigadier was definitely unhappy, as quickly became clear to me.

On Wednesday morning at 10.30 I was arrested while swimming in the Travel Lodge pool. A tattooed Fijian man wearing an open-necked blue polo shirt, casual pants and sandals simply whispered quietly to me,

'Mr. Christopher, security forces, please come with me. My boss wants to speak with you.'

Dressed in my bathing suit at the time, I insisted on changing into my suit. When I was dressed I picked up the bundle of Kava roots I had bought at the Suva market earlier to give Rabuka. Before leaving the hotel I put all my money on the bar and bought as many packs of menthol cigarettes as I could stuff in my pockets and told a number of hotel staff what was happening, gave them my wife's number in New Zealand and asked one of them to call her collect to let her know what was happening.

I was taken to the Queen Elizabeth Army Barracks in the back of a military Landrover together with my lawyer friend Tevita Fa. The normal rules don't apply when the army runs the show: we were not told if we were being charged with a crime, or even given any indication of what was going on.

We were imprisoned in cells measuring five feet by six feet. I was terrified when I first stepped into mine – the walls were covered with blood. Fortunately, it quickly became clear to me that this was not the result of assaults on prisoners, at least by our captors. Mosquitos fed upon me constantly, and the grisly mess was the result of the incarcerated squashing them on the whitewashed wall.

I felt like I was going crazy. There was nothing to do, no stimulation. I took my credit cards from my wallet and added their numbers, then I folded my visa receipts into playing cards and took myself for a fortune at poker, and I smoked when a guard would give me a light.

The guards strutted around pointing their rifles at prisoners and dry firing them. I repeatedly asked to go to the toilet just for a change of scene. The sports page from the *Fiji Times* was there and I must have read it ten times. I made inane conversation with my captors, knowing they were dangerous men but needing to talk with someone – prisoners were not allowed to converse with each other. Eventually they gave me some shoe polish and I amused myself by polishing my shoes for hours on end. I even resorted to sit ups and push ups, exercising until it hurt (this didn't take long).

Sitting in my cell I wondered if anybody in New Zealand would try to get me out of jail. The only person I thought might be crazy enough to try was the affable Auckland lawyer Lorraine Smith. When I was finally taken from my cell I passed the spot where Fa had been imprisoned and was not sure whether I should be pleased or worried by the fact that he was no longer there. I was worried. I was taken to see an officer who identified himself as Major Mataitene. He served me with an exclusion order signed by Rabuka himself, decreeing that I should be 'excluded forthwith from Fiji' on the grounds that I was a threat to the 'peace and good order of Fiji'. I was then taken to my cell, where I had nothing to do but listen to the Indian prisoners in the cells around me being interrogated by their intimidating guards.

The major had agreed that I could telephone my wife. I told the guards this and while they checked the legitimacy of my request I dozed on a foam rubber mattress, pillow and blanket they provided.

About midnight I was woken to speak to Philippa. She told me there was an Air New Zealand flight from Nadi leaving at five that morning. I checked with my captors, and it was agreed that I would be transported to that flight (Rabuka said I was to be excluded 'forthwith', and forthwith means *immediately*, I contended, and eventually they agreed).

But I did not make the plane that morning, without explanation. A new guard appeared at around two in the morning and suggested that I might see the Brigadier the next morning. I agreed, though my impression was that the choice was not mine to make.

The sun rose at 6.45 am and I spent the day being visited by guards and being told that we would be leaving shortly. At five that afternoon, it finally happened. But I was not taken to meet Rabuka, rather, I was escorted back to my hotel, where the security forces men with me insisted that I listen to an announcement on the seven o'clock news. The Brigadier publicly adopted the suggestion for an amnesty I had made in my letter to the Fiji Solicitor-General and cabinet. There would be an amnesty to allow those with guns to surrender them. The 21 men facing gun charges were to be released. My involvement with the gun-runners was over – against all expectations I had succeeded – or so I thought at the time.

Next, I asked my guards if they would get Fa so we could celebrate together – they had assured me that he was okay. He arrived at the room quickly, and we shook hands, laughed, and bought food and beer on room service to drink with the guards. Late at night Fa stumbled off with most of the security people, leaving two guards to stay with me until I flew back to New Zealand.

The *New Zealand Herald* reported the amnesty thus:

'In a bizarre twist the Fiji government last night announced a thirty day amnesty for illegal arms – a move advocated by a New Zealand barrister on Tuesday hours before he was detained.

The announcement follows the imposition by decree last week of draconian powers of search and indefinite detention without charge. . . Within hours of [Harder's] letter reaching the cabinet, security officers took him into custody.

Last night Mrs Harder said the whole affair had been very worrying but she now expected her husband home on Saturday morning.

I was held in my hotel, nominally under 'room arrest' while I awaited a flight from Fiji. In fact my guards were not unreasonable - I loitered around the hotel and Suva Harbour, I swam from time to time, listened to my Walkman, and exchanged innocuous pleasantries with the cautious hotel staff.

The New Zealand consul came to see me in my hotel 'at the request of the Canadian Embassy'. I did not have New Zealand citizenship at the time, and this was a source of some embarrassment to me because I was eligible for dual citizenship and had not taken it up (I had been concerned that my application might be opposed for political reasons). Nevertheless, I thoroughly appreciated the visit, and felt more confident that I would get back to Auckland in one piece.

I never got to meet Rabuka during my time in Fiji, however the night before catching my flight I did meet with Colonel Konrote, an intense, balding man in a khaki dress uniform covered in ribbons. My guards without explanation took me to him, and he spent several minutes venting his spleen to me about Gagaj Sau Lagfatmaro - Henry Gibson. He told me he would kill Gibson if he ever returned to Fiji, and asked me to pass the message on: I guess that was the purpose of me being taken to see him.

It was obvious that my involvement in the Rotuma sedition trial in Fiji was at an end. My primary concern at that point was getting back to my family alive, but I was worried about the fate of the Chiefs accused of sedition. I argued with Colonel Konrote that they were harmless men who had done little of significance and posed no threat to the regime.

I told him that releasing them was the sensible option to take. At this time he became very angry with me and said that the full force of the law would be used against these men. After I returned to New Zealand I kept a close eye on progress in this matter, and was pleased to hear that all the accused were eventually acquitted.

While talking with Colonel Konrote, I also voiced my concerns about some unsettling rumours I had heard that contrary to Rabuka's statement on the news the previous evening, the 21 men facing the gun running charges would not be included in the amnesty. I wanted to be reassured that this was not the case.

The colonel assured me the brigadier was a man of his word, and undertook to forward to me written confirmation that the amnesty applied to my clients and their co-accused. Typically of the military regime, he never delivered on his promise, but to my relief I was later able to confirm that the amnesty was applied to all.

I left Suva with my guards late in the evening and we drove through the night to Nadi airport arriving about three in the morning. I loitered with the soldiers for a couple of hours. When I readied to board my Air New Zealand flight I asked one of my guards what had happened to my kava roots. With a grin on his face he said, 'the boys had drunk it.' As I walked onto the plane I turned back and shouted, 'Tell them I pissed on it!' The purser was expecting me. He escorted me to my seat, gave me a copy of the *New Zealand Herald* then welcomed me home.

On the plane, a stewardess told me that Prime Minister David Lange had taken Fiji to task for interfering with a New Zealand citizen. I cringed: I was not a citizen at all. I had permanent residence in New Zealand but I had been travelling on my Canadian passport.

When I arrived at Auckland airport the media mobbed me. I felt drained but happy to be home safely, and hugely pleased to see my family again. I didn't want to answer questions at that stage, so put the reporters off with an invitation to call me at home after an hour or two. Later I spoke with them at length, describing what had happened in detail.

Eventually, I went so far as to write a book about what had happened. It goes into a lot more detail than the brief account I have set out here, and is called *The Guns of Lautoka*. The idea of setting out in print what happened first occurred to me when one of my guards made a chance remark about how embarrassing it would be for the regime if I did such a thing. I didn't know about that, but I do know that exposing bullies to the light always makes it more difficult for them to continue their offensive behaviour.

In the book I wrote a story about the Chief Justice told to me by a local lawyer. When the embarrassed Chief Justice received a copy of my book, as a Christmas present he went into his office on Boxing Day and typed me a letter advising me that I had been summarily struck of the Fiji Supreme court rolls for barristers and solicitors.

One of my reasons for writing the book was that my involvement in Fijian affairs did not end at that point. I was, at the time, involved in defending my Fijian associate Mohammed Kahan from extradition proceedings that sought to remove him from London, where he was living, to Fiji to face charges of gun running and treason. At the time Fiji had hanging as the mandatory punishment for anyone convicted of treason.

The Guns of Lautoka was an attempt to bring the nature of the Rabuka military regime in Fiji to the public's attention, and thus assist my friend's cause. In that connection a senior English barrister, Robert Roscoe, of Victor, Lissack and Roscoe, London, made it quite plain to me that had my account been published in Great Britain during Kahan's trial, I would certainly have been found in contempt of court.

The decision of the Bow Street Magistrate in London was to dismiss the Government of Fiji's application to extradite Kahan because he would face execution if he were returned to Fiji.

Kahan's plight was a messy affair. Amidst all the other complications, I was made aware of a terrorist plot to bomb a Japanese airliner flying to Fiji. I first passed the details of this to the Japanese embassy in New Zealand, and then to the New Zealand Police. In 1989 and 1991 while Rabuka was still Prime Minister I tried to return to Fiji. Both my efforts were unsuccessful but I would not give up. One day I would be able to return to Fiji.

A year after my last rejection from Fiji a young Fiji Indian girl came into my office. She had a problem with the University she worked at in relation to a tenure matter. I explained to her that it was not my normal line of work but she insisted that I help her. In due course I met with the University officials involved and the matter was resolved satisfactorily.

On this occasion, like many occasions before, I handled the client's case pro bono (for free). I did this because she could not afford to pay me, she seemed to be suffering an injustice and her case had some merit.

Two months after I solved the Fiji Indian woman's problem she bounced into my office and told me she had come to repay me for my help. Before I could say a word she handed me a letter.

The letterhead read Minister of Home Affairs, The Republic of Fiji. It was a typed letter addressed to me signed personally by the Minister of Home Affairs, Sitiveni Rabuka. In the letter he apologized for my recent rejection from Fiji at the Nadi International Airport. He said that it had been a mistake and that my name should have been taken off the prohibited persons list some time ago and that I was now welcome to return to Fiji.

I looked at the letter in utter amazement. 'Is this a joke?' I asked. 'No', she replied. 'Well how in the hell did you get this?' 'My best friend who is a Fijian is the personal secretary to Rabuka. I asked him for a favour. Here you are Mr. Christopher. What goes around comes around. Thank you for what you did for me!'

Two weeks later another Fiji Indian woman came into my office. She asked if she could hire my services to defend her father who was charged with murder in Fiji. My eyes lit up as she continued to explain her father's predicament to me.

Kalika Prasad had been charged along with his cousin Dhan Raj with the murder of Dhan Raj's wife's lover. Dhan Raj and his wife lived in a little hut on the property. Their marriage was not a happy one. His wife started an affair with her cousin who became her lover. On the night the lover walked up the mountain he was drunk and yelling out that he was coming up to see Dhan Raj's wife. Dhan Raj ran down the driveway to confront the lover. The lover's words provoked and enraged Dhan Raj so he confronted him. Kalika Prasad followed close behind.

The two could be heard screaming and fighting with each other. This was followed by a thud, a cry and another thud. Then all went quiet. Prasad and Raj returned to Kalika Prasad's house where they talked quietly throughout the night. Early the next morning Kalika Prasad drove his truck part way down the track and stopped next to a body. He and Dhan Raj then loaded the dead lover into the truck tray then drove to the seashore where they dumped the body in an irrigation ditch.

The body was found the next day. When the deceased's identity was established his family were spoken to. One member of the family told the police officer that his brother had been having an affair with the wife of Dhan Raj.

Two days later the police came to the house of Kalika Prasad. Prasad and Raj were not home but Raj's angry wife was. She had been crying all night. She told the police officer how she followed her husband part of the way down the drive way and how she had heard the two fight. She heard two noises that sounded like thuds and she saw Kalika Prasad go down the driveway a short time after her husband started yelling and fighting with her lover.

The wife was taken to the police station and a statement was taken and typed on an old style typewriter. In it she blamed her husband and his brother for killing her lover. The next day Prasad and Raj were arrested for murder. They appeared in the Lautoka Magistrates Court.

The Fiji Indian woman having explained her father's predicament pleaded with me to take the case. I agreed subject to her and her husband paying all my expenses including plane fare, hotel and food plus a $100 a day. I also explained that I would have to be re-admitted to the Fiji bar by the same Chief Justice who had previously struck me off the rolls. Only if I could get re-admitted would I be able to appear in court for his trial.

While I prepared my admission papers lawyer and friend Anand Singh would handle my Fiji client Kalika Prasad and he would act for Dhan Raj.

Finally I was back in Fiji. I walked up the stairs to the first floor of the Fiji Government building. I almost felt at home. Quite a relaxed atmosphere exists between the magistrates and lawyers. However, I was astonished to hear how harshly one arrogant and punitive judge spoke to two local Indian lawyers. The rudeness of this particular Sri Lankan judge reminded me of a scuffle I had with a local Auckland judge. Judge Bradford had only recently been transferred to Auckland. He was sitting in the old Number One court in Kitchener Street, when I appeared in front of him for the first time on behalf of a client in a drugs case in late 1987.

I stood up to address the court. 'May it please Your Honour, Christopher Harder, barrister, appearing on behalf of the prisoner.' The judge looked over the top of his glasses and bellowed, 'Is that a hyphenated name?' I looked at him and said, 'I beg your pardon?'

'Is that a hyphenated name?' he roared back. You could hear a pin drop, I quietly put my papers on the table and replied courteously, 'No sir, that is my first and last name'.

'I am not interested in your first name', he snapped back.

My blood was beginning to boil. Here I was being super polite, bowing in a traditional show of respect, calling His Honour sir, and he was bellowing like a stuck walrus. I saw red. Who did this rude old bastard think he was, I thought to myself.

'Excuse me Sir,' I replied, 'I would like to see Your Honour in Chambers, please!' 'You may speak to me in open court Mr. Harder,' he replied.

'No Sir,' I said. The court was full of lawyers. Policemen were everywhere and the press benches were overflowing.

'I wish to see Your Honour in chambers now! Sir.' My request was one that His Honour ignored at his own peril. I had had my share of rude judges. A young lawyer sitting beside me looked up in utter amazement. Kiwi lawyers did not normally stand up to judicial figures in this fashion but I could think of a handful that did, Peter Williams QC, Kevin Ryan QC and Michael Bungay QC.

My anger levels began to rise. I was sure the judge could see what was coming. 'I would like to see Your Honour in chambers, *now*,' I repeated.

With that, the judge declared the court as chambers and said, 'Go ahead Mr. Harder, what is it you wish to say?'

'No Sir,' I replied, 'I require the court to be cleared.' Chambers hearings were usually between the judge, prosecutor and the defence lawyer. By this time the judge realised he had bitten off more than he could chew. 'Clear the court,' he ordered. 'Clear the court!' he repeated. I stood my ground standing silently at the bar table waiting for the moment. My chest began to tighten. A blast was welling up inside me. As the last member of the gallery left the court I began to speak. When I had finished I left the judge in no doubt that he should not speak to me in that tone of voice.

It took me six trips to Fiji, and six visits to the Public Prosecutor's office to meet with the prosecutor in Suva before I finally convinced her that the appropriate charge for my client Prasad to plead guilty to was one of being an accessory after the fact and that Dhan Raj who was provoked should plead guilty to manslaughter. In the end my client Prasad received a 6-month jail sentence but was released within two months. Dhan Raj was sentenced to 5 years' prison for manslaughter and was released after 3 years.

11

The Lawyer's Golden Rule

The 'Golden Rule' in cross-examining a witness is simple: Never ask a question if you do not already know the answer, unless you want a surprise to ruin your case. This case is an example of this principle.

On 18 October 1984, three armed men held up an Armourguard van outside a Foodtown supermarket in Birkenhead, Auckland. They stole $294,529 in cash, forcing the three guards to lie on the ground before driving off in a stolen van. It was the largest sum ever taken in a New Zealand robbery, up to that time.

Initially three men were arrested for the crime. One was Charles (Chas for short) Thomas Willoughby. He was known throughout the criminal community as a master safe-cracker – perhaps the best in New Zealand. He was a cunning, persuasive Maori; with such a gift of the gab he could 'sell ice to the Eskimos'.

This gang of robbers had a high-adrenalin style worthy of a Hollywood screenplay. They were notorious and well known to the police. Often they were under informal surveillance. On one occasion the two safe crackers of the group were dining out in a restaurant. After a few drinks the two schemers started a ruckus in the restaurant, and the police were called. They soon arrived and the two villains' names and addresses were noted, along with the time of the incident.

Soon afterwards, the safe crackers leapt into their Ford

V8 and drove to Taupo at break-neck speed. Having previously established the location and type of floor safe of the supermarket they intended to burgle, the pair used a portable hi-speed drill capable of drilling the safe open. The two burglars were soon in possession of the cash, and wearing night-vision goggles and driving without headlights they dashed back to Auckland at near suicidal velocity. A trip, which normally took three and a half hours, was compressed into an impossible two-hour drive and a ready-made police alibi. When they arrived back at Auckland in record time the cheeky pair caused another scene at another bar, which was once again attended by the police and their timely alibi confirmed.

But the Foodtown robbery was a different matter altogether. The robbers had not established their alibis, and though the robbery was well planned, they left too many clues behind. It did not take the police long to get a fair idea of who might be behind the crime.

Chas Willoughby left New Zealand for Australia. When he arrived, he had a problem: a good deal of his cash remained in New Zealand buried in a hole in the ground at Puhoi, a little village north of Auckland.

Willoughby was looking for somebody who could retrieve his stashed loot from New Zealand. Then he ran into a man in Sydney named David Smaller. Smaller was a good man with a big heart. He was not the most intelligent person on the planet, but he would do anything for a friend. Willoughby befriended Smaller who later agreed to help out his friend Chas recover his 'untaxed money' buried off the main road near Puhoi, north of Auckland.

Willoughby offered Smaller $500 as payment for his trouble. He also promised him that when he had received his cash, he would repay Smaller the $1,600 that he had recently loaned to Willoughby.

David Smaller flew to Auckland, New Zealand, booked a rental car, and began following the detailed instructions Chas had given him. On his journey he took a camera, and at every step of the way took a photograph of what he was doing. He took a photograph when collecting his rental car; he took a photograph of the car itself; he took a photograph of the car by the side of the road, of the fence he had to climb, of the track he had to walk up, of the tree marked with an 'X', and of the old punga log pointing towards the exact spot that Willoughby had buried his treasure.

Digging up the spot in the ground Smaller proceeded to photograph the plastic bag containing three plastic ice cream containers packed full of bundled ten and twenty New Zealand dollar bills, dug up fresh from the ground.

Smaller was meticulous in saving every bit of paper as it related to his adventure. Having retrieved the cash from its hiding place, he returned to his hotel on Auckland's waterfront. Smaller opened the ice cream containers and spread the cash over the bed in his room, piling it neatly into tidy stacks of each denomination. There were 44 bundles of bills. He counted one and found it contained a thousand dollars, so he assumed that he had just unearthed $44,000. He then took a final picture of the money, which was to later cause much interest at his trial. The next day, Smaller made a visit to the Bank of New Zealand in Queen Street and deposited the money in his own name and transferred the proceeds to a Sydney bank without difficulty. He told bank staff that the cash constituted the proceeds of a rock concert for which he had been promoter.

Next, he flew back to Sydney. Smaller met his friend Chas at the airport and described his successful journey. How he had retrieved the money, and then transferred it to his own Sydney bank account without any problems. Smaller had done his job perfectly.

Then Smaller did something very stupid. He gave the film from his camera to his sister to have it developed. The pictures had hardly been produced by the processing machine at a pharmacy before the chemist was on the telephone to the New Zealand police representative in Sydney: the photographs were clearly of a journey to New Zealand, an expedition into the country and the unearthing of a great deal of cash.

The last picture on the roll showed an extremely well endowed naked man taking a picture of himself in front of a full-length mirror with a bed in the background covered with 44 bundles of money. The TV was on in the room and the photograph captured the Television New Zealand logo on the screen.

Before long David Smaller was arrested in Sydney then extradited. Smaller consented to returning voluntarily to New Zealand having been charged with receiving the $44,000 knowing at the time the money had been dishonestly obtained. Willoughby was also arrested and later extradited (after unsuccessfully opposing his extradition) to New Zealand to face trial along with his two other accused robbers.

The presiding judge in the High Court trial was Mr. Justice Pritchard. Eb Leary, one of the great criminal lawyers of his time, acted for Willoughby. Peter Williams QC acted for the second accused robber. My friend Aaron Perkins acted for the third accused robber. I acted for the alleged receiver. David Morris was the Crown prosecutor.

Morris was convinced that my client Smaller had taken his series of photographs as part of some pre-conceived plan to fabricate a defence in the event of anything going wrong.

Morris called Smaller's sister as a Crown witness to give evidence that her brother had given her the film in Sydney to have it developed. The police were weaving a circumstantial case against the four accused. Morris referred the photograph of the well-endowed Smaller with all the money in the background, to the Crown witness.

Then he asked the innocuous sounding question that blew the case wide open for the Smaller defence.

'Why did your brother take that photo of himself and all the money?'

When I heard this, I was ecstatic. I already knew the answer and was intending to ask it if Morris didn't. I had been praying 'my learned friend' would ask the question. Now I could hardly contain my glee.

Slowly with a slight grin on her face the sister began to explain. 'Well, my brother has always said that his girlfriend told him he had everything a woman could want except money. When my brother came out of the bathroom and stood naked in front of the mirror, he saw everything a woman could want – plus the money! He told me he just had to take a photo for his girlfriend.' The jury could not stop laughing at the answer because each of the 12 jurors had a photograph book with the amazing picture in front of them.

I swear that, in the photographs before the jury, Smaller's flaccid penis was at least thirteen inches long. Whether through pity or admiration, Smaller was acquitted. Willoughby was convicted. Aaron Perkins' client received a hung jury verdict because they could not agree on his client's guilt or innocence. Peter Williams QC's client was discharged under section 347 of the Crimes Act 1961 for insufficient identification evidence. After the trial had ended and the courtroom emptied the court crier uplifted the photo booklets given to the jurors. Each booklet had one photograph missing. Guess which one?

12

Rainbow Warrior Spies In DC

In May 1989, George Campanelli left Australia as discreetly as he could. He knew that if he stayed he would soon face charges relating to sales tax fraud: he had apparently been purchasing alcohol wholesale and selling it retail, without paying tax along the way. He was of Australian citizenship and Italian parentage and would soon be wanted in Sydney for an alleged two million dollar sales tax scam.

His first stop was Suva, Fiji where, being a wealthy man, he hired a senior Fiji Indian lawyer to help him try to buy Fijian citizenship. He hoped to avoid deportation to Australia. This attempt failed. From the South Pacific he flew to Los Angeles, California. It did not take Campanelli long to get in with the wrong company. Soon after his arrival, LA police arrested the wanted man when he was found in a drug dealer's mansion under police surveillance for alleged importing of cocaine from Bolivia via Antigua to California. Campanelli sat in the Fresno County jail minus his freedom awaiting probable extradition to Australia. All he could do was phone home collect.

Fortunately for Campanelli he had worked out a clever system to allow him to call anywhere in the world from the prison pay phone. By calling his brother's number, the charming Italian could call collect as many times as he wanted as long as he paid the next person a $100 note to step out of line for him. Each time he spoke to his brother he gave him another number. His brother would then divert the phone to the requested number. Campanelli did the rest.

One such call was to his former lawyer in Fiji. To help his former client pass the time in jail the Fiji Indian lawyer sent Campanelli a copy of a once prohibited book in Fiji, my book, *The Guns of Lautoka*. It was about my arrest in Fiji in 1987 for acting for a number of Fiji Indians charged with gun smuggling.

In June 1989 I was in the middle of New Zealand's biggest murder trial in the nation's capital, Wellington. The Queen v The Wairoa 18 gang-related murder was coming to a slow close. Campanelli had been pushing me for several months to take up his case and come to the United States. He had hired and harassed a battery of lawyers from Australia, Montreal and Rome and now he was trying New Zealand.

A very determined Campanelli called my legal chambers in Auckland, New Zealand where he learned I was in the middle of a murder trial in Wellington. Still he made telephone contact with me shortly after I walked into the lawyer's changing room at the beginning of the lunch break. The call had been diverted from Fresno to Los Angeles then Wellington, New Zealand. Call divert at its best.

This insistent person with the promise of money up front, asked me to travel to California, in particular Fresno, to see him as soon as possible because his extradition clock in the United States was fast running out. After reading *Guns of Lautoka* he had concluded I was the man that should go to Washington, D.C. to plead his case with the US State Department to see if he could be extradited to Italy instead of Australia. He believed he was less likely to go to jail in Italy.

There was one problem, although Campanelli's father was Italian and born in Italy, he was born in Australia, meaning he did not have Italian citizenship and would have to apply. To this end, he hired a bilingual lawyer from Montreal, Quebec to fly to Italy and try to have his Italian citizenship granted urgently at ministerial level. I could only speculate how this was to be achieved.

HIGH COURT, WELLINGTON NZ, JUNE 1989

Obviously a mission to Washington, D.C. for me had the

potential to be an expensive exercise, so I asked for a reasonable up-front non-refundable retainer. It arrived quickly by electronic bank transfer twenty-four hours later. Eager to go, I was obliged to do my closing address before I could contemplate leaving the trial and New Zealand.

With so many accused on trial the closing addresses from the defence counsel plus the Crown prosecutor meant this process could take three or four days. That was too long for my imprisoned Australian Italian client to wait. With the agreement of Peter Williams QC, Mike Bungay QC (God rest his soul), Mike Lane QC and the rest, I approached Chief Justice Eichelbaum, the trial judge, for permission to deliver my closing address before the others. I also sought permission to leave the trial after giving my address, entrusting senior counsel P.A. Williams, QC, to act as my junior on this rare and only occasion. I could do no more; my presence was required more urgently elsewhere.

WEDNESDAY 12 JULY, 1989, LOS ANGELES

I flew directly to Bradley International Airport at Los Angeles via Air New Zealand flight TE6 Economy class on Wednesday 12 July on a flight itinerary organized by prompt and efficient travel agent Susan Judd. I flew Delta Airlines to Fresno on the same day. First I checked into the Holiday Inn Centre Plaza hotel on 2233 Ventura Street, in downtown Fresno. Early next morning I made arrangements to visit the client at the County jail. I had to present my passport and meet with the Sheriff's deputy before I was finally allowed to see Campanelli. He was a short balding little man, with a hairy chest, muscular arms and a confidence that belied the fact he was in a little stainless steel interview room that echoed in an annoying fashion as I listened to what he had to say.

He quickly explained his situation. He was wanted in Australia, for sales tax fraud. So far he had resisted being extradited to Australia for seven months. He had spent most of his money on the local top-gun lawyer fighting, so far unsuccessfully, to try to defeat the extradition order.

Campanelli knew his time for removal was near. Only the

signature of the Secretary of State was missing from the warrant. Once that had been affixed he knew he was on his way back to Australia, and that could be anytime. The court had authorized his removal. My mission was to go to Washington, D.C. and get the State Department to extradite him to Italy instead. As a last option he was prepared to spy for the Americans in the South Pacific if they did not extradite him to Australia. He claimed to have connections in the area to make it worth the CIA's while.

My plane landed at Dulles Airport outside Washington, D.C. at 6:14 am Saturday 15 July 1989 – the weekend of the 200th anniversary of Bastille Day, US time.

I had requested an early check-in and a smoking room with a double bed through the travel agent. I was standing at the front desk waiting to be served by the elderly Indian gentleman speaking on the telephone to a guest. I cast my eyes across the smallish lobby with marble floor.

All of a sudden I caught a fleeting glance of a face in a small group walking by. A second later my eyes flashed back to the point in the crowd where I thought I saw a familiar face, but it was gone. I turned back to the front desk to check-in shrugging it off although the moment stayed in my mind as an unanswered question. Who was the blonde female with the face that seemed familiar?

I picked up my key for room 506 from the receptionist. I was tired from my flight from LA and I wanted a rest. At some stage I knew I had to telephone the District Attorney and the State Department official in relation to Campanelli's case but that would have to wait until Monday. From Fresno I had advised both of them that I would make contact with them once I was settled into my hotel in Washington, most probably Monday 17 July, still two days away.

I slept for five hours before I decided to get up and take the afternoon bus tour around Washington and visit the sights of this famous town. I toured around, snapping pictures of the White House, The West Wing, the Pentagon, the Treasury building, the Obelisk and other points of interest. It was only after I returned to the hotel that I worked out I had no film in the damn camera. I had neither the time nor the energy to traipse around the tourist spots again, so instead I went to the 7 –11 on the corner and purchased a wad of colourful postcards of Washington, D.C. to make up for my blunder.

I was sitting in the Ramada Inn house bar looking at my postcards. The bar was about 15 by 80 feet long with the bar at one end and fireplace and Chesterfield chair at the other end. I sat down in the chair by the fireplace and ordered an orange juice with grenadine and soda. It had been my main drink since I stopped drinking eight years before. For some reason I looked up from my postcards. Maybe it was to look at the barmaid at the other end of the room. Anyway, something else grabbed my attention.

I was suddenly very interested in the four men sitting at the table about fifteen feet away. For a moment I looked sideways at them: I could see three of the men face or side on. One had his back to me. It was not the best of light being in a bar but it was enough to trigger something inside my head. I recognized two of the faces. I was pretty sure from the first look who they were but my mind wouldn't really let it register. I had a very good memory for faces. This I knew from my years of experience working in the criminal courts in New Zealand.

One part of my brain kept trying to tell me something. Another part kept trying to suppress my observation and my preliminary conclusion. I cocked my head to one side again and tried to hear what they were saying but they were speaking at such a low level I could not pick up what was being said. I casually got up and left the bar heading for the elevator.

I tried to keep my mind blank till I got to my room. I wanted to get my camera and go back downstairs before anybody left. If what I was thinking were true nobody would believe me unless I got a picture. My adrenaline was really beginning to pump. I had to think.

I picked up the telephone and dialled the *New Zealand Herald* newspaper in Auckland, New Zealand. I spoke to a senior reporter, Malcolm Pullman with whom I had previously dealt and had a good rapport. I could trust him. Explaining I was in Washington, D.C. on an extradition case, I asked him to ask me no questions, and that in return I would tell him no lies. Can you fax me all the published photographs of the escaped Rainbow Warrior bombers that have been in the newspaper magazine, I asked. I was pretty sure I had seen these faces before in a book on the Rainbow Warrior bombing.

The book had pictures of all of the DGSE bombers and the support players. He asked why I was interested in the Rainbow Warrior bombers I said, 'Just trust me on this one. If you can fax me the pictures and something comes up, you will be the first to know.' It had been four years since French State sponsored terrorists had blown up the Greenpeace ship Rainbow Warrior and killed Fernando Pereira in Auckland Harbour on 10 July 1985. I gave him the fax number of the Ramada Inn. Next I picked up my camera, this time with film in it and went downstairs still wearing the grey striped suit I wore when I wanted to look authoritative.

I sat down at my table in the corner. I took a further look at the group just to be sure. They looked at me realizing that I appeared to recognize someone. Only three of the four-man group remained. When I believed I could get a clear shot of the one who I recognized I raised my camera. The other person I believed I recognized when I first sat down, the tanned one with the dark hair had already gone through to the dining room. I was to later identify this person as likely to be Dormond, the ringleader of the Rainbow Warrior bombing.

As I pressed the button and the flash activated, the men's hands flew up in front of their faces. It was this pose that finally convinced me that I wasn't imagining things. The last people I had seen trying to cover their faces in that manner were Dominique Prieur and Alain Mafart, the two captured French agents in that infamous pose taken by the *Sunday Star* newspaper photographer in New Zealand, then flashed all over the world. This was the first time two faces hired for French state sponsored terrorism had been displayed on the front page of newspapers around the world.

When I put my camera back on my lap, I noticed that some very hard stares were coming my way from the table. Suddenly their voices were raised and I could hear them speaking French now in very serious-sounding tones. I craned my neck forward to try to pick up any fragments of the conversation I could. There was only one word that registered with me as they continued to talk in raised voices and look towards me at the same time. 'INTERPOL'.

Although I had failed French at school I recognized the word INTERPOL as the French inspired, International Police organisation. If these gentlemen were who I thought they were, and they were now talking about me because I had just tried to take their picture, then chances were the conversation went something like this. 'Even if someone has recognized us (wanted French DGSE) they can do nothing unless they get the warrants from New Zealand through INTERPOL. There won't be enough time. We are leaving tomorrow.'

Suddenly the group got up and walked out of the bar across the hall into the dining room. I waited a couple of moments then got up and walked to the hotel front desk to inquire if any fax had come for me from New Zealand. 'No' came the reply.

Disappointed I returned to my room and called Malcolm Pullman again at the *Herald* newspaper in Auckland again. Had he sent the pictures I had requested? No, not yet. It would take some time to find them, he said but he would try ASAP. I then realized that if he sent pictures of the Rainbow Warrior bombers to the front desk of the Ramada Inn and hotel staff recognized them, anything could happen. I asked him to hold off sending me the pictures until I went across the road and booked a second room, this time at the Holiday Inn, so I could use it as a safe fax. It was agreed I would call him back with the number.

I was getting very excited. I had to stay close to the quarry. I went back downstairs. The group including the two I had previously recognized by face, but not yet by name, were sitting in the dining room. I quickly left the hotel running out the front door, across the road and down the street one block to the Holiday Inn.

Pulling out my Visa card I booked a double room for one night. The receptionist handed me my room key. Then I asked her to write down the hotel guest fax number. With a secure fax number in hand I rushed back to the Ramada Inn where I had left the suspects dining. Walking past the dining room entrance I could see them still eating. I quickly went back up to my room, phoned New Zealand again this time giving Malcolm Pullman the new fax number of the Holiday Inn.

After a brief time I went back downstairs to the dining room. I sat three tables away from the group I had under observation. I ordered a coffee and just looked at them. My presence must have made them feel uncomfortable because they declined dessert then got up and walked out of the restaurant. Naturally, I rose to follow them.

Walking through the hotel foyer the group of four men split. Three of them headed for the front door, while the fourth walked back towards the elevator. I decided to follow the three out the front door. I was no more than seconds behind them but when I got outside they had disappeared like puffs of smoke. Real spooky I thought.

Having lost the three I returned quickly to the elevator, where the fourth man was still standing waiting. I stood beside him for a moment looking at him. I had seen the face before. As I stood there I asked myself a question 'Do you really want to do this, Christopher?' Before I could answer the elevator door opened. My number two suspect stepped in first. I paused for a second then as the excitement of the moment got the better of me I followed him into the elevator. There was silence for a couple of seconds as the two of us stood facing each other.

The old lift struggled upwards. Then I looked 'my suspect' in the eyes and with my most authoritative voice with North American accent asked, 'Are you French?' He was startled by my question apparently eager not to have any problems. He quickly responded by raising his hands with fingers spread at chest level in a typical French gesture replying, 'Oui, we are leaving tomorrow.' He emphasized 'tomorrow'. At that the elevator stopped and the door opened at my floor. As I stepped out of the lift I could feel the hair on the back of my neck rise.

My heart was racing faster than it had ever raced before as the elevator door closed behind me and I walked back to my room then picked up the phone and called the Holiday Inn to see if a fax had arrived for Harder. No luck yet.

I knew that I desperately needed a decent photograph of the men I suspected were Rainbow Warrior bomber fugitives from New Zealand on the loose in Washington, D.C. Eventually I struck on an idea.

I went back downstairs to the house bar then wandered over and sat down at the bar making small talk with the African American woman standing behind the bar. I introduced myself as Christopher. Her name was Natasha. She looked to be in her mid twenties. I explained I was a Canadian but that I lived in New Zealand and that I was in Washington as a criminal defence lawyer in relation to an extradition case. I explained that I desperately needed to get a picture of the men that had just left the bar.

The barmaid said they had been around for three or four days. She had served them a number of times. Natasha warmed to the challenge especially when I introduced a US $100 bill. She suggested she get her sister, who also worked at the hotel as a waitress, to stand in front of the targets and get a picture that way. I agreed handing her my Kodak. I strongly suspected two of the group were faces I had seen before. I then left the Ramada Inn and went across the road to my second temporary residence in Washington at the Holiday Inn.

From my temporary second Washington residence I placed a call to newspaper reporter David Hellaby at *The Dominion* newspaper in Wellington, New Zealand. We had worked on various stories from time to time, he as the reporter, and me as the defence lawyer. He knew me well. I asked him for a big favour. Again I requested he ask me no questions but could he fax me any published photographs of the escaped Rainbow Warrior bombers. Why? Asked the inquisitive Hellaby. I told him if he faxed me the pictures then something panned out, I would call him.

The barmaid from the Ramada Inn, Natasha knocked on my hotel room door at the Holiday Inn at 2am. She had finished work and had brought me my camera and film. For the next two hours we tried to find a film-processing place to get the film developed but we were unsuccessful. We even called the *Washington Post* and *Times* looking for a wire photo machine to send the pictures to New Zealand.

About four in the morning I finally received a fax from David Hellaby of *The Dominion* newspaper in Wellington, New Zealand. He definitely won the Rainbow Warrior photo Derby as far as I was concerned because I was yet to hear from my contact at the *Herald*. Hellaby had faxed me two pages with eight photographs on one page and five on the other page out of one of the Rainbow Warrior books. I thought it could have been barrister Colin Amery's book, *Ten Minutes to Midnight*. I knew I had previously seen these very same pictures only a clearer set. The two pages had come from a book published on the Rainbow Warrior bombing in New Zealand. This coincidence no doubt helped me recognize a number of the group in Washington because I had seen their pictures in a group before.

The first faxed page had the header *'Agents of the French Secret service involved in Operation Rainbow'.* The first picture was of Roland Verge, the skipper of the *Ouvea*. He had escaped. Next came Jean-Michel Bartelo, combat swimmer, also escaped. Christine Cabon, the spy who infiltrated Greenpeace offices and befriended a *Herald* reporter, also escaped. The fourth picture was of Gerald Andries, a combat swimmer, also escaped.

At the bottom of the page but not least were the classic *Auckland Star* pictures of Mafart and Prieur with their hand in front of their face in an effort to hide their identity. On the right side of the page there was a picture of a man with a distinctive face, wearing a helmet while water rafting in New Zealand after the bombing, he was known to police as Jean-Louis Dormond.

When Natasha looked at the fax pictures she first identified Roland Verge and Jean-Michel Bartelo, then to my surprise she pointed out the picture of Major Alain Mafart. I had not seen this person myself. She said I have a picture of him on the film in your camera. She was particularly certain it was Mafart when she looked at the fax photo.

I recognized who I believed was Roland Verge, skipper of the *Ouvea*. He was very tall. 6' 2" but now he had a beard of sorts. He had the same curly dark hair. Dormond, chief of the underwater combat school for the French DGSE Secret Service was the first male of the group I recognized sitting at the table in the house bar. The man I followed into the elevator looked like Jean-Michel Bartelo, an underwater combat man and a frogman.

Looking at the faxed copies of the pictures they were not as clear as one would like but I had seen the better copies of the pictures before. I had retained them in my subconscious. When I looked at the Christine Cabon picture, I wrote beside her picture 'glasses, blonde.' This was the face with the blonde hair (wig) I believe I saw in the crowd when I first checked into the Ramada Inn early on Saturday morning 15 July.

Next, at 4.30am, I attempted to call Detective Inspector Allan Galbraith in Wellington, New Zealand. (18 hours ahead.) He had been the officer in charge of the Rainbow Warrior bombers caught by the New Zealand police back in July 1985 and initially charged with murder. Under pressure from France, New Zealand buckled and agreed to a plea bargain accepting two guilty pleas from Mafart and Prieur for manslaughter. They were each sentenced to ten years in jail but soon after, because of a French threat to veto New Zealand produce from the EEC, the two spies were transferred to Hau Atoll, a French Protectorate, less than two years into their sentence

When I first called the Wellington New Zealand Police the telephone just rang and rang. I called back and finally did get the operator. Some hours later I received a collect call from Detective Inspector Galbraith. He was calling from his home telephone after-hours. I explained to him that normally I wouldn't call him from half way around the world in Washington, D.C. unless I had come across something I considered very important. Likewise I explained I was not one that liked to have egg on my face and that what I was about to say, although at first it might seem incredible, had a credible explanation due to what I had personally observed at the Ramada Inn. Then I told him I was fairly certain I had accidentally stumbled across some of the escaped Rainbow Warrior bombers in a hotel in Washington, D.C. coincidentally on the weekend of the 200th Anniversary of Bastille Day 1789.

The Detective Inspector was remarkably calm about the whole thing. I described to him what had happened, what

I had observed and the descriptions of the people I had seen. He said he would have to dig out the files, double-check the descriptions I had given him to see if they fitted, but that from his recall my descriptions were consistent. I gave him my telephone number and room number at the Ramada Inn. I didn't need the Holiday Inn fax anymore.

I asked him to go as fast as he could because the Frenchman I followed into the elevator, who I later identified as Bartelo, had said they were leaving tomorrow. The weekend in Washington and the weekend in Wellington, New Zealand overlapped. The Inspector said he would see what he could do. He told me he would probably have to get cabinet approval or at least some political input before he could set the wheels in motion to have the murder warrants sent to Washington because of the sensitive nature of the subject.

The inspector asked that in the meantime I should try and confirm my identification. I explained to him that I had paid a barmaid to take some pictures but that as it was five o'clock in the morning in Washington and I had, as yet, been unable to see if she had captured any of the bombers on film. It would be several hours yet before I could get the photographs developed. Patience.

At 6.45am, after less than an hour's rest, I got up. I couldn't sleep. I decided to have a quick shower then go back to the Ramada Inn to see if anybody had come down for breakfast so that I could make comparisons with the fax pictures. In my right hand I carried my black briefcase. Inside it were the two pages of Rainbow Warrior fax photos sent to me earlier that morning.

As I walked into the dining room there, sitting bold as brass was the lady with the unusual nose, Christine Cabon, the woman who infiltrated the Greenpeace offices in Auckland before the 1985 bombing. She looked exactly the same as in the picture, except now she was wearing glasses. I sat no more than 6 feet away from her with my brief case up and open on my lap so that I could look at her and her photo. Same lips, same nose and exactly the same haircut and black hair.

This confused me because I had earlier written 'blonde'

and 'glasses' when I first looked at the fax pictures hot off the fax, and in particular at the picture of Cabon, because I had written 'glasses and blonde' in regards to the familiar face I had recognized in the hotel lobby when I first checked into the Ramada Inn. Anyway at this point in time I had absolutely no doubt I had identified Christine Cabon. Of this I was certain. Natasha identified Mafart. I did not see him but we both picked Verge and Bartelo.

The Cabon woman was totally unnerved by my presence because by now it was logical they all knew they had been recognized. While she was eating and I was watching Verge came down for breakfast, took one look at me and walked straight out of the dining room and out of the hotel. Christine Cabon wolfed down her Eggs Benedict then quickly left the restaurant taking the elevator to her room. I waited a little while thinking that somebody else might come down but no such luck. After about fifteen minutes I left to go back to my room.

I waited by the elevator. When the door opened a woman walked past my nose. I recognized her face, but something was wrong. Then when she was about fifteen feet away I realized it was the Cabon woman. She was wearing the same clothes as in the dining room except now she was wearing a blonde wig. Hence the reason I must have written blonde beside her photo from my first sighting of her. She went out the front door. I followed her but by the time I got out the door she, like the others, had vanished.

The clock in the lobby showed 8:05 am as I rushed out the door and hailed a Yellow taxi. The trip to the Columbia photo lab at 1133 15th St. NW Washington, D.C. took less than 10 minutes.

I was at their front door as it opened at 8:30 am in the morning. I explained the urgency. The middle-aged man behind the counter suggested I drop back at 9:15 am and pick up my prints. In the meantime I took the taxi back to the Ramada Inn.

Again I walked into the dining room to see if I recognized anybody having breakfast. Sure enough, there was the little man with those eyes and lips I first saw sitting in the bar the previous afternoon. He looked similar to a not so good helmeted picture of Dormond, head of the underwater combat school for DGSE agents. His picture had been taken accidentally by a tourist standing on the river bank while 'the leader of the pack of French terrorists' went white water rafting in the South Island after the Rainbow Warrior bombing in Auckland.

Shortly after 9:30 am I returned by taxi and picked up the pictures taken the night before by Natasha. I took the taxi back to the Holiday Inn to examine the pictures and compare them with the fax photos. I quickly realized the pictures were too small to compare and that I needed to get the heads enlarged. Two hours later I had my blow up shots in my hand. Although the quality was not 100% rather somewhere between 80% and 90% it was, in my view, a picture of Mafart (a big surprise) sitting beside whom I contend is Dormond, the organizer and Verge, captain of the *Ouvea* yacht used to take the fleeing bombers out of New Zealand, most likely meeting up with a French nuclear submarine and returned to France without a trace until the July 14 weekend in 1989 in Washington, D.C.

I got up early to make an appointment to see Stanley Ifshin of the State Department. Before I left the hotel I called the New Zealand Embassy in Washington. At first I could not get anybody to listen to me but I did, after a time, get to talk to a Dr. Adams at the Embassy. No doubt the call was tape-recorded. I believe he found my assertions incredible and not worthy of serious consideration.

I told him I had pictures that I believed the Embassy might find interesting. What a fuss would be made if French Rainbow Warrior bombers were captured in Washington, D.C. and New Zealand asked for their extradition. Later that morning I telephoned the New Zealand Embassy again and left a message for Dr. Adams to the effect I had left some pictures at the front desk of the Holiday Inn addressed to the New Zealand Embassy, if they wanted to send somebody over to pick them up.

I enclosed the following notes written in my own hand.

Dr Adams, New Zealand Embassy
Enclosed 4 photos and 3 blow-ups plus two pages of faxed copies of pictures supplied by the Dominion newspaper.

(The photos are numbered according to how they were grouped on the sheet of faxed photos.)

Photo Cabon – certain I.D. this a.m at breakfast. Six feet between chairs for 5 minutes fax photo at table (wearing glasses). First sighted, (blonde). Note scratched out 'blonde'. This morning dark hair like photo. Observed her gulp breakfast and go. Sighted leaving hotel 10 minutes later with blonde streaky hair (wig) and wearing same clothes as at breakfast.

Photo Dillais (Dormond) sat directly opposite for ten minutes with fax photo. Would bet the 'bank' same as blow up. Yesterday he mentioned "INTERPOL" in French, after I attempted to take photo of bar background (not developed)

1a Verge, picked as person now wearing moustache and beard, (full). Tall, 6'2" +

Skipped breakfast when he saw me. Have not sighted with fax photo. Pretty certain. Picked by the barmaid and me from fax photo.

Face to face in elevator yesterday, without fax photo. Spoke briefly, question,

"Are you French?" A nervous Frenchman answered, "Oui, we are leaving tomorrow." Bartelo. Barmaid recognized him as the person who had been drinking tonic.

5. Barmaid picked from fax photo. I have no comment unless man on far (blow-up) with waiter in background? (Mafart)

Andries possibly

Bartelo covered face with hand like Mafart photo (5) when I took bar photo yesterday.

It can't all be simple coincidence. For your consideration. As a lawyer, do not think this is a wild goose chase.

When I returned from the State Department and from visiting the District Attorney General concerning my Australian/Italian client I was in a bad mood. I had been unsuccessful in shifting any ground as far as having Campanelli deported to Italy as compared to his being extradited to Australia. This was so because he did not yet have his Italian citizenship although he believed it was only days away.

Nobody from the New Zealand Embassy had called about the pictures so I decided to call a taxi and deliver them myself to the Embassy. To my surprise the trip was less than five minute's drive from my hotel. Obviously they were not keen.

I was like a cat on a hot tin roof. I walked up the road to the 7-11 convenience store down the street past the Ramada Inn. I wondered if 'my murder suspects' were still staying at the hotel or had they left as had been suggested to me by Bartelo in the elevator. I was waiting on the New Zealand Police and the Government to send the murder warrants to Washington via INTERPOL and for something to happen. I bought a 7-11 ham sandwich in one of those plastic containers sealed with plastic. I also purchased a can of Cherry coke and then I walked back to the hotel.

A loud knock at the door woke me. It was 8 o'clock Tuesday morning. "FBI" boomed the voice. I got out of bed, got half dressed then took the chain off the door and let the FBI agent come into the room. He showed me his ID and told me his name was Alan Maxwell. He asked me to have a seat on the bed. 'I'll sit on the chair by the table so I can take a few notes if you don't mind,' he said. 'No not at all,' I replied.

'Well what can you tell me about these Frenchmen you spoke to Inspector Galbraith about?' asked the FBI agent.

'I told Inspector Galbraith the full story, here, I have tape recorded it.' I picked up the micro cassette recorder and handed it to the agent. 'Do you simply want me to play it back for you?' 'No, I'd rather you tell me again from the beginning if you don't mind.' I had observed the standard practice of policemen around the world asking a suspect to repeat a story over and over to test the variations of the alleged incident.

FBI Agent Maxwell said they would have to interview hotel staff at the Ramada Inn seeking verification of my identification. He asked for my home address and phone number in New Zealand. He also asked if he could have some of my pictures. He thanked me again, and then advised me that I should leave the matter in the hands of the FBI from that point on. I can't say I was unhappy to do so.

Then before we parted we had an informal chat and he revealed that he had been a criminal defence lawyer in Louisiana before he joined the FBI. With that we shook hands and parted company. I made immediate plans to fly to Pittsburgh and then on to Hamilton, Ontario to visit an old school friend before flying on to Vancouver, British Columbia to meet up with my wife, then have a little holiday in Hawaii before returning to New Zealand and the daily grind of the criminal law.

Before I left Washington I went back to the State Department. When I advised the State Department staff member of my sightings of the French Rainbow warrior bombers in my hotel, he showed little interest. New Zealand was off America's best friends list because of our anti nuclear stance taken by a brave David Lange. I also met again with the District Attorney handling my client, Campanelli's case. His last appeal had been heard. The Secretary of State had signed the removal warrant. Unless that was revoked Mr. Campanelli would shortly return to Australia.

This was all the more certain when Campanelli's Montreal lawyer called from Italy to say his citizenship had not yet been granted and might not be for a while yet. This information effectively torpedoed my mission on behalf of my client.

I stayed at the Holiday Inn that evening, too unnerved at this point to return to the Ramada Inn.

I left Washington very shortly after that, and did not see my French 'friends' again. As you are no doubt aware, the escaped Rainbow Warrior bombers were not arrested in Washington DC. In a telephone conversation with FBI agent Maxwell some weeks later he confirmed that they had obtained a positive I.D. from the hotel staff and that the suspects had been traced back to a travel agency in New York. By the time the New Zealand murder warrants had arrived in the United States the French had already left the country. Despite Detective Inspector Galbraith's best efforts bad timing meant the bombers got away again.

My client Campanelli was ultimately extradited back to Australia where he pleaded guilty. Due to the time he had spent in custody in the United States he was released on bail within months of his being sentenced to 18 months in Pentridge Prison.

Twelve years later on July 14th 2001, Bastille Day, the *New Zealand Herald* published the following story;

French Agents "seen in US"

A new book claims four saboteurs wanted by New Zealand met openly in Washington, says Eugene Bingham.

An Auckland lawyer may have sighted French secret agents wanted for the Rainbow Warrior sinking in a Washington, DC hotel four years after the bombing, according to claims.

Christopher Harder will claim in a book to be published this year that he stumbled across four fugitive agents during a visit to the United States in July 1989.

Inquiries by the Weekend Herald have confirmed that New Zealand Police faxed copies of the arrest warrants to the Federal Bureau of Investigation, but none of the Frenchmen could be located.

Authorities were unable to confirm or discard Mr Harder's claim about their identification.

Up to 11 agents of the French Secret Service, the DGSE, were implicated in the fatal mission to sink the Greenpeace ship in the Waitemata Harbour in July 1985.

Only two, Captain Dominique Prieur and Commander Alain Mafart, were arrested and faced New Zealand justice. They pleaded guilty to manslaughter and were sentenced to 10 years imprisonment, though both were home free in France by 1988.

Mr Harder said that he was in Washington dealing with an extradition case when he saw a group of French people in his hotel, the Ramada Inn.

"Two of the faces I recognised from somewhere" said Mr Harder. "I knew instantly who they were, but my mind wouldn't really let it register."

He went upstairs to fetch his camera, and then snapped a picture of the group in the hotel's bar. They were upset by the attention and moved to the restaurant.

Later, he followed one of the men out of the restaurant and asked if he was French. "He replied, Oui, we are leaving tomorrow," said Mr Harder.

After asking friends in New Zealand to fax over photographs of the wanted agents, he coaxed a barwoman to take more pictures for him. He also contacted the head of the police investigation, Detective Superintendent Allan Galbraith.

The next morning, he sat near a French woman at breakfast in the Ramada. Mr Harder identified one of the faxed photographs as Christine Cabon, who infiltrated Greenpeace in Auckland under the alias Frederique Bonlieu.

He claims the other people were DGSE agents Roland Verge, Louis-Pierre Dillais and Jean-Michel Bartelo or Gerald Andries. A man photographed by the barwoman could also be Marfart, said Mr Harder.

Mr Galbraith told the Herald he had asked the American authorities to investigate after taking a call from Mr Harder.

"We got a response some time later that they had a look at it and had not found them, which was not unreasonable," said Mr Galbraith.

"To the best of my recollection, the Americans were not able to actually confirm who they were."

The FBI agent who dealt with the case has since left the agency, but it is understood that by the time he traced the French diners they had left the country.

The Herald requested copies of police documents relating to the incident but they have not been able to be found.

Detective Inspector Maurice Whitham, who was on the investigation team, said copies of the arrest warrants for Verge, Andries and Bartelo were faxed to Washington but the French people were never located.

Mr Whitham said he had doubts about the alleged sighting because it was difficult to identify people from photographs.

A plastic surgeon that has given evidence in court about identification based on computer comparison techniques has analysed the pictures. Dr Chris McEwan said he had looked at the photographs of the people alleged to be Marfart and Dillias and, while there were problems with the quality of the pictures, there were similarities in facial features between the pair in the photographs and confirmed pictures of the agents.

"I could not be absolutely certain it was them, but there's enough there to be strongly suggestive," said Dr McEwan.

Even if the four were the wanted agents, however, it is not certain they would have been brought back to face charges. Two years after Mr Harder's encounter, Andries was arrested in Switzerland.

But after police headed by Mr Whitham had prepared a case for Andries extradition the Government decided not to pursue it and he was freed.

Three weeks after my return to New Zealand I received a letter from the Chief Justice, Eichelbaum J. For a moment I felt trepidation, because of my departure immediately after finishing my closing address at the Wairoa murder trials, but remembered His Honour had given me permission to do so. Opening the letter, I was pleasantly surprised. Dated 1 August 1989, Chief Justice's Chambers, Wellington, It read,

It was good of you to send me a copy of your book, The Guns of Lautoka. I am looking forward to reading it when I take a break shortly. It will be a pleasant memento of "The Queen v 18" You will have been rightly pleased with your client's total acquittal.
With good wishes, yours sincerely,
Thomas Eichelbaum.

CHRISTOPHER HARDER 129

Above: Christopher's father Lloyd Jacob fishing with his brothers (L to R) Brian, electrician and union official, Paul, marine biologist & sculptor, and twin brother Gregory, self employed in computer sales.
Right: Christopher and wife Philippa.
Below right, Grandfather Jacob Henry Harder, and Left, grandfather and grandmother, Margaret, with Lloyd as a young child & his sister.

Back Row - l to r: Justices Henry, Smellie, Tompkins, Robertson & Temm
Middle Row: Justices Wylie, Hillyer, Anderson & Thomas
Front Row: Justice Barker, Chief Justice Eichelbaum and Justice Thorp

Above: Renee Chignell outside High Court, 1989, *Auckland Star*. Right: Neville Walker with detective Colin Mitchell

Left: A clearly relieved Neville Walker after being released on bail on 23 December 1990, following seven bail applications. *Auckland Star.* Right: My childhood mentor Silas Huckleback from Lynn Valley, B.C. Canada.

Below: the Rainbow Warrior bombers in Washington DC. Alain Mafart is at left.

132   THROUGH THE LEGAL LOOKING GLASS

Detectives on the Plumley-Walker case, Ron Cooper (left), John Dewar and Crown prosecutor Simon Moore (right). *Auckland Star*

Below: Neville Walker, flanked by defence counsel Jim Boyack and Chris Harder (right), briefs reporters after being found not guilty of murder

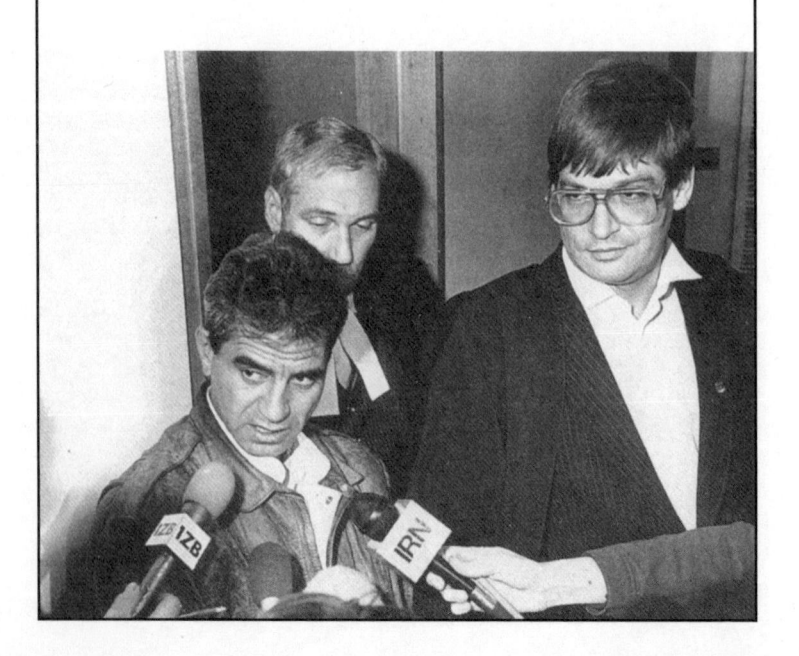

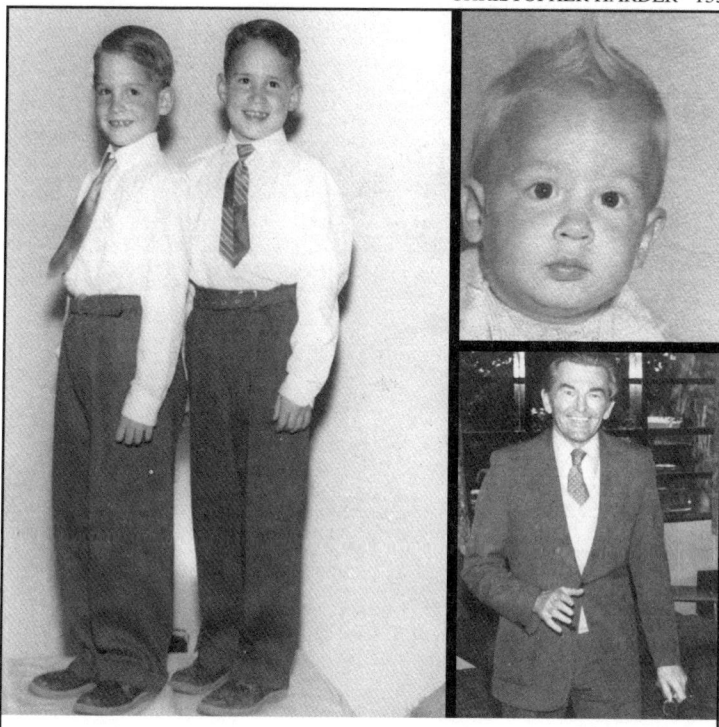

Above left, Twins Christopher and Gregory; Right, top, Christopher as a baby; Below, Best friend Len Simpson;
Bottom: My father, Lloyd, and mother, Elma (<u>El</u>izabeth <u>Ma</u>rion), holding the twins.

134 THROUGH THE LEGAL LOOKING GLASS

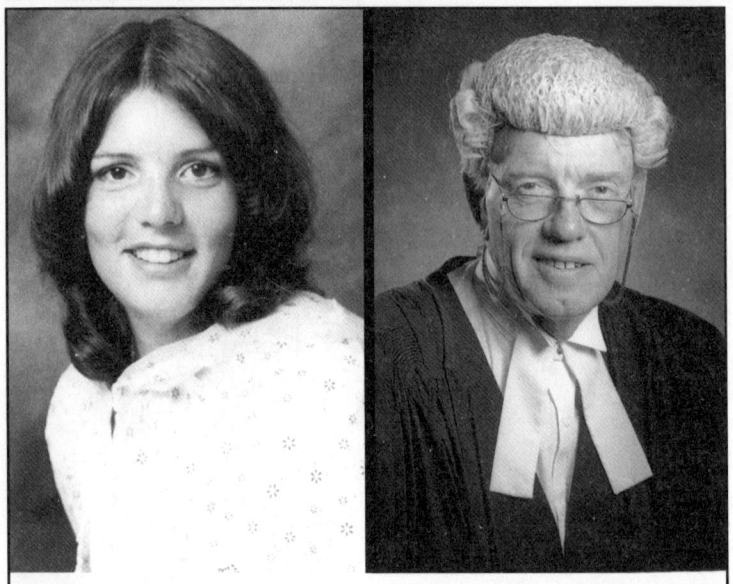

Top, left, Yvonne Bennett. Right: Justice David Morris, the former Auckland Crown Solicitor; Below, Warwick Bennett, later found guilty of Yvonne's murder. *NZ Herald*

13

The Plumley-Walker B&D Saga

Peter Plumley-Walker was a 56-year-old accounts clerk who worked with a Queen Street travel agency in Auckland. He was diligent. He spoke with a plummy English accent and wore an extravagant white handlebar moustache. In his spare time he umpired club cricket matches, and was secretary of the Auckland Cricket Umpires' Association. The public face of Peter Plumley-Walker was conservative to the point of being stuffy.

On Friday 27 January 1989, Peter Plumley-Walker disappeared. That afternoon he had been divorced from his wife Pauline. Plumley-Walker had always been very committed to his family, had regularly spoken about his wife and children with his few close friends and associates, but seldom discussed the fact that he had separated from his wife in 1980, and lived in a small Herne Bay flat by himself.

The uncontested divorce proceeding had been brief, taking from 10.00am to 10.15am before the Family Court. Peter stumbled from the court with tears in his eyes, and his now ex-wife described him as 'more upset than I have ever seen him in his life'.

On the 28 January, Peter Plumley-Walker's car was found burned out in Ellerslie, a suburb of Auckland. His daughter and brother were notified, and after failing to locate him they reported him missing. On Thursday 2 February a jet boat driver found a body a couple of kilometres downstream of Taupo's Huka Falls. The feet were tied together, there was a rope around the neck, and the hands were tied behind the back. Within 36 hours the corpse was identified as Peter Plumley-Walker.

In a small, conservative country like New Zealand, this was big news. The dead man had not been a luminary in the community, but many knew him. Newspapers were full of the story and it was not long before details of Peter Plumley-Walker's private life began to come to light.

Suspicious bruising on the body tended to confirm the stories that were circulating that the umpire had been an enthusiastic practitioner of bondage and discipline. Auckland's underground sex world wanted nothing less than a rapid police investigation to avoid close scrutiny of their activities – all involved were therefore more than happy to help the investigators conclude their inquiries quickly.

It quickly became clear to police that the dead man was heavily involved in this shady scene, so chances were the death was either the accidental result of a bondage session gone wrong, or was a deliberate murder. When it was confirmed that Plumley-Walker had been dumped over Huka falls weighted down by a concrete block, the investigation began to focus on murder.

I followed the scandalous death of the Auckland cricket umpire with interest. In early February 1989 shortly after the body was discovered, there was a knock on my door from a husband and wife who ran a tow truck business in West Auckland. She had been involved in bondage and discipline because she had a kinky side to her personality. To attract other 'sex players' she had advertised in the *Truth* newspaper. When the police searched Plumley-Walker's Herne Bay flat, they found this woman's number, along with the name, Renee Chignell.

First of all, the investigating officers searched the couple's home and their tow truck yard with a search warrant. At the house they found all manner of bondage gear including leather clothing, sex toys, pornographic books and hardcore sex videos.

The police also found some blood on a curtain in the lounge that the couple could not explain. In a trailer on the property the police found a concrete block very similar to a block that was found below the Huka falls. Rope was also found on the property of the same type as the rope found tied to the concrete block at the bottom of the falls.

The couple had no alibi, because, they claimed, they had driven from Henderson, where they lived, to a motel just south of Hamilton on the day Plumley-Walker disappeared, to arrange a bondage session there that was to be organized by mobile phone. For some reason the other party did not make contact and the B & D session fell through.

Because the couple never made further contact with or met the anonymous client, they had no way of verifying their location on that day. In the wife's appointment book police found a potentially damning entry for the day Peter Plumley-Walker disappeared: 'Peter, 2pm, $200.' The suspects claimed this related to another client, but the last sighting of Plumley-Walker on the day he disappeared had been at the Ponsonby Bank of New Zealand withdrawing $200 at 2pm. The police told the couple they were in trouble and that they should get a good lawyer. They came to me.

At the time I genuinely believed they might be the responsible parties, and that their denials were just for show. At first glance there appeared to be a growing pile of evidence pointing to their involvement, but the couple were adamant that they were innocent, so I started poking around. Slowly, things began to unravel. First, it turned out that the rope found at their home wasn't the same as that found below the Huka Falls.

Next, an explanation emerged for the blood on their curtain – the woman's visiting mother had suffered a nosebleed, but not mentioned it to the couple. The big break, though, was when we worked out that while the wife had been conducting her bondage session with 'Peter 2pm $200' in a motel in West Auckland, the husband had been waiting idly for his wife in a nearby park. He had stopped and chatted with an off duty policeman walking his dog. Miraculously, this man remembered the incident: The off duty police officer effectively gave my clients an alibi taking them out of the suspect pool and me out of a high profile murder case.

The police eventually identified alternative suspects from a service station security videotape, recorded near Taupo during the early hours of 28 January. Reasoning that it was possible Plumley-Walker was taken to Taupo in his own car; investigators scoured the security tapes from every service station between Taupo and Auckland. A recording obtained from the Wairakei service station showed Plumley-Walker's distinct gold station wagon with two passengers – a short, teenage girl with blonde hair, and a man with grey hair in his late 20s or early 30s, wearing a distinctive Triumph motorcycle singlet with a picture of a Hog riding a Harley Davidson motorcycle.

The blurry videotape pictures roughly matched the appearances of two people who had already been questioned in connection with the case: Neville Walker and Renee Chignell. During the initial search of Plumley-Walker's flat police found a piece of paper with the name Renee along with phone number and address and what looked like an appointment time for 4 pm. While Walker and Chignell had openly admitted that they ran a bondage and discipline business from their Remuera home, they denied knowing the dead man.

The police were not satisfied with the initial responses they received from the couple so they went back and questioned them again: their outright denials continued. Investigators searching their Remuera home found the distinctive Triumph Singlet worn by Walker shown on the videotape.

When this information was passed onto Renee Chignell, she began to crumble. Walker's denials of any involvement continued, but Renee Chignell changed her story. Peter Plumley-Walker had died in bondage, she said. He was midway through a session he had pre-booked with her, and for which he had paid $200. She did not know what had caused his death, but once she and her boyfriend had established that he was dead, they knew they were looking at some serious trouble so they decided to take the body to Taupo in Plumley-Walker's car and dump it over the Huka Falls.

Upon returning to Auckland the couple parked Plumley-Walker's car at the back of a warehouse in the industrial area of Ellerslie where they poured petrol on a newspaper then set it alight inside the car.

Renee Chignell wanted to make one thing perfectly clear

to her police interviewers. She said she always told her clients if they felt anything going wrong during a session all they needed to do was say, 'mercy, mistress, mercy', and she would immediately release them. Plumley-Walker had not said the magic words.

On 16 February 1989 Renee Chignell and Neville Walker appeared before the district court at Auckland. Chignell was charged with the murder of Peter Plumley-Walker at Auckland, and with wilful damage to his car. Walker was charged with being an accessory after the fact to the murder at Auckland, as well as with wilful damage. They were both bailed from Mount Eden prison within a week, but the time Chignell spent there – and what she said to a fellow inmate, soon to be called witness A, was to later be of crucial importance during the murder trial.

On Saturday 29 April 1989, before the lower court proceedings had moved any further forward, Renee and Neville each received an unexpected shock. When they reported in to their local police stations, as per the conditions of their bail, they were told that the pathologist had delivered his report on Plumley-Walker's body. Gravel had been found in the corpse's stomach. The police interpreted this to mean he had been alive when they threw him over the Huka Falls.

The two were then re-arrested and held in custody overnight. Chignell was now facing a charge of murder at Taupo, not murder at Auckland, but for Neville Walker the development was more serious. Instead of him being tried as an accessory after the fact to murder at Auckland, he now found himself facing a charge of murder at Taupo.

While he was waiting in the holding cell a little weed of a person, later identified in court as witness B, was placed in the custody cell with Walker. Initially 'B' had been arrested for the theft of a cash box from the nightclub next to the Wharf police station. He denied he had taken it. When he was searched he was found to have several hundred dollars in his underwear. When asked where he got the money he told the officer Detective Marty Ruth had given him it. He said he was a police informant. Soon after 'B' appeared in court the next morning along with Walker, he was released on bail.

Once outside the courthouse 'B' beat a fast track to the Auckland Central police station where he met Ruth. He then proceeded to tell Ruth how when he was in the cells, he had met Neville Walker. He informed Ruth he had befriended Neville Walker who told him he was in for murder.

'B' also claimed Walker told him (a complete stranger) that when he and Chignell threw Plumley-Walker's body over the Huka Falls the body was still twitching, the inference being Plumley-Walker was still alive when he was thrown over the falls. 'B' was then put on the witness protection programme. He was to be used as a witness of truth against Walker to support the Crown case that death occurred at Taupo by drowning. From the police and the Crown's point of view this equalled murder. 'B' was now a very important witness.

By the first week in September 1989 I had a new 'civil' client. A retired, Jewish businessman named J had called at my office to ask me to take on his case, He wanted to sue his neighbours for trespass and nuisance.

J's wife had died of cancer and he claimed his neighbour's children had deliberately destroyed his wife's peace and quiet the last year of her life and he wanted to make them pay. I explained that this was not my normal line of work. He insisted. He said he wanted me because I had a reputation of being a mean bastard and just the fact that he had hired me would give them a fright. I tried to dissuade him again by naming a high fee. I said to take on a case like that I would require him to agree to pay a significant pre trial fee and that I would want at least half of it upfront. Instead of frowning and walking away, he smiled and said, 'I will put a cheque in the mail this evening.'

I contacted Karen Soich, by then an intellectual property and entertainment lawyer. I would engage her to help with J. The client gave one instruction. He wanted the papers filed and served before Christmas. We began to work on the case. The balance of the pre-trial fee would be paid once the papers had been served on the neighbours.

Three weeks later I was sitting at my desk reading a client's file when the telephone rang. My secretary Debbie took the call. It was a clerk from the Auckland District

Court offering me a little legal aid job – the charges were driving under the influence and refusing to accompany police officers. In general I am not enthusiastic about legal aid work, and it was most unusual for the District Court to call and offer me a legal aid assignment, but because I did not want to offend the court staff, I said yes.

'Make an appointment for the client within the next couple of days,' I told my secretary before I returned to reading the file on my desk. A moment or two passed before I suddenly asked Debbie to repeat the name of the new client.

'What did you say his name was?'

'Neville George Walker,' came the reply.

Suddenly something clicked. I had heard that name before on the radio in relation to the Peter Plumley-Walker murder case. I turned back to my secretary. A big smile broke across my face.

'Call him right now!' I insisted. 'Let's get him into the office today.'

Renee Chignell's father had retained (hired and privately paid) Stuart Grieve and Paul Davison, two of the top criminal barristers in town, to represent his daughter as soon as he learned she was charged. Ray Parmenter, on the other hand, represented Neville Walker, courtesy of the Government paid legal aid.

If Walker felt the need to see another lawyer about a driving charge, perhaps all was not as well as it should be so far as Mr. Parmenter was concerned. Maybe my involvement with the Plumley-Walker case was not over yet after all. Little did I know at the time just how involved I was fated to become, and at what massive cost to me personally and financially.

Neville Walker was a man in his 30s of medium height with dark hair heavily streaked with grey. When I first met him at my office in Remuera he wore a moustache. Talking with Neville Walker it quickly became clear to me that he was not the brightest boy on the block, yet he seemed to have a streetwise cunning. He took a long time to respond to some of the questions I had put to him, and his understanding of the legal process and legal concepts was rudimentary to say the least.

Instead of sitting and talking in my office I decided to take Walker for a long walk around Remuera while the two of us discussed his overall legal situation. Walker was not happy with Parmenter because he had told him to go off and get another lawyer on legal aid to deal with his most recent traffic charges. This made Walker feel unwanted and resentful. Just as day follows night the conversation moved on to the murder case.

'If Ray Parmenter is acting for you on the murder charge, why isn't he doing this as well?' I enquired of Walker.

'I went in to see him when it happened, but he just told me to go get legal aid, and the clerk from the District Court told me to see you, so here I am.' It was clear to me that Walker's relationship with Parmenter was less than solid. It was obvious to me that Walker's case would be a 'major' performance that would require a great deal of time and effort. This was all the more so when one realized that senior Crown prosecutor Roy Ladd was leading the prosecution. Ladd, who was reputed to have a heart of ice, liked high profile murder cases, and he seldom lost. And this case was definitely going to be high profile.

After spending several hours with Walker he innocently asked me if I wanted to do his murder case. I gave a prompt 'yes' in reply. To that end I helped him write a letter that he signed and sent to the Registrar of the High Court advising that he wanted to change his lawyer from Parmenter to Harder.

Immediately the system reacted negatively to the request despite the fact that the legal aid rules allowed a person charged with murder to have counsel of his choice. I guess it was no real surprise and I should have expected the opposition given Parmenter's high standing in the legal profession against my maverick background. Parmenter made a complaint to the Law Society. Past President Colin Nicholson QC was assigned to interview Walker and to find out who he really wanted to defend him at his murder trial. This whole proceeding smelled a bit funny to me, as if the 'establishment' was trying to stop me taking on this high profile case, so I asked Walker to take a tape recorder with him to the meeting and to record what was said to him by Nicholson QC.

When Walker first met the Law Society appointed barrister, Walker told him he wanted to tape their conversation. The reply was sharp: 'You don't need to do that!'

Despite that advice Walker acted on my instructions and turned on the tape recorder. This limited the vocabulary Nicholson QC could use in relation to me. In the end Walker convinced Nicholson QC that he wanted me, and that was the end of the matter.

Roy Ladd had been a senior Crown prosecutor at Meredith Connell in Auckland for years. He expected one day to be *the* Crown solicitor, and further down his career track, a High Court judge. To some, Ladd seemed a pompous, arrogant man. I remember one occasion when Peter Williams, Kevin Ryan and I were conducting a murder trial in the old High Court on Eden Terrace (now Auckland University's Law School). During the afternoon tea break, Williams discovered we had no milk for our afternoon tea.

'Go and borrow some milk from the Crown room, Harder' blurted out Williams. I was the junior lawyer of the three, so that sort of thing fell to me. I walked the short distance down the hall to the Crown room. There in the middle of the room stood Roy Ladd surrounded by five junior prosecutors.

Normally the young prosecutors were quite friendly towards me whenever I walked into the Crown room. Today, with second to 'top dog' Roy Ladd present, the junior lawyers ignored me. Roy Ladd had significant mana to some, and he exuded authority.

'Have you guys got any spare milk?' I asked. Then without waiting for a reply I walked over to the fridge and opened the door.

'No, we don't!' replied Roy Ladd. As he said that, I could see six bottles of milk in the fridge but I said nothing.

'Okay.' I replied with a straight face. 'Sorry I didn't realize you were so short of milk.' This was despite evidence to the contrary. I left the Crown room empty handed but my mind was working overtime on revenge. 'I'll fix that mother...!' Williams and Ryan were forced to drink their tea black. 'Don't worry boys there will be plenty of milk tomorrow, I promise!'

That night I plotted my revenge for the humiliation I

faced in the Crown room at the tongue of Roy Ladd. I called my sister-in-law Rosemary Sharp, then a design lay-out artist. I asked her to do up a special clever design for me on short notice. I supplied the copy. Then I bought twelve crates of milk (it still came in bottles, back then). Once the labels had been printed out on the computer the two of us cut them out. Next I glued each label by hand on to each of the one hundred bottles of milk I had purchased for Roy Ladd.

Early the next morning I parked my car loaded with crates of milk outside the High Court. The normal court milk run had already been made. The time was 6:45 am. Then carefully, without witnesses, I replaced the daily supply of milk for court staff and judges with my specially labelled brew. When the building was finally unlocked I swooped upstairs carrying two crates at a time into the unlocked Crown room. Bad security. I put the bottles from the first two crates in Roy Ladd's fridge. I then went back downstairs and carried up the two remaining crates. These I left in the middle of the Crown room. I had a big grin on my face as I walked quickly out of the unguarded Crown room.

Roy Ladd was apoplectic when he discovered that all the milk available at the High Court sported bright pink labels illustrated with an anatomically approximate rendering of a cow's udder. He was even more distressed when he read the *Auckland Star*'s account of the incident:

> **Counsel would not be cowed**
> *The cream of the criminal bar has sprung a surprise on Crown lawyers at the High Court in Auckland – of a dairy variety.*
> *No fewer than 100 bottles of milk were delivered to those gentlemen the other morning, complete with labels reading: "Roy the Boy Big (Udder) (including a picture of a cows teats) Dairy (Sharemilkers) Company – Official supplier to the New Zealand Criminal Bar."*

Word had got around the court that a defence lawyer's request for a bottle of milk from the Crown Prosecutor's fridge had been turned down. There wasn't enough to go around, and that counsel (Harder) who had been so told, arranged for an early morning milk delivery that left the Crown room overflowing with a fridge full of milk plus several extra crates sitting squarely in the middle of David Morris' Crown room, then under the temporary control of Roy Ladd.

Colleagues said, 'Mr. Ladd was as surprised (and dismayed), as they were. They are advising defence lawyers to pull the udder one.'

In 1989 Stuart Grieve and I concluded that a meeting Ladd and the police had with the pathologist in Rotorua had the potential to turn Roy Ladd into a defence witness. This was because the pathologist initially gave a preliminary finding consistent with 'death by hanging at Auckland' and then seemed to switch his finding to 'death by drowning at Taupo.'

Grieve (acting for Chignell) wrote to the Crown Solicitor, David Morris demanding that Ladd be taken off the case. I had a witness summons drawn up and signed by the registrar. Next I arranged for an attractive blonde legal clerk named Denise from my office, to serve the summons on Mr. Ladd when he came out of court for the day. When he finally emerged Denise handed the summons to Roy Ladd.

For a moment Ladd looked like a stunned mullet, then he turned and stormed off. Inside the Crown room he could be heard swearing, 'That bitch in pink from Harder's office just served me with a witness summons!' In due course Ladd was replaced with another prosecutor, one from Wellington. His name was Bruce Squire. He was not then a QC but he was a good friend of the Solicitor General. In hindsight I believe the unorthodox action of the defence summonsing Crown Prosecutor Roy Ladd effectively removing him from the case caused serious back room ructions.

First trial

At the first trial the Crown used two secret witnesses – 'A' and 'B' as the main thrust of its case. Witness A was an attractive blonde who had been arrested and jailed, bail being refused, in relation to heroin importing charges. While at the women's division at Mount Eden prison, she had befriended young Chignell at the behest of a prison guard who asked her to look after the young dominatrix charged with murder.

Witness A was to later tell her lawyer that Chignell had confessed to her that Neville Walker had actually beaten Plumley-Walker when he was tied up in bondage with a dog chain around his neck attached to the ceiling and his arms and legs strapped spread-eagled against the wall, and that he had died.

Witness A said she came forward as a witness because she didn't think it was fair for Chignell to get the blame if Neville Walker actually did the deadly deed. Under cross-examination she admitted that it was only after she told Detective Colin Mitchell of the alleged admission she claimed Chignell made to her, did the police drop their opposition to her bail.

The initial prosecutor Roy Ladd had signed his consent to the bail memorandum allowing Witness A be released on bail despite strenuous previous opposition on repeated occasions by the police. The Crown alleged they had a strong case of heroin 'import and party to supply', against her. The detective she had 'sung' to was the same Colin Mitchell who was tasked with looking after witness B.

B gave evidence at the first trial that Walker had told him in the Auckland District Court custody holding cell that Plumley-Walker's body was still twitching when he and Chignell threw it into the water. This made B the key Crown witness. The question was, could the jury believe him? Had the jury been told everything so that they could make an honest assessment? The Crown submitted they had. Grieve and I disagreed. Something was being hidden. Both Grieve and I had a field day in cross-examining B.

B had a long list of dishonesty offences but he still insisted he was telling the truth about what Walker said to him. He also stated under oath that he had not received any money or other benefit from the police. I was certain this was a lie I just couldn't prove it. B said he was giving evidence because it was the 'right thing to do'. 'What happened to Plumley-Walker shouldn't have happened,' he said.

Prior to the start of the trial I made a written request addressed to the Crown asking that they supply me with a copy of the complete witness B file. I was advised that no such file existed. Despite that, Grieve and I both thought that we had done a fair job of destroying B in the witness box. Time would tell.

Next Grieve cross-examined the detective who interviewed Chignell. The detective alleged Chignell had confessed to him that she had pulled the chain hooked around Plumley-Walker's neck and attached to the ceiling tight so that his toes could barely touch the floor. The detective stated Chignell told him that she had left Plumley-Walker hanging like that when she left the room to answer the front door bell.

Surprise, surprise. Her mother had shown up unexpectedly with fish and chips for dinner. When her mother finally left the flat Renee and Neville went back into the secret dungeon where they found Plumley-Walker's limp body hanging. His face and hands had turned blue. The rest is history.

Grieve's job was to discredit the police officer so that his evidence was not believed or relied upon by the jury. Grieve used details contained in a newspaper article I had given him the night before. It reported that police had found a wallet and other items along a road near the Huka falls. This part of the article was attributed to the police officer Grieve was presently cross-examining. The police officer agreed with the facts. He also agreed he had given the reporter those details. Grieve continued to use details from the article with which the police officer had associated himself.

When Grieve put it to the officer that details of the sexually explicit photographs of prominent people found at the flat and mentioned in the second part of the article, had also been supplied by the witness, he categorically denied he had been the source of that part of the story.

This was now a major credibility issue. If Grieve or I could show the detective had lied, it would be a big score for the defence. I leaned over to Grieve and told him to drag out his cross-examination of the detective until 5 pm so that he could be kept in the witness box overnight. I told him I knew the reporter who wrote the story and would call him to see if the officer was telling the truth.

I spoke to the reporter later that evening. I explained the significance of the story and the denial by the critical witness who stated under oath that he was not the source. I asked him straight 'was he your source?' His response was immediate. 'Yes, but off the record at the Ponsonby police station. I've got the whole conversation in my notebooks. I'll call you back.' The reporter did indeed call back and confirmed his earlier story. He read his notes out to me on the phone. Then I softly cross-examined him to be doubly sure. Then came the hard question. Would he give evidence for the defence?

The reporter was very reluctant to do so until I re-emphasized the critical nature of this new information and the importance it could have on the witness's credibility. Finally he agreed to testify if he was summonsed, then no one could accuse him of favouring one side or the other. I agreed. I quickly had a summons drawn up and served on him. Then the shit hit the fan.

The deputy editor of his paper called me. He yelled and he screamed at me. I could not get a word in edgewise. He cited freedom of the press, protecting sources, and more, about why I should not have served the summons, especially without first discussing the matter with him.

The next day the newspaper hired Julian Miles QC and instructed him to have the witness summons set aside. I was served with a copy of an affidavit in which the reporter denied having had any such conversation with me. One hundred percent total denial of the conversation. I was furious. By the early hours of the morning I had boiled over. I was so angry I picked up the phone and called the reporter at home. I obviously woke him up. I said,

'You can't swear that affidavit and put it before the court, because it's total bullshit. I've got a tape-recording of our fucking conversation, you asshole!'

The next morning I called the newspaper's 'hired gun' and told him the same thing. That afternoon the Plumley-Walker trial judge adjourned the criminal trial to deal with the newspaper's motion to set aside the witness summons. The judge moved next door to another courtroom then announced he was putting on his civil jurisdiction hat.

That didn't seem fair to me. I thought the rule was that 'justice must not only be done but must be seen to be done'. His Honour dismissed my witness summons without Grieve or me getting an opportunity to cross-examine the reporter. I felt like somebody was trying harder than normal to protect the credibility of a critical Crown witness who just happened to be a police officer.

Grieve and Paul Davison were desperate to get some information to discredit witness A. The investigator in me went to work once again to discover the truth about witness A. Without going into detail, I learned there was a police letter asking whether the drugs and medication witness A was on could affect her memory and reliability. I phoned Davison and told him I had scored and that it was important I should meet with him and Grieve. Davison suggested we meet at his house in Parnell. I explained what I had learned. They, like me, were jubilant. Another piece of undisclosed information found by the defence. Bruce Squire would be angry. I knew we would need a copy of the letter and the medical file.

Suddenly I got an idea. I asked Davison to lend me his big briefcase. I have a plan, I explained. I left, leaving Grieve open mouthed. An hour later I was back at Davison's house with a copy of the letter in my hand. The two senior barristers stared in disbelief.

After my success, Grieve came up with a brilliant late night tactic. We would write a letter to Squire and Moore stating that we knew there had been less than full disclosure made to date. Now we were demanding the police and Crown make full disclosure in regard to witness A. A deputation of three, made up of Grieve, Davison and I drove to one of the prosecutors, Simon Moore's house, to deliver the letter at midnight.

Davison sat in the back of the car with the internal light on which made it look as though he had a halo around his head from where I was standing. Grieve stood at the end of the carport while I rang the sleeping prosecutor's doorbell. When, in his bathing togs, dripping wet from just climbing out of his spa pool, Simon Moore finally opened his front door, I quickly handed him the jointly signed letter with a cheeky grin. The letter did not reveal what we had found just that we knew full disclosure had not been made.

The next day when Grieve cross-examined Sergeant Dewar alleging full disclosure had not been made, prosecutor Squire, red faced, turned to Grieve and in a voice full of panic demanded to know if Grieve was suggesting that he had not complied with full disclosure. Up until this point Squire and Grieve had been friends. When it was revealed in court for the first time that the defence had somehow accessed witness A's medical file, Squire became apoplectic and a police investigation was begun into how we actually obtained the documents. I declined to be interviewed by the police. When it became obvious the Crown had not yet made full disclosure in relation to witness A, my co-counsel Geoff Wells and I decided to take exceptional unorthodox action. To that end we arranged a witness summons from the High Court registrar (subpoena duces tecum – bring with you specified papers) then served it on a prison officer requiring they bring witness A's medical file to court.

Once the prison officer arrived at court Wells requested to look at the file and arranged for it to be photocopied for Davison and Grieve to use in cross-examination. Now that Davison had a legitimate copy of the letter he could use it in court against A and the Crown. When the prison officer was not called as a defence witness Squire screamed like a banshee that we had improperly used the witness summons as a search and seize warrant.

Grieve, Davison and I gave the Crown witnesses heaps. We thought we were on a roll. The Crown closed its case to the jury alleging that Chignell and Walker had murdered Plumley-Walker at Taupo *or* Auckland, either by hanging at Auckland *or* by drowning at Taupo. Prosecutor Bruce Squire seemed to want a bob each way. I was sure he was wrong. Only time would tell. Davison and I closed to the jury on the unreliability of witnesses A and B.

In His Honour's summing up to the Plumley-Walker jury, he tried to counter defence allegations that certain police officers had lied in the witness box. He did this by adding a 'deadly one liner' to his summing up. He said:'Ladies and Gentlemen of the jury, can you really imagine a police officer doing something like that (lying) and risking his everything?' The effect it had on the jury was demonstrated when on 23 December 1989 Chignell and Walker were convicted of murder then sentenced to life in prison with a minimum non parole period of ten years.

I spent the Christmas holidays working on Neville Walker's appeal. I knew deep in my heart that witness B was a corrupt witness. I just hadn't been able to prove it yet because I still didn't have the Witness B file.

By the 15 of January 1990 I had filed Walker's appeal against conviction and a motion for a Court of Appeal authorized inquiry into my allegations of corrupt practice by certain police officers in relation to witness B, and my civil client dismissed me claiming I was no longer the winner he had hired.

Unbeknown to me at the time, Crown Solicitor David Morris fumed in private at my filing a motion with the Court of Appeal alleging police corruption in relation to witness B.

Some days after, Morris called and spoke to the Solicitor-General John McGrath QC to complain about my putting a witness summons on the first Plumley-Walker prosecutor Roy Ladd 'without apparent justification'. He also complained about me obtaining a confidential file from a prison officer, pressure I had put on the pathologist to try to get him to acknowledge that he had changed his opinion after consultation with the police and the Crown as to cause of death, and the fact I was writing a book about the case.

Morris was one who would defend the New Zealand police integrity with the last drop of blood in his body. This I was to learn in no uncertain terms. Best friend, worst enemy bar none, or so I thought at the time!

My motion for a Court of Appeal supervised inquiry into circumstances surrounding witness B becoming a witness of truth was heard in <u>March 1990</u>. The Court acknowledged some of my points but I was advised to leave it until the appeal hearing. Obviously I had not yet put sufficient information before the court. I would need more ammunition if I wanted to sway the judges into taking the most unusual step of granting bail to my client who had been convicted of murder, before his appeal hearing in July.

In continuing my search for the truth in relation to witness B and his involvement in the Plumley-Walker case as a secret witness I decided to visit B's ex-wife. I found her name and address and phone number in a police job sheet.

When I went to her Mt Wellington home where she had lived with witness B, she said she had already discarded all of B's possessions and papers after he had caused her so much anguish.

She gave me permission to look through the house. After giving it the once over, I explained that I wanted to systematically search every square inch of it, including the ceiling.

I looked in every drawer and cupboard, under the beds, under the mattress, behind the curtains, looked in every book and magazine, only to find nothing. I searched every room. Nothing was left to chance.

I found nothing. Finally I searched the dining room dresser, pulling out each of the four drawers, seeing nothing I closed them. There was nowhere else to look. I walked into the living room and sat down on the sofa.

For some inexplicable reason, I stood up and walked back into the dining room. I pulled the top drawer of the dresser right out off the runners, bent my head down and peered underneath. There, stuck to the underside of the drawer cavity was a piece of bluish white paper folded in half. I pulled it out and looked at it. It was a criminal information charge sheet revealing that B had been charged with driving while disqualified on State Highway One, south of the Bombay Hills in January 1989.

I sensed something was not quite right about it but I was not sure what exactly. The next morning I phoned the Otahuhu police prosecution and asked them what they could tell me about the driving while disqualified charge in relation to B. A short time later the prosecutor returned to the phone and told me the file had been transferred to Rotorua and dealt with there. He told me the file had been retained in Rotorua by police prosecution. Because the officer in charge of the case and the second in charge were both from Rotorua, warning bells went off in my head. I asked who had sent the file to Rotorua and he replied, 'Detective Colin Mitchell!' Now the bells were clanging!

Mitchell had been assigned to look after both Witness A and Witness B from the time they first became secret witnesses (jail cell informants) up to when the first trial in December 1989 had ended with Walker and Chignell being convicted for murder.

Having been told that the traffic file was still in Rotorua I called the local prosecutor who told me there was also a theft charge from a nightclub in Quay Street, Auckland. He said B had pleaded guilty to all charges and was sentenced to six months periodic detention. I asked for copies of the summary to be faxed to me. He apologised and said, as it was almost ten o'clock, he had to get to court. I sensed that the sergeant had picked up that I was onto something in relation to the Plumley-Walker case and that he would be less than co-operative. Desperate to get the information in the summaries I calculatedly waited ten minutes until I was sure the prosecuting sergeant was in court.

Then I called back and spoke to his secretary and asked had she faxed those papers through to me yet? When she expressed no knowledge of what I was talking about, I explained that there was a file on the sergeant's desk in relation to B and could she fax those up along with any other supporting documents. I hung up the phone and waited nervously to see if my ruse would work. Two minutes later the fax machine whirred into action and the information I required was at my fingertips. I noted that B had been ordered to carry out his sentence at the Otahuhu PD centre. On enquiring, I was told he had never attended.

When I pursued the matter I learned that Detective Colin Mitchell had told B's PD warden that B was a secret Crown witness in an important homicide case and he had cancelled B's PD with a simple phone call.

Now I had something new to show the Court of Appeal. It was obvious B was getting special treatment from the police and the justice system as a secret witness.

I continued to use the bail hearings as a way of spoon-feeding the Court of Appeal pieces of new information, bit by bit, of the police malfeasance I had discovered in the Plumley-Walker police case. By the time I had made my sixth bail application three weeks out from the July 10, 1990 appeal date, the President of the Court had had enough of my bail applications. He instructed the Registrar to refuse any further bail applications from me. I would not to be put off that easily.

Following the Court of Appeal hearing in March into my motion for an inquiry I requested the Registrar have the evidence of the various police witnesses who gave evidence before that inquiry typed up and forwarded to me. In those days evidence in the Court of Appeal was tape-recorded but typed up only if requested and authorized by the President of the Court. Here it had been so authorized.

However when I read the typed version of what each police witness said back then, I uttered an expletive under my breath at the President, but now I was smiling. Here in the court transcript was everything the President (Justice Cooke) had said during the hearing. The more I attacked a police witness, the more disparaging the President became towards me.

On a number of occasions he blurted out that I was wasting the Court's time. Now I would use the words the then President used against me to make a claim that His Honour was biased against me, and claim that he should not sit on the appeal. I suggested his remarks had shown a predisposition for prejudging my claims of police malfeasance and I would be obliged if he was taken off the case.

A week later I was advised that the make up of the Plumley-Walker Appeal Court had changed. Chief Justice Eichelbaum would now head the court that heard the appeal. I filed a further motion for bail and discovery in relation to benefits paid to witness B by the police and the Crown. Within 24 hours the Registrar advised me that the Court had agreed to hear my motion for discovery.

On the day, without fanfare, a very fair and principled Chief Justice ordered that the New Zealand police disclose within nine days all benefits paid to or given to witness B in a sworn affidavit.

When the affidavit was finally faxed to my office it came like a bombshell. It revealed that witness B was a secret police informant and that he had been paid thousands of dollars by the police over time for various bits of information. I put this new information alongside all the material co-counsel Geoffrey Wells, fellow Canadian David Cardinal and I had already located about charges the police had dropped against B and how various courts had been misled. I included the fact that Detective Colin Mitchell had cancelled B's court ordered periodic detention with a phone call.

Appeal

The appeal started on the 3 July 1990 . Grieve did an excellent job at the appeal, basing his main submission on the fact that the Crown case was put to the jury on the basis that Chignell and Walker had committed murder either at Auckland OR Taupo. He made the point that the trial judge had misdirected the jury when he told them they could bring back a verdict of murder even if some jurors found Plumley-Walker had been murdered in Auckland and other jurors found he was murdered at Taupo.

Grieve made the point that this must be wrong. Both accused were charged with murder at Taupo, but at the end of the trial Squire put the Crown case as murder at Taupo *or* Auckland. Grieve and I both believed Squire was dead wrong. Again time would tell. Grieve made the further point that when the jury returned its guilty verdict, the basis of their decision was unclear. Unanimity of jury verdicts is a vital component of the New Zealand legal system.

As the Chief Justice stated, 'Hypothetically speaking, because we don't know how the jury voted, on the instructions of the trial judge, they could have voted six for murder at Auckland and six for murder at Taupo in coming to their verdict but clearly that would not be a unanimous verdict.' On that note the three-day appeal hearing came to an end with the court reserving its decision.

Six weeks passed and still no decision from the Court of Appeal. Then something unusual happened. My wife Philippa took our black, Newfoundland dog Nell to the vet. In the course of the discussion he told her that his son had been on the Plumley-Walker jury. I telephoned the vet and we talked. I explained how we were waiting for the Court of Appeal to give its decision.

I also explained that one of the key points the Court was interested in, in a hypothetical fashion, was, what if some of the jurors voted for murder at Auckland and others voted for murder at Taupo. The father of the juror told me it was an interesting point. That was the end of the discussion. The next day the vet's son, the ex juror, called me and said in fact the jury had been split six, six.

The moment I heard this I telephoned Grieve. Then I sent a fax to the Court of Appeal asking them if they wanted me to get an affidavit from the ex juror. I received no reply to my fax inquiry but the very next day the Registrar sent Grieve and me a fax advising us that the Court of Appeal would give it's decision in 48 hours.

When the decision was released on <u>August 3rd 1990</u> the appeal was allowed on two grounds. The judgment pointed out that the court could not be certain that the jury was unanimous in reaching its verdict in light of how Squire had presented the prosecution case to the jury. On the further ground that there had been inadequate police disclosure in relation to Witness B, the court found as follows:

(a) *The details of payments to witness B for previous information, comprising sums of $200, $300, $500, $500, $200, $400, $400, $200, $300, $300 on various dates between March 1987 and June 1989 had not been disclosed.*

(b) *Charges brought by the police against witness B which were subsequently withdrawn, namely theft, obscene telephone call, offensive weapon, disturbing by telephone, and assault (two), these being in respect of occurrences between May and August 1998*

(c) *Charges of threatening to kill and disturbing by telephone, brought in respect of events in December 1998 and February 1989, which were dismissed.*

(d) *Various traffic charges; witness B's traffic list not having been made available to defence counsel before trial. The significance lay not so much in the charges as in the manner of their disposal. In April*

1988 warrants for arrest issued in respect of charges of driving while disqualified, exceeding the speed limit, excess breath alcohol and failure to supply name and address were issued but never executed. A charge of driving while disqualified in respect of a December 1988 incident was withdrawn in March 1989.

(e) On 19 June 1989, three days before witness B gave his evidence at depositions, a police inspector, in the course of a discussion over "the perceived threat level when he gave evidence" informed witness B that the police would relocate him in Rotorua, pay his accommodation, and give him an initial food grant to last a period of three months when it would be reviewed. On 20 June witness B received an advance of $200 for food.

(f) On 27 June the police paid for the witness' air travel from Auckland to Rotorua and provided him with groceries and cash to a total value of $200. In July/August there were further payments relating to motel accommodation at Auckland and Rotorua totalling over $900, as well as cash advances of $200.

(g) After witness B returned to live in Auckland, on 26 July 1989 he was provided with transport to and from Auckland airport, and airfares to enable him to attend a court hearing at Rotorua. On 28 August he was again provided with transportation and air fares for the same purpose.

(h) The last mentioned court appearance at Rotorua resulted in a sentence of three months' periodic detention on a charge of driving while disqualified. On or about 1 September a police officer arranged to have witness B excused from attendance at the periodic detention centre.

(i) In or about September a police officer was instrumental in disposing of a complaint made to Telecom in respect of toll calls which witness B had charged to the telephone account of the mother of his de facto wife.

(j) In September 1989 witness B was charged with assaulting his de facto wife and child and incidental

> *offences. Following enquiries by an officer who was a witness in the Plumley-Walker case the complainant decided she did not wish to proceed with her complaint; all charges were withdrawn.*

The same police officer, Colin Mitchell, was involved in incidents (e) through (j). The Court of Appeal omitted to name him. On both appeal points a retrial was ordered.

At 9:00 am <u>7 August 1990</u> I sent a fax to Simon Moore. I wanted to talk to Bruce Squire about the Crown withdrawing witness B from the second trial. He would not return my calls. The cover sheet read, 'Please read and consider. Obviously Squire is no longer up to prosecuting this case, he failing to communicate with this defence counsel over important matters. Is Squire deliberately being a rude and unprofessional S.O.B. or has the mental stress affected his ability to communicate in accordance with the Law Society Code of Ethics.'

Simon Moore, second in charge of the Plumley-Walker prosecution, finally advised me that witness B would be withdrawn from the case and not used as a witness of truth again. The re-trial was to be held in <u>October 1990</u>. Robertson J was to be the judge but Grieve, Davison, and Squire were all unavailable. I was all but broke having borrowed on my house to help fund my campaign against secret witness B and I needed to get the trial on and over with. My worst nightmare was soon realised when the retrial was put off until <u>March 1991</u>. I felt this was a plot against me at the time but I could never prove it.

On <u>23 October 1990</u> Squire wrote to me stating, *the attached facsimile to Mr Moore at the Auckland Crown solicitors office and, on its face, copied to the Solicitor-General has been drawn to my attention. I regard the contents as insulting and unprofessional. He demanded I write to Moore and the Solicitor-General making suitable withdrawals and apologies. He gave me 14 days to respond or he would be obliged to pursue the matter further.*

I ignored Squire's letter.

On <u>26 November 1990</u> Squire wrote to the Secretary of the Auckland District Law Society about my S.O.B. fax asking them to take the appropriate action.

<u>In December 1990</u> I filed a 347 application to have the

murder case dismissed for insufficiency of evidence now that witness B had been withdrawn from the case. My efforts failed to impress Justice Robertson. His Honour declined my application complaining that it should never have been brought.

On <u>21 January 1991</u> I replied to the Law Society's letter re Squire's complaint. I wrote that I accepted the tenor of my communication was inappropriate but went on to explain that I thought Squire's behaviour towards me had been out of line. Then to try to make my point I included paragraphs (a)-(j) from the Plumley-Walker Court of Appeal decision to try and demonstrate to the Society where the real injustice lay in the matter.

Second trial

Justice Robertson presided at the second trial in February 1991. At the time I was unhappy with both the judge and jury. I felt his Honour was interfering too much as well as being too officious; I also felt we had a bad jury. This was not going to be an easy retrial.

After the first trial I heard a rumour that on the day of his death, Plumley-Walker had experienced not one, but two bondage sessions. If this was true, it was the key to the accused winning the trial. This was because the Crown was using the bruising found on Plumley-Walker's buttock to establish that he had still been alive some nine to fourteen hours after he had first been whipped in the bondage session.

The session with Chignell had started at 4.00pm. If the timed bruising was caused by the Chignell session, and Plumley-Walker was dumped over the Huka Falls at midnight, *then Plumley-Walker was still alive when Chignell and Walker disposed of him.* Manslaughter would have been the best outcome available in these circumstances.

On the other hand, if there had been a previous bondage session earlier in the day, then the bruising might have started hours before his session with Chignell, supporting the defence assertion that Plumley-Walker had died accidentally during his second session.

During the second trial I was still trying to track down the rumour of a prior bondage session. To that end I worked my way through most every massage and bondage parlour in Auckland city interviewing whoever I could get to talk to me, carrying Plumley-Walker's picture with me to try to jog memories.

My investigations paid off. Ultimately I found a parlour where Plumley-Walker's distinctive appearance was recognised by one of the staff. Next, I found the name of the bondage mistress she believed had previously had a session with Plumley-Walker. Next I spoke to a girlfriend of the missing bondage mistress. Night after night this woman and I tried to find her friend but with no luck.

Then out of the blue I received a phone call telling me that the woman I was looking for was overseas with a prominent businessman on holiday. After some cajoling she told me the name of the client. The rest was easy. I obtained the client's phone number for his private line at work then I called it.

'Hi, is John there?' I asked. 'It's Christopher Harder, lawyer calling.'

'Sorry Mr. Harder, John's in Singapore at the moment.'

'Well I urgently need to talk to him. Do you have his contact details?'

Thus I obtained the telephone number of the appropriate hotel in Singapore. He denied the woman was with him but said that she was staying at a nearby hotel. The telephone and fax numbers were duly obtained.

I tried to telephone the blonde without success. Eventually I resorted to having hotel staff slip a facsimile under her door encouraging her to take my call. This worked, and I took the opportunity to talk through my situation and how she might help. She recalled the session with a man who matched Plumley-Walker's description. A picture of the deceased was then sent to her by facsimile, and she identified him without hesitation. Initially, she offered to provide an affidavit, but after some convincing agreed to fly back to New Zealand to appear as a witness.

'I'll pick you up at the airport. What do you look like?' I asked.

'You'll recognize me when you see me.' I did.

The surprise witness from overseas testified at the second trial, giving excellent evidence for the defence. So much for the Crown's bruising theory establishing Plumley-

Walker was alive when he was thrown over the falls.

Sir Brian Barratt-Boyes the world-renowned heart surgeon also gave evidence for the defence in relation to Plumley-Walker's health. He stated that the microscopic slides he had examined indicated the deceased was suffering from heart disease and a severe narrowing of the arteries. Sir Brian said the stress of a bondage session might well have contributed to Plumley-Walker's collapse and ultimate death.

By the end of the second trial I was not confident at all. The judge was against us. And the Crown still had their pretty blonde secret witness A. The jury never warmed to the defence.

In those circumstances I concluded that drastic action was called for. Go for a hung jury, and then get a different judge and jury next time. After all a life sentence, serving a minimum of ten years with the rest of your natural life subject to recall to prison if you committed even a minor offence was a very long sentence. Hung jury and retrial it would have to be. Towards the end of my address to the jury I played the hung jury card:

'...If but one of you have a reasonable doubt, then it is your duty to say not guilty. If that is your view, then you *stand fast till hell freezes over.*'

Predictably, Justice Robertson reacted interrupting my address to tell the jury I was wrong to suggest that a juror stand fast till hell freezes over. He then told the jury he would have more to say about my 'stand fast till hell freezes over' comment in his summing up to the jury.

When Justice Robertson's turn came, boy did he get stuck into me. Again he repeated to the jury it would be wrong of them to stand fast till hell freezes over. His Honour concluded by telling the jury that my comments were wrong and unprofessional. Then the jury retired. It was just after noon on a Friday.

The jury considered its verdict that day and well into the evening. About nine o'clock the judge asked the jury if they were making progress. They said they were. The jury then retired to a hotel for the night before restarting their deliberations at nine on the Saturday morning. All day the jury deliberated. Finally just after five o'clock in the evening the jury foreman passed a note to the registrar to be delivered to the judge. It advised His Honour that the jury was unable to agree upon a verdict and that the jury was hung.

After the jury was dismissed by the judge counsel met with His Honour in chambers. The crown applied for a new trial and the judge granted the request. I then applied for bail for Walker. The judge looked at me with disdain. I had gotten my hung jury but at what cost. 'I'm sorry Mr. Harder, if I gave your client bail now it would be a media circus. Anyway I want to get home and watch the six o'clock news. I have never given a barrister such a bollocking in front of so many members of the press and I want to see what they are going to do to you!' he said with a big crocodile smile on his face.

As the lawyers stood to leave the judge's chamber, I remembered some advice given to me by Charles Hutchinson QC many years earlier. I had purchased his desk and book shelves when he retired from the law and used him as a sounding board from time to time before he died. He said if you ever want to be discourteous to a judge, 'don't yell at them Christopher, just remember, when you bow, make sure you bow *really* low'. With that advice in mind, just before I took my leave, I bowed very, low to this bollocking judge.

I too rushed home to watch the six o'clock news. I turned on TV3 news then sat down nervously knowing that the lambasting I had taken from the judge in court was about to be blasted across the country on the national news. I was home alone. At least I didn't have to share my anticipated public humiliation with my family. The TV3 Plumley-Walker logo came up on the screen. Headline News. Then the newsreader trumpeted, Plumley-Walker trial judge tells jury to 'stand fast till Hell freezes over', and they did.

I fell out of my chair and onto the floor in front of the television laughing so hard I almost died because for a moment I could not get my breath and there was nobody to pat me on the back to help me start breathing again.

On the Monday I arranged a telephone conference with the prosecutor and the judge so that I could apply for bail.

When Justice Robertson came on the line the first thing he said to me was, 'Mr Harder, it looks like the joke's on me.' I think I replied, 'We all have a turn'. Walker was then granted bail pending his third murder trial set down for hearing in June 1991 some two months away.

On <u>15 February 1991</u> Squire wrote to Margaret Wong of the ADLS refusing to accept my apology, believing it to lack sincerity.

On <u>11 March 1991</u> I wrote back to the Law Society and said it was too bad Squire had refused to accept my apology. I suggested that should Squire desire to continue with this matter by insinuating my complaints against him lacked any specific content, then I would advise that specifics would no doubt be made clear in the subsequent enquiry that would surely follow the second retrial in the Plumley-Walker case.

Over the following months formal complaints were made to the Law Society about me by ex-Plumley Walker prosecutor Bruce Squire, the Commissioner of Police John Jamieson, Detective Inspector John Dewar, second in charge of the Plumley-Walker case as well as the officer in charge, Inspector Ron Cooper.

Prior to the third trial the Crown tried to introduce two further secret witnesses who had been in prison with Neville Walker for a time. Both had a story to tell. Walker had allegedly told them he had beaten Plumley-Walker with an iron bar as he hung, apparently lifeless in Renee Chignell's bondage and discipline room. Both witnesses had outrageous lists of criminal offending. The Walker defence opposed the calling of the two new witnesses.

Justice Anderson spoke to the Crown prosecutor and me. 'Mr. Harder if the Crown is so foolish as to call these two witnesses then the consequences of them doing so is on them, but I would be surprised if after due consideration the Crown chose to call these two extra secret witnesses. I need say no more.'

In due course the Crown chose not to call the secret jailhouse witnesses C and D but they still intended to call witness 'A' who gave evidence against Chignell and prejudice against Walker.

Third Trial

At the third trial in June 1991 New Yorker turned New Zealander Jim Boyack, poet extraordinaire, joined me as co-counsel. Justice Anderson was the trial judge. He was recognized as the fairest of all the judges. He knew how to run a trial in a proper fashion. He displayed no arrogance or contempt from the bench even if defence counsel were dogged about a point. He was a straight down the middle judge with good commonsense and a huge amount of compassion for his fellow man.

When Boyack and I finally stood up with the two accused (Davison and Grieve remained sitting) to take the verdict at the third trial, my heart was racing faster than it had ever raced before. One thing I knew for sure, if the jury said 'guilty' I was positive I was going to have a heart attack right there in court. When I finally heard those two lovely words 'Not Guilty' repeated twice, the adrenalin rush I experienced on the spot was greater than anything I had ever experienced in my life. It was just the best. This was all the more so because for over two years judges and QCs (doesn't always mean Quite Clever) had been telling me that the best I could possibly do for my client was to obtain a manslaughter verdict.

Following the sweet victory of the Plumley-Walker saga I began to write my book about the case with gusto. I knew it was only a matter of time before I faced the Disciplinary Tribunal over this case.

I knew the book would be my defence and my salvation when my day came to appear before a tribunal, and it was written with that in mind as well as the historical documentation of the case from a defence lawyer's perspective.

I finished writing the book by early October 1991. HarperCollins published *'Mercy, Mistress, Mercy, The Plumley-Walker Murder Saga'* with the speed of light having it in the bookstores by mid November 1991.

The publication of the book was to have huge ramifications for me and not in a positive sense. Not only did I not make money out of it, it ended up costing me hundreds of thousands of dollars. Some saw it as me taking the main chance to capitalise on the salacious details of Plumley-

Walker but that was far from the truth. It was an exposé of some of the outrageous activities that occurred during the three trials involving defence, judge, Crown and police.

On 5 December 1991, I had a television interview with Paul Holmes about the book. In the course of the interview he asked me if there was corruption in the Plumley-Walker case. I said yes.

A week later on 11 December 1991 Police Commissioner John Jamieson wrote to the Law Society about my 'corruption' comment made on the *Holmes* show. He made a complaint alleging I was guilty of professional misconduct for alleging 'police corruption' on the *Holmes Show* and in my book. Law Society counsel Stuart Ennor was asked by the Complaints Committee to read '*Mercy, Mistress Mercy*' to see if a misconduct charge could be made out against me.

On the 23rd December 1991 I wrote to the Auckland District Law Society in response to Police Commissioner Jamieson's complaint.

'Now having considered the matter over the weekend, can I suggest you reply to the Commissioner of Police that maybe he should read 'Mercy Mistress Mercy', and then reflect on his letter of 11 December, with a view to assessing my allegations in light of the Police and Crown actions in the Plumley-Walker case.

If the Commissioner of Police is correct in his interpretation of my public comments then it would seem only proper that I should be charged with criminal libel and be given the opportunity to defend myself in front of a New Zealand jury. Can I suggest you pass this consideration on to the Commissioner of Police.'

In January 1992 Law Society President John Moody asked me to apologize to the Commissioner of Police. I refused but offered to meet with the Commissioner, the Solicitor-General and John Moody to try to work out matters but they all refused.

On 18 February 1992 the Law Society wrote to inform me that Mr. Jamieson's complaint was not about my book, but about comments I made during the *Holmes* interview.

On 19 February 1992 I wrote to and then met with Stuart

Ennor, who was then handling the Law Society prosecution against me. I outlined the background and my perception that some 'secret force' was operating against me but I just could not prove it.

On <u>20 February 1992</u> I wrote to the Commissioner of Police enclosing a videotape of a television commercial I planned to run to promote my book. The commercial was to close with, 'the book the Commissioner refuses to read, *Mercy Mistress Mercy the Plumley-Walker Murder Saga*'

On the <u>2nd March 1992</u> Commissioner Jamieson wrote to Margaret Wong again detailing his formal complaint.

Complaint 1 was made up of three parts.

1) Allegations that the Police are 'corrupt' and involved in 'fitting up evidence'

2) Allegations that the police pay witnesses (as opposed to informers) and the deliberate confusion Mr. Harder has sought to create.

3) The use of the '*Holmes Show*' and other media outlets to promote his book and his own singular and unsubstantiated views about the police handling of the Plumley-Walker case.

Complaint 2.

Alleged that I had provocatively used information to generate further publicity for my book and grossly distorted a statement I made that I had not read the book and had no wish to read it.

Try Harder advertising which is apparently a commercial production house operated by Mr. Harder produced a television commercial to promote his book in which it was stated that, 'This was the book the Commissioner of Police refused to read'

He closed with the comment; '*The society has now had my original complaint for almost three months. I look forward to your earliest resolution of this and my further complaint.*'

On <u>March 10 1992</u> I was asked to reply to the complaints of the Commissioner of Police before 23 March 1992 when the complaints Committee next met.

On <u>March 11 1992</u> I wrote back to the Law Society and suggested to Ms Wong that the Commissioner of Police read my book Mercy, Mistress, Mercy. Then he can apologize to me for his police officer's gross breach of the rules in relation to discovery, or RESIGN, 'because if he doesn't I look forward to defending any action he or the Auckland District Law Society might be foolish enough to initiate.'

My goal was to try to stop the Law Society juggernaut before they ground me down and bankrupted me out of the law with costs I could ill-afford to pay, to say nothing of the collateral damage that was done along the way to my practice. The ongoing Police Commissioner's complaints caused indescribable stress to my family and my work environment.

On 23 March 1992 Ennor met with a secret sub-committee of four of the Complaints Committee. He advised them that the Law Society could not sustain a case against me in relation to my 'police corruption' comments made on the *Holmes Show*, or on anything he had read in my book. He also recommended that a number of the charges against me be dropped, that some be tested in the High Court, and the remaining charges dealt with at the District level and not the NZLPDT. His advice was ignored and the ADLS Complaint's Committee withdrew Ennor's instructions with the backing of the council.

On 7 May 1992 President John Moody wrote to Commissioner Jamieson seeking a meeting with him in Wellington on 18 May about me, having failed to 'find him at home' on a couple of previous occasions.

Moody wrote to the commissioner again on 19 June 1992 still trying to arrange a meeting, this time for 25 June. '*I have tried on a number of occasions to visit you when I have been in Wellington but unfortunately without success.*' Moody wished to discuss the 'above' issue, namely me.

For some months the Law Society carefully looked for a new and suitable prosecutor. First the Committee sent my file to barrister Roger Haines QC to consider. After a week he returned the file citing his workload. Subsequently the file was sent to Colin Carruthers QC but he also returned it after a week, claiming his work schedule was too busy. Finally in August 1992 the Law Society instructed Howard Keyte QC to prosecute me before the New Zealand

Law Practitioner's Disciplinary Tribunal.

By now I had become angry and frustrated at the length of time the Law Society investigation of the Police Commissioner's complaint was taking. I had been trying since February to find out what the Law Society's attitude was going to be but I could get no adequate response from the Professional Standards Director Margaret Wong. The delay in finalizing that matter had been a big stressor on my family, my work colleagues and me.

The police complaint was hanging over my head. Finally in a telephone call I initiated on 10 September 1992 Margaret Wong of the Law Society casually told me that the Complaints Committee did not consider it had sufficient grounds to proceed with the Commissioner's complaint and that I could expect a letter from the Law Society to that effect shortly. I received my clearance letter *five months* after the decision had been made not to charge me, but I was never told.

Two years and two Tribunals later, I was stung in excess of $67,000 in fines and costs. In relation to Tribunal 2, Paul Holmes made an editorial comment on *Newstalk ZB* expressing shock and disdain at the penalty I had been given. He said words to the effect that, 'So the Law Society has seen fit to fine lawyer Christopher Harder $32,000! $32,000! For what? For yelling at a judge and a couple of other misdemeanors! Who do they think they are? For my money, if you were in jail on a serious charge and Christopher Harder appeared at your cell door and agreed to take your case, you would get down on your knees and thank God, wouldn't you?' (Wasn't that nice of him?)

The allegations that were made in *'Mercy, Mistress Mercy'* were, (and now repeated in this book) against certain police officers in the Plumley-Walker case are not levelled at the New Zealand Police in general. I accept that the Plumley-Walker case was an aberration and hopefully unique in New Zealand's legal history.

14

A Knife In The Heart

Mary S was a Maori woman charged with the murder of her Pakeha (European) de facto husband. They had three children – one to the couple, and two to Mary's previous partner. Her de facto husband had a habit of going to the pub and drinking after work and not coming home until very late. It put a real strain on their relationship.

One day Mary told him that if he was going to go to the pub after work, there was no point in him coming back. He went anyway, and returned home much later, only to find his clothing had been thrown out of the house and into the front yard. He tried to get into the house. Then he forced open the aluminum screen door and walked in the front door. He stood behind the couch with his hands on the backrest. Mary was standing in the kitchen, having had a few drinks. She picked up a knife from the kitchen counter and waved it in the air, shouting at him to go.

Mary walked up to the couch and tapped her partner a couple of times on the backs of his hands with the sharp side of the knife blade. These taps caused slight cuts and bleeding, but she succeeded in backing him out the door, down the stairs, and up the path onto their driveway. It had been raining, though it wasn't at the time. He was slightly drunk. She continued to tell him to get off the property and not come back. Suddenly Mary's partner came forward and the knife, still in my client's hand, pierced him in the heart.

I defended the matter before a judge and jury. At the end of the trial my client was found not guilty of murder, but guilty of manslaughter, and sentenced to five years in prison. The basis for the decision was reasonable doubt as to intent. Justice Anderson handed down the sentence. I thought it was harsh, but then you always do when it's your own client. Mary's children were traumatized to find that their mother was going to jail.

A year after she was sentenced, Mary showed up on my office doorstep. I couldn't figure it out, because it was a crime of violence and she should have served two-thirds of the five years, namely three years.

'What are you doing here?' I asked.

'I need your help, Christopher, I need your help.'

Oh no, not that line. I let her in and sat her down, still startled by the fact that she was here in my office instead of in prison where she should have been.

'How are you here?'

'Well, I got told last November that I'd be going to the parole board in June. I went before them and they told me that I'd be released on parole on the 27th of September.'

That was my birthday.

'How did you end up here,' I asked, 'this isn't the 27th.'

'I got called into the superintendent's office last week and told that a terrible, terrible mistake had been made.'

'What do you mean?'

'Well, when they sent me from the High Court to the prison after I was sentenced, the committal warrant referred to the section I was sentenced under, not the manslaughter section.'

'So?'

'Well, when it went to the receiving office, they had a list of sections. If you had been charged under these sections, you were prohibited one-third parole. The manslaughter section was listed there, but because it didn't appear on my committal warrant, they put me down for one-third parole. When they told me I could go home in September I told my kids and everything. They're all excited, they've got a party organized and everything.'

'So what do you want me to do?'

'Well, I accept that getting out is impossible, but I want you to tell my kids. I can't tell them.'

'You want me to tell them? What do I look like? I'd rather move a mountain! Wait a minute ... what did you just say?'

'I know that it's impossible for me to get out now, but ..'

'Yeah, hold on.' An idea was germinating. 'Shane?' I called out. Shane Cassidy was a lawyer who worked in my office. 'Come here. Now say that again.'

'I know it's impossible for me to get out now, and I've got to go back to jail, but I don't want to tell my kids.'

Tears were running down her cheeks. I looked at Cassidy and he looked back with just the hint of a grin on his face and a wink. Impossible, eh?

'Just let me have a think about it,' I said. For the next 10 minutes I walked amongst the trees in the back yard then walked back into my office. Lighting a cigarette, I picked up the phone and dialed the number for the Secretary of Justice, Mel Smith. The receptionist put my call straight through to her employer.

'Mr. Smith? Christopher Harder calling. How are you sir?' I asked.

'I haven't had to call you in ten years, sir, but I'm calling you now. I've got a bit of a problem. Does the name Mary S mean anything to you?'

'Oh no, not that one! Yes, I know it well. Christopher, that one was a complete cock-up. We have tried everything we can to resolve it.'

'Yeah, it sounds like a mess. Now I have your problem. Listen, I've got Mary S sitting in my office as we speak. She's refusing to leave until I agree to go and tell her children that mum's got to go back to jail for two years. Understand this, Mr. Smith, I'll do that shortly before hell freezes over, you know what I mean. Somebody has screwed up bad, and there must be a resolution to this somehow, and soon.'

'We've tried,' came the response.

'Well, let's go back and try again. What are the theoretical sections under which my client could be outside of prison?'

'She could be on work release, but that won't help her

because she is in prison in Wellington and her kids are in Auckland.'

We went through the various sections to see how far they could be stretched. There seemed to be no way around it.

'Only if we had a release from the Minister of Justice would she be eligible for work parole, then we'd have to transfer her to Auckland,' said Smith.

'Well, I'll draft up the letter, you just make sure it's on the Minister of Justice's desk this afternoon. I'm sure this isn't the first time women have been let out of prison on one-third release following a manslaughter conviction. I'm not making an issue out of it, but I'm not telling my client's kids she's going back to jail for two years. I don't wish to be the Bogeyman today, sir. I'm sure you can understand that.'

By mid afternoon my letter pleading for Ministerial intervention had been placed on the Minister of Justice, Doug Graham's desk. Within 24 hours Mary S was officially free – she had been transferred from Wellington's Arohata Prison to the roster of women's division of Mt Eden Prison, but out on work release, never to have to go back if she was a good girl. She had served a total of fourteen months on the day she walked out the prison gate for the last time, into the waiting arms of her jubilant children.

15

The Shower-Nozzle Sex Case

Sex allegation cases are by far the most difficult to deal with from a defence lawyer's point of view. First there is the automatic prejudice that attaches whenever such a charge is made then laid. Then there is the key question: If the allegation of sexual abuse is untrue, why is the complainant lying about the matter?

In this case, my client was a Scots-New Zealander in his early thirties whom I will call Jock. Jock carried a cane and walked with a limp. As well, he had a grumpy personality. Four years earlier, Jock had married a 22-year-old Filipino mail-order bride, whom I'll call Sue. When Sue first came to New Zealand to marry Jock, she brought her four-year-old daughter, Lisa, from a previous relationship with her. Jock adopted Sue's daughter.

By the time Lisa was eight, her mother and stepfather had produced three young children of their own, but the relationship was strained. The couple frequently argued. Sometimes during the course of these arguments Sue would run naked into the back yard of their South Auckland home, climb the well-established apple tree and scream at her husband for hours. I have no doubt that Jock was a difficult man to live with, and suspect that he may on occasion have beaten his wife. Eventually, Sue left Jock, taking Lisa with her but leaving the three other children in the care of her husband.

Two weeks later Sue approached the local Social Welfare office, having run out of money. She was told that no financial assistance would be made available to her until she applied for custody of her children. The Social Welfare official directed her to a legal aid lawyer, (a free lawyer paid for by the government for people who cannot afford to pay for one) who assisted Sue in completing the appropriate forms. While Sue was being interviewed, the lawyer asked her if there had ever been any instances of sexual abuse within their family. She hesitated for a moment then replied: 'Yes.' After that the police became involved.

Sue described a day when eight-year-old Lisa had been in the shower. She described how she opened the bathroom door to see Jock on his knees in front of the shower with his fingers penetrating her daughter's vagina. She then describes how her husband got up off his knees, picked up the shower nozzle then pushed it up Lisa's bottom.

Jock subsequently faced two sex charges on the word of his former partner and her young daughter. The accused man approached me and then pleaded with me to take this unappealing case. He told me emphatically that he was not guilty of either charge!'I didn't do anything wrong Mr. Harder!!' More often than not, the standard response of a person charged with a sex offence is: I didn't do it!

The trouble with sex allegations is that independent evidence is rarely available to help establish the truth. Often an accused person has to rely solely on his lawyer's cross-examination skills in the hope of raising a reasonable doubt in relation to the police evidence. After all it is for the Crown prosecutor to prove the case beyond reasonable doubt but still there is that extra prejudice that goes with a sex charge involving young victims.

I was first approached to take Jock's case just two weeks before the trial. After an in-depth interview, my client admitted to me that he had used the shower nozzle as described, and that he had put his fingers inside his adopted daughter's vagina, but that his wife was twisting the facts to make him look guilty.

On the face of it Jock's admitted behavior seemed repugnant, but I have found over the course of my career that behind every story there is more often than not another story. Sometimes, if the legal process works, as it should, a jury trial can provide an opportunity for the truth to come out, but not always.

Both Sue and Lisa gave evidence before a jury. It is sometimes suggested that being cross-examined by defence lawyers is an ordeal that complainants in sexual abuse cases should not have to endure. This case is a demonstration of the importance of why careful cross-examination is critical.

Based on my client's explanation to me for this, at first impression, criminal behavior, my questioning was very precise. Under cross-examination, the girl's mother agreed, that on the morning of the day she alleged she observed this criminal behaviour she had taken her daughter to the doctor. The child had been diagnosed as having a thrush infection in her vagina. The doctor wrote a prescription for an anti-fungal cream that had to be applied internally to the daughter's private parts.

As I continued my cross-examination the reality of the situation started to become clear to the judge, Ron Gilbert, formerly the top criminal lawyer in Dunedin before his elevation to the bench. Jock had done the *actus reus*, the physical act necessary to allege sexual abuse but he did not, in my view have the necessary *mens rea*. In relation to my client touching his stepdaughter's vagina, he was simply administering the prescribed medication because his wife refused to apply the cream to her daughter's private parts, claiming that for cultural reasons it was taboo for her to do so.

In the circumstances it was necessary for Jock to do what he did. Mum wouldn't do it, and the child couldn't do it because she was suffering from a condition known as psoriasis of the skin on her hands. Both hands had been wrapped in gauze at the time to prevent her from doing any further scratching.

And in relation to the second charge my client did not have a guilty mind because he was doing no more than cleaning the eight-year old's bottom because she had a habit of not wiping herself properly. My client had no sinister motive behind his actions.

Under further cross-examination it became clear the motive for the mother lying about what she had observed was motivated by her need to obtain custody of all her children before Social Welfare would give her any financial assistance.

When I finished my cross-examination the judge turned to the prosecutor and asked 'Madam Prosecutor? Do you really want to continue with this case?

At that point, the trial - and my client's nightmare - came to an end when Judge Ron Gilbert directed the jury to acquit the accused in light of the various revealing matters disclosed in the defence cross-examination of the Crown's key witnesses.

The Donnelly Murder Case

Michael Donnelly was a young man from West Auckland. He was charged with murder. There had been a history of animosity between Donnelly and a couple of other West Auckland men who believed he had informed to the police about some illegal firearms. The night before the killing someone had poured petrol on my client's car and then set it alight.

On the night of the shooting Donnelly saw someone on his property and, leaning from his back porch, fired a series of shots from a .22 calibre automatic rifle at a person who, the police alleged, was 50 feet up his driveway running away at the time. The victim was hit nine times – seven times in the back. One shot pierced his heart and he died. Such was the Crown case.

Donnelly claimed that the man had been carrying something that looked like a rifle, so he had fired in self-defence. An iron bar was found at the scene. The case for the prosecution looked tight, at first glance. Bail was opposed, and Donnelly was remanded to the security block at Mt Eden prison - a hellhole at the best of times.

The first trial was set down in the High Court before Justice Peter Hillyer who had been such a help to me in the past. I had unfortunately in my early years of practice had several run-ins in court before His Honour and this had strained our understanding of each other.

On one occasion when Hillyer and I disagreed I was defending in a rape case. My client had been accused of abducting a prostitute from Karangahape Road in Auckland, sexually abusing her in his car, then driving off with her. As the car turned from Karangahape Road onto Newton Road, the complainant jumped from the car and rolled on to the roadway as my client's car continued on. Seconds later a service station attendant who worked on the same corner picked up the hurt young woman and carried her to the sidewalk. An off duty nurse also stopped and attended to the hurt woman sitting on the sidewalk. The attendant wrote down the licence number of the vehicle and gave it to the police who later used it to track down my client.

The defence was that my client had had consensual sex with the prostitute, he had given her some cannabis to pay for the sex, and that he was giving her a ride to a girlfriend's house when she jumped out of the car. He said she had been very stoned and was behaving very strangely.

The crux of the case was the credibility of the complainant. Was she telling the truth about her rape and abduction or had the sex been consensual, and her subsequent exit from the vehicle the result of her drugged state and erratic behavior?

After the complainant had completed her evidence the judge released her as a witness and told her she was free to go. My client who was sitting in the dock leaned over and told me he was disappointed I had not cracked the witness. He reiterated to me the fact that the complainant was a 'spaced out lady' at the time and that she had not told the truth. I told the client to relax, I could do no more with the witness because she had finished her evidence and been released.

I believed my client but how could I prove it? That evening I re-read the various police job sheets in relation to the case. The service station attendant had picked the complainant up off the road after she had jumped or fallen out of the car. The job sheet referred to a nurse arriving on the scene and attending to the complainant. The injured complainant told the nurse she had been abducted and raped by a man. At the trial the complainant identified my client as her attacker. The nurse was called as the 'recent complaint witness.'

Normally this witness is the first person the complainant talks to about the alleged sexual attack. As I continued to read the job sheets I noticed that the service station attendant had not been interviewed by the police or called as a witness. I guessed that was because he had only been on the scene for a few seconds before the nurse came to the rescue.

I decided to double check. I drove to the Caltex service station in Newton Road and tracked down the Good Samaritan petrol pump attendant. Explaining who I was I asked him to run through his recollection of the events of the night in question. Without hesitation he began to explain. He had been watching a car turn the corner into Newton Road from Upper Queen Street when suddenly the front passenger door flew open and a young woman wearing a leather jacket rolled out onto the road. He ran over to her and helped her to her feet. He picked up her broken high heel shoe then assisted her to the side of the road.

'What happened?' he asked.

'There were two of them – they tried to rape me!' she replied. This was totally different from what the girl had told the police and the jury– there had never been any suggestion that there were two attackers. Either she had lied to the police or, as seemed more likely, she really had been so stoned and freaked out on the night of the incident that she couldn't recall anything with any accuracy. In any event this new evidence was very damaging to the complainant's credibility and vital to our defence. Now I needed to have the complainant recalled to the witness box so I could put this new allegation of two rapists to her for comment.

Unfortunately for my client after the complainant had completed her evidence she flew to the South Island for a skiing holiday. In light of the previous disagreements I had had with His Honour, I was not confident Justice Hillyer would order the recall of the witness.

To bring the complainant back to Auckland from the South Island so that she could be re-examined would first require a helicopter to fly her from Mt. Hutt ski field to Harewood, Christchurch's International airport for a connecting flight to Auckland.

Initially the judge was opposed to my application to recall the witness but after some discussion in chambers His Honour accepted that my application had merit and the witness should be recalled. After a delay of a day the complainant was back in the witness box. When I put the conflicts to her she could not adequately explain why she had told the petrol attendant there had been two attackers but told the nurse there had only been one attacker. It did not take the jury long to acquit my client. Another win!

Having this particular judge presiding over the Donnelly murder case was therefore not an auspicious beginning to this critical trial. In those days, a court stenographer who sat next to the judge typed up transcripts of proceedings. No audio recordings of evidence were made in these days. In the late '80s judges could do incredible things with the tone of their voice and facial expression when addressing a jury. If a judge favoured the prosecution, the defence faced a hard task. Of course the Court of Appeal never heard, saw or experienced any of these invisible biasing actions that a skilled judge could use to influence the jury against an accused in the old days.

Compounding my problem, Aaron Perkins was the Crown prosecutor. He and I had been good personal friends for a number of years. Back in the mid '80s a man named Peter Fulcher faced multiple charges of importing heroin using attractive women as drug couriers. Now the couriers were turning on him.

This was a major trial. Perkins was my junior counsel. Perkins and I made a good team. On no less than thirteen occasions during that three-week trial, the Crown prosecutor David Morris, Aaron Perkins and I marched up the seventeen steps and 43 paces down the back corridor and were escorted into the judge's chambers. Of course you never entered the judge's chambers without an invitation from his associate. Some thought Perkins and I an odd pair. Aaron stood about 5'4" with his high heels on. I stood 6'2 $\frac{1}{2}$'". His size was deceptive. Perkins had big balls and a better than average brain, as he demonstrated to everybody in the Fulcher drug case.

On each occasion the two of us would tag team Justice Tompkins and David Morris concerning the admissibility or otherwise of certain aspects of the evidence. The judge would listen to our arguments. First he would hear from the Crown, then us. Perkins and I both recognized Morris as being the wiliest prosecutor to wrangle with. Unbeknown to anybody David Morris reminded me of my father. In my younger years I had a very testing relationship with my father so that background made it easy for me to challenge Morris in the manner that I did.

On every occasion in chambers the judge would let each of us speak and then he would give his ruling. Four of these applications were of little note to the defence but nine of them were very important (to allow the evidence complained of in each situation to be given before the jury would be very prejudicial to our client's case). Unfortunately the consequences for Fulcher were such if he was convicted, that we could not just blindly accept the judge's initial 'No' ruling.

So on every occasion we argued the point in chambers I ignored the practice and protocol of having just one bite of the cherry. Instead I continued to try to make my point clearer. Although His Honour had said 'no' on nine occasions – on each of those occasions before he could pick up his pen and write 'No' on the court file - Perkins and I continued to argue the point. The end result was that we changed nine 'No' rulings to 'Yes' rulings by sheer perseverance.

The client was convicted of some of the heroin import charges but not others. Unfortunately for Fulcher, halfway through his offending the legislation was changed raising the maximum sentence for importing class 'A' drugs (the most serious) from 14 years to life in prison. The real contest for Perkins and me was to ensure that Fulcher was not convicted of the charges that carried a life sentence. Fortunately the defence was able to discredit the key crown witness. She was an attractive blonde who was forced to admit in the witness box that she was having sex with her police minder. This meant she was likely to be a biased witness. On the critical import charge Fulcher was acquitted. After the jury had been discharged and the prisoner remanded in custody for sentencing at a later date I began to pack up my books and papers. Suddenly I felt a tap on my shoulder.

'Mr. Harder,' said the judge's associate, 'I have been requested by the judge to ask you for a copy of your Canadian dictionary.'

'What do you mean?' I asked.

With a big grin on his face he said, 'The judge wants to see where in Canadian it says *no* means *yes!*

I looked at Perkins. For the next five minutes neither of us could stop laughing. Two weeks later David Morris hired Aaron Perkins as a prosecutor.

Perkins took his vacations in England where he would compete in the Isle of Man motorcycle races. He was a formidable racer with nerves of steel. On the occasion of his return from one of his overseas trips, I composed a press release. It detailed how Auckland Crown prosecutor Perkins, on holiday in London, had been cheered as a hero. The release told of a heroic exploit where Perkins had crossed a London Electric Power Board Workers Union picket line, then climbing 150 feet up a power pylon in a raging storm to rescue a tiny, shivering, stranded kitten.

At the end of the press release Perkins was asked why he had risked his life to rescue the kitten? The fabricated quoted response I mischievously attributed to Perkins at the end of my pretend release read, 'Wouldn't you, for a little pussy?'

For a joke I faxed a copy to a reporter friend in Wellington. The release had NZPA typed on the bottom. This stood for 'New Zealand Press Association'. To my surprise and horror the release was taken seriously. Throngs of reporters suddenly wanted to interview my hero friend Perkins just back from London.

The next day I received a call from the Law Society asking me to explain the circumstances of my sending a fax under the initials of the New Zealand Press Association without authority to a Wellington newspaper. Peter Williams taught me early in my career to always 'piss on the bushfire' quickly before it turned into a forest fire. With that advice in mind I quickly flew to Wellington where I profusely apologized and groveled to the president of the NZPA not to pursue his complaint against me with the Law Society. Since this incident, and after Perkins became a prosecutor, we have unfortunately clashed in court a number of times.

At the start of the first Donnelly trial, the two of us spoke little. He was set on prosecuting and convicting my client and I was intent on defending and winning. Our past friendship meant nothing now.

Perkins gave the opening address for the prosecution. He characterized my client as a cold-blooded murderer who had shot the deceased man nine times – seven times in the back at a distance, as he was walking away from the house, down the driveway according to the Crown's theory.

His address was a brutally unsympathetic presentation to the jury taking no account of the fear my client would have been experiencing at the time. As I heard Perkins make these comments my blood began to boil. Perkins ignored the fact the deceased had been carrying a bar that could have looked like a rifle in the dark.

When the 11:30 morning tea break came Perkins had not yet finished his address to the jury. Justice Hillyer told the jury to take the morning break then he retired from the court. When the jury rose and began to walk out of the jury box I leaned over to the prosecution table and said in an audible voice 'Hey Perky, you ever heard of self-defence?'

He looked at me with dagger eyes. How dare I call him by a familiar name in front of the jury! And self defence? It wasn't his job to raise self-defence! Sad to say he was probably right: my behavior was not appropriate. The prosecutor asked to see the judge alone before the jury returned. He then complained about the comments I had made in front of the jury.

I was still mad though, and blurted out to Perkins in front of the judge:

'Well, you know what it's like to be in fear for your life – when you've been threatened!

His Honour criticized my behavior but he said the trial was to continue. The main prosecution witness was a man who had been with the deceased on the night of the killing. The two had come to the house armed with metal bars and knives. The witness said they had left these on the verge of the road before making their way on to the defendant's property.

I cross-examined the witness. He was adamant that the

deceased had been shot when he was halfway down the driveway as he was running away. He would not be swayed on this crucial point.

Came five o'clock, the judge urged me to finish my questioning. Although he offered to keep the court after five o'clock that day, I insisted that I would need time to study the witnesses evidence and that I would continue my cross-examination in the morning. His Honour was not pleased, but he had no choice but to allow me to resume next day. I would not be cowed – it is always an advantage to keep a witness in the box overnight.

Begrudgingly, the judge adjourned the court for the night. As is usual for me, I asked him to warn the witness that he was not to discuss his evidence with anybody overnight. He was under cross-examination. This warning should be given to all witnesses with regularity when cases are adjourned overnight but often it is not.

The next morning at about eight o'clock I received a phone call from a former client of mine. She was a woman of the world, with a big heart and supplied me with information from time to time – she had her ear to the ground, when it came to events in the Auckland underworld. Her name was Carolyn. I had helped one of her sons out of a spot so we had a very good relationship. She was also a potential witness for the defence in Donnelly's case. The evidence she could give would demonstrate the atmosphere of animosity and fear that had existed at the time Donnelly and the deceased had their fatal clash.

On the phone, she said: 'You're not going to believe what just happened!!! I just saw (the prosecution witness). He comes here lots of times. He came here at seven o'clock this morning. He told me he had been in the witness box last night and he had to go back to court this morning. He told me about all the lies he told in court when you were asking him questions.'

'I beg your pardon?'

'When he denied setting Donnelly's car on fire, and all that other threatening behavior days before.'

'And he told you *he told lies in court?*'

'Yes.'

I took her statement before returning to court and resuming my cross-examination. I spoke softly.

'Do you recall last night you were told by the judge that you weren't to talk to anybody about this case?'

'Yes.'

'And have you?'

'No.'

'You're sure?'

'Yes.'

I turned to the judge.

'Your Honour, I'd be obliged if I could have name suppression for the person I am about to refer to.'

Earlier in the trial the judge had granted name suppression for a *New Zealand Herald* employee who was identified as the gay boyfriend of the deceased. The application had been treated, as a formality, a matter of course, so I was confident this would be treated equally liberally, given there was no objection from the Crown. I continued my examination without pause.

'Now witness, isn't it true that this morning at seven o'clock..'

I was just about to take the witness's head off in the witness box in front of the jury when Justice Hillyer interrupted me.

'Mr. Harder, I'm sick and tired of these name suppression applications you continue to make! I felt the judge was trying to disrupt my questioning of the witness. By this early stage of the trial I had concluded that I had an unsympathetic jury, judge and prosecutor. If the trial continued my client would be convicted of murder.

Suddenly I inappropriately exploded at the judge, regretting it immediately, but the damage had been done.

This is not something you do to a judge like this one in front of the jury. The trial went down hill from there. The judge sent the jury out. Immediately Perkins asked Hillyer J to abort the trial because of defence counsel's inappropriate behavior. The prosecutor and I both got our wish.

Needless to say, David Morris and Aaron Perkins wrote to the Law Society about my trial behaviour. Although both prosecutors complained of my behavior to the judge, His Honour did not complain.

After the first trial had been aborted pressure came to bear from several quarters on the Donnelly family to change Michael Donnelly's defence lawyer. Fortunately for the client and me the family decided to stick with me.

On 6 April 1993 the Solicitor-General once again wrote to the Law Society, this time to the President Mr. Salmon. In his letter McGrath laid out various complaints in relation to my conduct in the first Donnelly murder trial that was aborted.

In his letter he complained that I had 'suggested the Crown was not fairly putting its case in Perkins opening, that I had made reference to a well known criminal in my cross-examination without a proper basis, that during my cross-examination of the key crown witness I had been disruptive of the hearing and abusive to the judge'. Last he complained that I made a statement to the press about Perkins that I should not have made. He ended his letter stating,

"The material I am sending you in view shows Mr. Harder went well beyond the permitted bounds to the extent that Mr. Perkins, in my opinion, rightly had to ask for the trial to be aborted. Paragraph 2(d) above indicates such unprofessional behaviour is likely to continue in the form of a public attack on prosecuting counsel. For these reasons I have decided to make this complaint to your society". Signed JJ McGrath QC, Solicitor-General.

To be continued in Chapter 20.

17 Whangape Maori Protest

At first glance, Whangape – a tiny harbour settlement north of the Hokianga – doesn't look much like Waco, Texas. For me, though, there are great similarities. The two locations represent to me opposite sides of the same coin: Waco was a tragedy while Whangape was, in its own small way, a triumph. In some ways I see the resolution of the New Zealand situation as a personal vindication – I took what I learned in Texas a few months earlier and applied it locally.

In 1993 a man called Robert Buchanan won Lotto. He collected four million dollars, the biggest prize at that time in New Zealand history, just two days before he was due to apply for the Domestic Purposes Benefit. Buchanan had trained and practised as a district nurse, but the phenomenal resources suddenly at his disposal put him in a position to realise life-long dreams. As a young man he had farmed for a time, but gave up because he could never see himself being able to buy land. With enough money to set his own path, it did not take him long to purchase 839 hectares of sheep and cattle country in the far North for $715,000.

The vendor was a man called Frank Geddes. Ngati Haua opposed the August 1993 sale passionately: the iwi argued that it should have had a first option on purchasing the land, due to its significance to the tribe.

Buchanan's occupation of his new farm was rocky, to say the least. His relationship with local Maori was confrontational. Both sides arguably displayed belligerent behaviour. A sign was painted high on a rock face near the property stating - 'Lotto buys Misery' - and a protest encampment was set up at the main entrance to the farm. Everyone entering and exiting had to run the gauntlet, which sometimes resulted in nails appearing in vehicle tyres. There was a mysterious fire in Buchanan's woolshed. Rails disappeared from his stockyard. His letterbox was axed.

There was some national interest in the situation, and locally it was very high profile. The Kaitaia police made a point of clearing marijuana plots, their owners unknown, from the farm's gullies. The local newspaper editorially raged against the protestors. The Far North District Council tried to use the force of its bylaws to compel the removal of the camp. Talk among farmers in the area was that vigilante justice might be a practical solution to the problem - breaking a few Maori arms and legs might just be a way of solving the problem.

On December 29 1993, matters came to a head in a dramatic and violent fashion. Details of the events are somewhat sketchy, and vary depending on who tells the story. We know for sure that the owner returned to the property through the farm entrance - protestors claim that he sped through at a dangerously high speed, endangering the nearby children. The vehicle was stopped at a roadblock, where it was attacked. Its windows were smashed and Buchanan was allegedly punched.

The escalation from passive to active confrontation transformed the situation from a local sore point to a real focus of national interest. The prospect of Maori challenging the ownership of privately held land frightened many; especially rural landowners, and the protest now had a reputation for violence. The Whangape Valley was a microcosm in which issues of significance to the nation were being played out, and matters were not being resolved peacefully.

The police laid charges against four of the protestors. Some of the matters alleged were fairly serious - assault with a weapon carried a potential penalty of five years imprisonment. The Ngati Haua were resolute in their desire to win back the land so rich in their tribal history, and the looming prosecution did nothing to lessen their commitment to the protest camp. Both sides were angry and neither seemed willing to be flexible. Needless to say, the court action was highly political, and intrinsically linked to the ongoing protest at Buchanan's gate.

Ngati Haua called me to defend the accused men. They probably chose me because of my previous involvement with Keina Murray, a member of the iwi. Murray had been disqualified from driving, but was driving his car home anyway at one o'clock one morning when he had difficulties with it. He stalled in the middle of the road, and then had problems starting the vehicle again. When he did manage to get the engine running once more, he found that the car moved by bunny hopping along the road. All this made a lot of noise and attracted attention to him. Someone called the police.

A junior constable, new to the force, arrived at the scene. At the time he was chasing another Maori man. The fugitive fled from his pursuer through Murray's car, passing in one of the rear passenger doors and out the other. It was alleged by Murray (although not accepted in court) that during the pursuit the policeman was shouting insults at his target, calling him, among other things, a 'fucking nigger'. My client said that the situation scared him, so he ran from his car onto a nearby cricket pitch. There he came across the constable again, the two struggled and the officer drew his pistol and shot Murray four times.

The population of Kaitaia, especially local Maori, was incensed by this incident. Tempers were close to flaring, and the situation was genuinely dangerous. In these circumstances I appeared on television with Murray's mother and effectively poured oil on the troubled waters. Our approach was conciliatory and forgiving, and in our comments and attitude we took great care to say nothing that might be interpreted in any way provocative. This was my first dealing with Ngati Haua, and the resolution achieved was to the satisfaction of all involved.

I also suspect that the publicity (much of it attracted unwittingly) associated with my trip to Waco in 1993 caught their attention. There were some disturbing parallels with the situation developing in Whangape.

The charges were due to be heard in the Kaitaia District Court on Monday 17 January 1994. I spent the day before, in a hui with the Ngati Haua. The primary purpose of our discussions was to agree trial tactics for the following day, but I knew that there was a greater significance to the meeting – the situation had escalated to a stage where the authorities were hell-bent on enforcing the rule of law, and the protestors were becoming fanatical about their stand on principle. I had seen this in Texas (although it bears noting that the Northland iwi's principles were more rational by degrees than those of the Branch Davidians), and was painfully familiar with the eventual consequences of intransigence. This hui was my chance to try to inject some common sense into the equation. Fortunately, staunch and heartfelt as their position was, the Ngati Haua proved to be a people with the wisdom to see that escalating their conflict would not lead to its resolution.

We spent five hours speaking, and during that time my personal adventures in Fiji and Waco paid their dividends. In Fiji I had found when under house arrest that given a captive audience and the opportunity to talk with them at length, I could present the perspective of an objective observer. Not having an emotional investment in the situation, I could effectively explain the high price that often attaches to stands of principle, and propose options from 'outside the box' that were orientated on results, not on positions.

It was clear that the focus of the potentially incendiary Whangape situation was the protest camp. Although there was no direct link between the prosecution and the protest, the two constituted different aspects of the same issue. Criminal charges aside, given the circumstances, it seemed likely that the continuation of the camp would lead to further violence.

The five hours of talk were draining for all involved. The iwi was passionate in its attitude to the land, and committed to continuing the protest. Their emotional investment had, predictably, been increased rather than lessened by recent developments. There was a general reluctance to even consider abandoning the camp. I talked a lot, as I am wont to do when given the opportunity, and my attitude to the hui was more respectful than it has, at times, been to the courtroom (perhaps because there was more wisdom in that iwi than I have seen in some courts).

As we reached the end of the day I knew that I had made my points as well as I could. My arguments for common sense and compromise were on the table facing the passion of the Te Rarawa connection to the land, their sense of injustice and their pride in the stand they were taking. I wanted to hammer home the potential consequences of unwillingness to compromise. The Ngati Haua knew that I had been in Texas, and everyone on the planet was familiar with the tragic loss of life that had eventuated there.

I opened my briefcase and took out a cap that I had purchased from a vendor by the entrance to David Koresh's doomed compound in Waco. The lettering on it read WACO – We Ain't Coming Out. I held the hat before me so all could see it and said, 'Who wants to wear this?'

No one spoke up. I sat down, talked out, and waited to see what would happen.

Hone Harawira, Otere Halkyard and Glass Murray were some of the staunchest protestors and men of the highest principle. It was these three men who spoke then. Eloquently conveying their pride, making clear that the ultimate goal of regaining tribal land remained unchanged, they suggested that to avoid continued conflict something new could be tried.

I was moved, and responded by quoting an old adage that a friend had taught me that had left an impression on me.

'Whatever you can do, or dream you can do, do it now. For boldness has genius, power and magic in it.' (Author unknown)

The hui decided that the protest camp should be abandoned.

The headline of the news report of the court case in the New Zealand Herald, 22 April 1994, read:

All Charges Dismissed

"Charges have been dismissed against four people accused of assaulting and intimidating a millionaire lotto winner during a Northland land dispute.

The charges arose out of a protest by Ngati-Haua members against the sale of a farm at Whangape to the lotto winner, Mr Robert Buchanan.

Raymond Trevor Murray, aged 31, a sickness beneficiary of Whangape, appeared before Judge Martin Beattie in the Kaitaia District Court charged with assaulting Mr Buchanan.

James Phillip Murray, a contractor of Whangape was charged with the unlawful intimidation of Mr Buchanan.

Hone Paul Tamati Harawira, 39, of Awanui, was charged with assaulting Mr Buchanan with a crowbar and unlawful assembly.

Otere Halkyard, 32, unemployed of Whangape, was charged with assaulting Mr Buchanan with a hammer, assault with intent to use a weapon, intentional damage to Mr Buchanan's vehicle and unlawful assembly.

All the offences allegedly happened on December 29 last year.

Judge Beattie dismissed the charge against Raymond Murray at the start of the trial on Tuesday.

The charge against James Murray was dropped after an application from the defence lawyer, Christopher Harder, that there was no case to answer following prosecution evidence.

The charges against Halkyard and Harawira were dismissed at the end of the trial. Whangarei lawyer, David Sayes represented them both.

Judge Beattie said he found the evidence of the defence witnesses to be credible, and the testimony of Mr Buchanan could not be relied on."

18

The Papal Knight Drug Case

I was in Canada on holiday and my colleague Shane Cassidy was in charge of the legal office when a new client made an appearance. While in Vancouver with my parents, I received a telephone call from Cassidy. A client had walked in off the street, having been charged with possession of cannabis for supply.

Cassidy told me that X had been using a QC but his fee was too expensive so he changed his mind and now he wants to hire us.

'Yeah, that's cool,' I told Cassidy.

'Get an instructing solicitor just to cover our asses, then get a retainer – see if you can get five grand. Tell him I'll see him when I get back.'

I finished my holiday and returned to New Zealand, then arranged for the client to come to see me. X arrived with all the relevant legal papers. I asked for the details of what had happened.

X explained that he had rented a lock-up storage garage. The police had searched it and found two large garbage bags with dregs of cannabis in the bottom, together with two boxes of the tubes from which plastic bags are dispensed. All the plastic bags were gone. On the basis of this circumstantial evidence, the police inductively reasoned that approximately 800 bags must have been filled with cannabis and distributed from the garage. In the summary of facts the 800 bags were noted, the value of the drugs was set at $250,000, and the situation was characterized as, 'major cannabis dealing'. X took me to the site and showed me the garage, the alarm system, and the padlock. I questioned him in great detail about who else might have had access to the storage space.

'I'm the only one who knows the alarm combination and I'm the only one that has the key. People work for me, but I let them in and out.'

No obvious defence there. His previous counsel had taken X through depositions on a hand up basis, which meant that the maximum penalty went up from one year (as it would have been in the District Court), to seven years. X and his wife were extremely concerned that a jail sentence might be imposed on conviction. They wanted to know if I would take the case, and what I would charge.

'Thirteen or fifteen grand, something in that neighborhood.' They had already paid five. The couple explained that they had very little money. The accused man had an idea: 'I guess I'll have to sell the wife's car to get some money.'

Later, X returned with his wife to discuss how my fee would be paid. Mrs. X was a big woman, without being fat, and my assessment was that she was in charge of the pair. X announced that he would sell his wife's car to pay the fee, but Mrs. X was not at all happy with this. Sell *her* car to pay for *his* problem? And then give the money to a bloody *lawyer*?! A domestic incident was developing in my offices.

I didn't care how the couple resolved their differences. I certainly cared about my fee.

My objective in defending the case was clear: X and his wife were adamant that avoiding prison for him was the goal. I agreed that I would work on that. For the next three months I worked on the Crown, gradually convincing the prosecutor to reduce the seriousness of the charge, despite resistance. Eventually, I succeeded. The brief would be altered. Reference to the 800 bags and value of $250,000 would be removed, and the situation would be described as 'cannabis dealing', not '*major* cannabis dealing'. I felt confident: as it originally read, the brief of evidence clearly suggested a jail term would be an appropriate punishment. Now altered, the seriousness of the matter was greatly diminished. I told X: 'this is the best I can do. You plead guilty to this summary and you'll be okay.'

X pleaded guilty as I advised him to do. The judge remanded him on bail while a probation report was prepared. When a report is called for, an officer interviews the offender and discusses the persons past and the offence he is to be sentenced for. Normally the probation officer will indicate to the client the sentence he is going to recommend to the court, be imposed.

Two days later I was sitting in my office in Remuera, downstairs from my house, when suddenly Mr. and Mrs. X burst in. They were hysterical with anger. 'You lied to us! You deceived us! You bull-shitted us!' Mrs. X was doing most of the yelling.

'Stop, stop, stop! What are you talking about? What do you mean? Whoa! Whoa! Whoa! What's the problem?'

'We went to the probation officer this afternoon and we sat down at his desk and he looked at my husband and the first thing he said was 'You're going to jail.'

'Wait a minute, that's bullshit, he . . .'

'That's what he said! We're getting ourselves another lawyer! You deceived us! You lied to us! . . .'

I tried to interrupt, to win a pause in the stream of abuse, to tell them that something was clearly not right, but to no avail. I pride myself on being able to handle others' anger, but was disconcerted in this instance I could have no effect. My clients wanted their money back, they wanted the file, and they wanted to find themselves another lawyer, and this time a GOOD lawyer! Then they stormed out.

I was not happy. The case had seemed to be going well, I had put a great deal of work into it, and I didn't want to lose the client. I called the probation officer immediately.

'Hey, my client just came into my office with a mad as hell wife screaming at me. Seems you told my client he was going straight to jail!'

'That's right Mr. Harder, I did.'

'What the hell did you say that for?!'

'Have you seen the summary of facts? '$250,000', '800 bags', 'major cannabis dealing.'

'For fuck's sake! You've got the wrong summary of facts! All that stuff is out. It has been deleted. Obviously you have been given the incorrect summary of facts.'

'Oh! Well that's different!' said the probation officer.

'That would just be PD.' (Period detention)

'Fax me through your report that it would just be PD, quick.'

It was too late. That same afternoon I received a phone call from X's new lawyer, David Reece. He had taken over the case, and was preparing an application for X to change his plea from guilty to not guilty. The accused man had lost confidence in me and had no interest in listening to anything I had to say.

At the same time Mr. and Mrs. X had applied for a costs revision of their bill (a process conducted through the New Zealand Law Society). They wanted their money back. I argued that X had been charged on an 'agreed fee' basis, that I had completed my part of the deal, that there had been a misunderstanding, and that X would not go to prison (and so my client's goal would be reached) if I kept the case. No matter what I said, the couple was not interested. The costs revision was completed. I lost. I was ordered to return most of the fee. I appealed the costs revision to the Registrar of the High Court (who is assisted by a barrister in costs revision appeals). The determination was that the costs revision had been fair: I still had to pay. I appealed to the High Court.

The matter was set down for hearing, and I was worried. I was working on a case in Whangarei, and could not personally attend court in Auckland. Shane Cassidy appeared on my behalf. Two days before the hearing date, I called the court to find out which judge would hear my appeal. Paul Temm, QC. A vivid recollection of a young lawyer receiving his practising certificate flashed through my head:

'If I ever catch you without an instructing solicitor I'll see that you're struck off the rolls!'

To that point, the issue had been the fee charged. In front of Temm J, the question of having an instructing solicitor suddenly assumed vital significance.

'Who was the damned instructing solicitor?' I asked Cassidy – this was a full year after X had first spoken with him.

'I'm sorry, Christopher, I genuinely, genuinely can't recall.'

My nightmare was beginning to come true. Temm J would be able to see from the papers no reference to an instructing solicitor. If Cassidy and I could not produce one, a career might well end.

The day before the hearing Reece took an affidavit from X. This set out in detail how I had sworn in his presence. Mrs. X had been very upset, he said.

'My wife rang Mr. Harder's *instructing solicitor*, [my emphasis] Robyn Harre to complain about his behaviour and seek her advice.' On the eve of my appearance, I couldn't stop laughing.

Rescued by the opposition.

19

Hong Kong Triad Kidnap Case

Let me tell you about my involvement with a seventeen-year-old Chinese I'll call Johnny Low. Johnny was born in Hong Kong, but lived in Auckland with his mother. His father was a businessman who still ran several companies in Hong Kong and worked from that city, visiting his family in Auckland every few months.

I travelled to Hong Kong to look after the interests of this teenage client, who had been charged in New Zealand with kidnapping and demanding money with menaces – serious matters for one so young, and especially unusual considering the accused was a 'clean skin' with no previous convictions. This case started from a small incident in an Auckland restaurant.

A sixteen-year-old Hong Kong boy named Charlie, living in New Zealand on a student visa, went to a Karaoke bar with some friends. At one table sat a number of youths claiming to be members of the 14K Triad, a Hong Kong gang, in Auckland. At another table sat a group of Taiwanese students. A fight broke out between the two groups. The police were called but before they arrived the fight was over and the parties had dispersed.

Two days later Charlie was contacted by a 14K Triad gang member and told to go to the address of another gang member. Charlie was familiar with the address because he had previously loaned his computer to one of the men who lived there. Arriving at the property, he was confronted by one of the men involved in the fight, who accused him of talking too much about the brawl. Over a period of ten hours Charlie was detained against his wishes. Two men from the house beat him, then forced him to agree to pay them money.

Charlie was eventually released after promising to pay $1,000 as a penalty for talking out of turn. Subsequently he ran into Johnny, the boy who would become my client, at a badminton court and told him of these traumatic events. Charlie asked Johnny for help in solving his problem. Johnny agreed to help because he was on speaking terms with those who had detained and beaten Charlie the night before.

After Johnny agreed to help, Charlie asked him to recover his computer from the address where he had been beaten. Johnny duly did so and returned it. Sometime after the computer was returned, the leader of the 14K Triad (nicknamed 'Elephant Man') told Johnny and Charlie to meet him at a pool hall. The two friends were then assaulted because 'Elephant Man' believed my client and Charlie had demanded $800 in 'computer hire fees' from one of his gang. As a punishment the Triad leader required Johnny and Charlie to come up with $5,000 that night. When the pair realised they couldn't raise such an amount in one evening, my client Johnny made contact with Elephant Man, who compromised by demanding a $1,000 penalty.

A week later members of the 14K gang were having dinner at a local Chinese restaurant. By chance Charlie, his home-stay friend and Johnny attended the same restaurant. Charlie had been planning to fly back to Hong Kong the next day to escape his tormentors. Unfortunately for him one of Charlie's friends informed Elephant Man of his plans. When he learned of this deceit Elephant Man told his boys to take Charlie to a motel and look after him until morning when he could go to the bank and get the $5,000.

The group told Charlie they were going to have a party at a local motel. Charlie contributed $50 for beer and cannabis, while Johnny and another boy were sent to get the beer and the drugs. While my client was away three 14K members threatened and assaulted Charlie. One of the youths held a knife in each hand waving them around and threatening Charlie that if he did not pay he would cut his arms off.

After a time Charlie went into the bathroom, and emerged a short time later with a plastic bag containing $5,000, which he gave to one of his kidnappers. He then asked to be released. Charlie was told to stay in the motel until the morning. The $5,000 was taken downtown and handed to Elephant Man, who waited in a deserted hotel car park.

The gang members returned to the motel, angry with Charlie for not paying up earlier. They demanded another $3,000 for holding out on them. Over the next two hours they made Charlie phone his mother in Hong Kong. Charlie explained that he owed some people money and he must honour the debt before he left for Hong Kong. His mother suspected the boy was in trouble because she could hear male voices telling her son what to say.

'If you are in trouble,' she told him, 'then say uh-huh.'

Charlie promptly replied 'uh-huh.' His mother told her son she would call his uncle in Auckland and ask him to arrange the money in the morning. Eight hours later the New Zealand Police armed offenders squad surrounded the motel and called on the occupants to come out with their hands up. Four youths, including my client Johnny, were arrested and charged with kidnapping (punishable by fourteen years imprisonment) and two counts of demanding with menace (each punishable by seven years). Johnny was also charged with possession of cannabis.

I went to Hong Kong to research this case, and specifically to talk with Johnny's father. I found flying into Hong Kong in the dead of night on Friday 13 December 1996 a little hair-raising. As we approached Kai Tak airport the Singapore Airlines 747 swooped from the clouds into a canyon of high-rise apartment buildings and downtown skyscrapers. This unnerving experience was offset by the view of Hong Kong lit up at night - a sight never more splendid than in the week before Christmas. Hong Kong is a city to rival Las Vegas or Acapulco for night-lights and in the festive season neon artists outdo themselves.

Johnny's dad put my private investigator Brian Rowe and me up in the prestigious Nico hotel - in a suite on the 14th floor, overlooking Kowloon harbour - and left us to settle in and work in our own time.

I had been hired with a handsome retainer to look after, and defend if necessary, the interests of this teenage boy. No expense was to be spared. As well as spending time with Johnny's father, Rowe and I were hoping to interview the mother of the sixteen-year-old complainant.

After six days in Hong Kong we concluded that we could do no more to advance my client's defence in Hong Kong this trip. Unfortunately for the defence, the police inspector I first spoke to in Hong Kong was less than helpful when I requested his assistance in speaking to the complainant's mother.

Sergeant Day, the New Zealand officer in charge, agreed with the defence that the mother was a critical witness in the case. Twenty-four hours after my first request to the inspector I telephoned him back seeking a progress report. He advised me that he had spoken to the mother and that she did not wish to speak to me. Once my request had been turned down, Sergeant Day made a similar request to the Inspector to interview the mother himself. However, because the inspector had already succeeded in dissuading the witness from talking to the defence, he also inadvertently dissuaded her from talking to anyone else, including the New Zealand police. Unbeknown to the inspector this refusal to be interviewed actually helped the defence. Without the mother as a witness the police case in relation to the kidnap allegation was considerably weakened.

We had one last discussion with my client's father over a cup of coffee in the mezzanine lobby of the Nico Hotel before we left Hong Kong. I explained to him the unexpected advantage that might later flow on to his son's case because of the New Zealand police having also been denied an interview by the mother.

By that stage I was also pretty sure that a trip to Peru was on the cards. To protect my new, well paid brief from wandering off to another lawyer working over the holiday while I went to South America, I dropped a comment into the conversation to the effect that I might go to Peru and Cuba for a week over January. For the past fourteen years I had worked the Christmas/New Year break and throughout January when most lawyers were on holiday.

This way I started off the year with some 'new blood' and a bit of a financial cushion for the first couple of months. I had to ensure the clients continued to come. I seldom did legal aid work - my clientele were mostly private paying, and expected results.

Johnny's father asked:'Why do you want to go to Lima?'

'Because of the hostage drama.' I replied. 'I think I can negotiate a plea bargain.'

A puzzled look appeared on his face.

'For how long?' he asked.

'A week, ten days' I said. 'And I might go to Cuba after Lima, but I'll just have to wait and see how things develop.' The mention of Cuba caused my client's dad to break out into a smile.

'Could you pick me up some Cuban cigars?' he asked eagerly.

'Of course I would! It would be my pleasure!' I replied. I had been a bit anxious he might object to me travelling overseas on an unrelated case. My anxiety reduced when I interpreted his request as a signal he did not object to my holiday travel plans as long as I returned to New Zealand within a reasonable time to work on his son's kidnap charge.

With our business finished in Hong Kong Brian Rowe and I packed our suitcases in preparation for our return to New Zealand. As we boarded our aircraft I felt a tinge of sadness leaving Hong Kong. The excitement of Christmas in Hong Kong was infectious. I would miss the hustle and the bustle of the Christmas crowds, the live fish and snake restaurants and the vast selection of reasonably priced electronic goods available in what was then one of the last colonial outposts of the British Empire.

Early in the case my private investigator had interviewed Johnny, who denied being a member of the 14K Triad. This was a complicated and already complex case. By the beginning of May we were back on the case in earnest. I prepared detailed submissions outlining why I thought the police should drop the charges against my client. Sergeant Day refused.

'The complainant says your client is 14K. If that is so he is a party to the kidnapping and demanding with menace at the very least.'

I was determined to find the key to Johnny's case, despite the fact that at first glance it looked impossible. To persuade the police to drop a charge before trial I found it necessary for the defence and police to agree on the facts. Once that is done it is easy enough to see which way the case is likely to go.

My next option was to ask the police to re-interview the complainant. In his first statement he denied buying any drugs or contributing to the cost of the motel. I insisted he be re-interviewed. These aspects were more consistent with a party than a kidnapping. After all, the boy's mother had not been interviewed. Without her, the kidnap case would weaken, though the demanding with menace charge was strong against all four.

Charlie was subsequently re-interviewed. He admitted he hadn't told the police that he contributed money for the drugs and the cost of the motel room. Good. But Charlie was insistent that all four accused claimed they were 14K, including Johnny. Later, in the presence of Johnny's father, I explained that there was a credibility issue between the complainant and what Johnny had told the police and also my private investigator.

'Johnny, I need to know the truth. I know you don't want to admit to being a 14K member because your father will be angry but let me tell you if you are convicted because you don't tell me the whole truth you can't come and complain to me later,' I told him.

'I have spoken to your father. He promises me if you tell me the truth he will not beat you or disown you. Do you understand?'

Still the boy sat mute. 'Father,' I said 'would you please leave the room for a moment.' Closing the door I turned to my client and explained.

'At present you are a party to the kidnap because you were found in the motel with the complainant. You also face a strong case of demanding with menace because when you came out of the toilet you told Charlie that he could pay $1,500, rather than the $5,000 the others were demanding. So you see, Johnny, the case can't be any worse than it is. Were you a member of 14K?'

After a long pause he finally replied.

'Yes, but do you have to tell my father?'

'Relax. Everything will be okay. Dad? You can come back in now.'

'Well?' asked the father.

'Your son has admitted to me he is 14K. Now I have assured him you will not get angry here or at home. Is that agreed?'

'Yes' replied the father.

'Then this is how we defend from this point on. There are two parts to a crime, the *actus rea* (the physical act) and the necessary *mens rea* (guilty mind). Your son appeared to be a party to the physical kidnapping or detaining as well as the demand with menaces. But I am no longer so sure he had the necessary guilty mind to convict him of kidnap or demanding. Charlie had approached Johnny knowing at the time Johnny was 14K-related, which was why he asked him for help. Sir, the truth may well set your son free!'

At the lower court deposition hearing - where the evidence is tested to see if it is sufficient to go to trial - I cross-examined Charlie. I established he had seen a fight, then was later beaten and forced to pay money by a group of 14K gang members. Charlie agreed and also confirmed that Johnny was not involved in this incident. Charlie said he approached Johnny and asked for help on the basis that he believed Johnny to also be a 14K member. Johnny agreed to help. The complainant confirmed that Johnny and he were punched by Elephant Man and his gang, and then told to find $5000 that same night to pay the extortionists. He also confirmed that Johnny had been at the motel, but that he had never hit or hurt him. Charlie also agreed that when the other three were demanding an extra $3,000, Johnny had them reduce it to $1500.

The end result of the case saw the deposition hearing adjourned after my cross-examination. I pointed out to Sergeant Day that my cross-examination had demonstrated Johnny did not have a guilty mind in relation to either the kidnap or the demanding with menaces. 'I suggest you drop the kidnap charge. The mother is not here. Your case is weak. The other three should plead guilty to demanding with menaces.'

'No,' replied the sergeant 'All four must plead to demanding.'

'No way,' I replied. 'On my cross-examination my client will walk.'

'Well, what are you suggesting your client plead to if it is not kidnap or demanding?' he asked. 'Intimidation,' I replied.

It sounded serious but intimidation was only a summary charge with a maximum penalty of three months in prison and/or a $500 fine.

'Who is going to pay back the $5,000 taken from the complainant?' the sergeant asked. 'That should be the responsibility of the other three accused,' I suggested.

The lawyers for the other three refused to pay the money. After a time the sergeant lost his patience when the lawyers seemed unable to agree. To break the logjam I offered to pay the $5,000 restitution on behalf of my client. Finally we had a deal. The four accused and the lawyers marched back into court. The other three accused pleaded guilty to one count of demanding and were remanded on bail for sentence. The police withdrew the kidnap charge against all four. The Justices of the Peace were informed that both the kidnap and demanding charge against my client were to be withdrawn once my client had pleaded to a minor summary charge of intimidation for following the complainant around, because the police wanted a charge to clear their file.

Adeptly I distanced my client from the other three accused. I knew the judge was likely to make an example of them, because New Zealand was not used to Triad gangs threatening and demanding money from those in their own community. I manoeuvred my client, now facing very minor charges of intimidation and possession of cannabis, to the number one court. There I explained to sentencing judge Michael Lance QC the background to the case. After two hours of argument with truculent prosecutor Mark Treleavan the sentencing judge finally gave in to my request and discharged my client without conviction.

The three other accused were not so lucky. Two were sentenced to prison, one for eighteen months, another for twelve months. One accused received six months periodic detention because he was only seventeen and not as deeply involved.

Outside the court my client and his family were elated at the outcome. My client had no criminal record. Now his family could apply for valued New Zealand citizenship and remain here.

The Donnelly Re-trial (Part 2)

Before the retrial started, I forced the police to investigate whether the witness committed perjury. When questioned, he admitted it. It was more than a year before he was charged, (begrudgingly), by the police.

Things went better the second time around. The lying witness was called again, but was understandably less credible now. I cross-examined the armourer called by the prosecution. A semi-automatic rifle fires a shot every time you pull the trigger – you don't have to work a bolt action or even wait between shots. I put it to the witness that nine shots could be fired from a .22 semi-automatic in 1.89 seconds. We had tested this, so he couldn't very well disagree.

It was also helpful that there was a photograph of an iron bar lying beside Donnelly's house. The prosecution claimed that it had been left there after the shooting by the deceased man's accomplice – the lying witness – who had used it to smash car windows after the killing and then abandoned it. The defence took a different message from the bar: It corroborated Donnelly's description of seeing the deceased man carrying what looked like a rifle.

The defence contended that the two men were armed with knives and bars when they ran down Donnelly's driveway. Donnelly, sitting on his porch with his .22, saw an intruder carrying what he thought was a rifle, and in fear of his life fired a series of shots from a distance of about ten feet as the man turned to run towards the door of the house. Two shots hit the man in his front and side, seven in the back. The defence case was that the deceased continued to run for about 25 feet after he had been shot, just as a deer will run on for a few seconds after it has been shot in the heart.

After we had led this evidence, there was a trial break. Things were going well, but we were still not certain of an acquittal. During the break, however, new evidence came to light. Halfway between the house and the spot where the body fell, a .22 calibre bullet head was found. It was logical to suppose that this had entered the body or clothing of the deceased, and then fallen to the ground. This fact was very supportive of our contention that Donnelly had shot at an intruder very close to his house, and tended to disprove the Crown case that he cold-bloodedly gunned down a man 50 feet away, running to get off the property.

The bullet head on the ground was photographed and the jury saw it. On the basis of that photo, and the Crown's witnesses, I made the brave call not to call evidence. This is extremely unusual where self-defence is pleaded, and the client has given no statement to the police claiming self-defence. But the bottom line was that if the defence were to call evidence, it would have been the same evidence called by the prosecution. I had the Crown witness admitting he committed perjury at the last trial. My ploy not to call the defendant worked and Donnelly was acquitted.

Two days after my client had been acquitted I bumped into Justice Henry, the re-trial judge in the elevator. He congratulated me on my win then looked at me with a half sad look on his face before he said, 'Too bad you didn't get a manslaughter verdict for your client Christopher.' I understood what he meant. Now that I had won and rubbed the police and the prosecutor's noses in the mud of the Donnelly case I knew the prosecutors would soon turn the heat up on the complaints that they had made against me to the Law Society.

Then for greater impact Crown Prosecutor David Morris and Plumley-Walker prosecutor Bruce Squire somehow persuaded the Solicitor General to look at the charges against me more closely. The police officer in charge of the investigation forever blamed himself for the acquittal. He believed that one of the police officers involved in searching the site must have accidentally kicked the bullet from a spot 50 feet up the driveway to where it was eventually found, very close to the house. I don't know the truth of the matter, and suppose I never will. In a sad postscript some years after his acquittal Donnelly drove his motorbike into a ditch. He was paralyzed from the waist down.

Almost a year after Donnelly was acquitted of murder the star Crown witness was finally charged with perjury and he pleaded guilty.

I attended his sentence with my mother who was visiting from Canada at the time. Newly appointed High Court Justice Silvia Cartwright was tasked with sentencing the lying Donnelly Crown witness for his perjury. As I sat beside my mother at the back of the court the judge sentenced the witness turned accused to three months in prison suspended for six months. Immediately I stood up at the back of the court. 'Excuse me Your Honour but you can't do that!' I said. I tried to explain but was cut short as the judge adjourned the court without a further word. My mother was telling me to sit down. She was most upset at my behaviour. I did not seem to have changed much since I was a young boy. I continued to vent my spleen on the prosecutor before he left the court but he too ignored me. I felt like the die was cast.

The next day I wrote to the Solicitor-General and complained that the sentence Justice Cartwright gave the accused for perjury was an unlawful sentence. This was because the law only allowed a judge to suspend a sentence of imprisonment if the term is not less than 6 months and not more than two years imprisonment.

The Body In The Woods Case

Yvonne Ann Bennett disappeared on Monday 19 April 1982. She vanished from an air force home at Hobsonville she shared with husband Warwick and daughter Vicky then aged five. She was 24 years old.

Mrs Bennett worked in Kelston as a part-time receptionist at the Westward Ho Tavern. She left work at 4.30pm on the Monday, taking with her a typewriter and stock books, which she promised to return the next day. Driving the family's green, wood-trim Morris Mini Traveller van, she called on a friend at Waitakere Hospital about 6pm, but details about her activities for the rest of the evening were confusing.

As a matter of habit Yvonne would take her dog, Sasha, for a walk, then stay up late to watch *Dallas* on television. Mr. Bennett was an air force sergeant – a loadmaster. That night, he told police, his wife was baking when he went to bed, and when he awoke the next morning she was gone. Leaving a note to let Yvonne know she should not worry, he took Vicky (his wife's natural daughter whom he had adopted) for a six-day holiday. They visited areas he had previously visited with his wife during the course of their 30-month marriage.

Yvonne Bennett's parents, Alan and Patricia Landers, had almost daily contact with their daughter. When she neither called beforehand nor appeared in person at their regular bingo night at a south Auckland hotel, the parents became worried. Phone calls went unanswered and the air force police could not locate Yvonne Bennett, so Alan and Patricia Landers called the police and reported her missing.

After they had confirmed that Mrs Bennett was indeed missing, the police search was extensive. Teams checked the upper Waitemata Harbour, swampland and bush near Hobsonville, and even a rubbish dump in the area. It is clear from their search patterns that foul play was suspected from the earliest stages of the investigation. There was no reason for Yvonne to have run off and no money or extra clothing was missing. Even if she had left of her own volition, her relationship with her parents was very close, and it seemed very improbable that she would voluntarily disappear without telling them anything.

Warwick was an obvious suspect. When he returned from his holiday with Vicky the next Sunday, he could not provide any assistance. Bennett proceeded to make a series of bizarre and newsworthy remarks to the police and media. There were widely publicised pleas through Auckland newspapers for his wife to come home, but he also publicly suggested foolishly that perhaps Martians had abducted Yvonne. Overall, there was insufficient evidence to tie him to any crime.

A year after Yvonne Bennett's disappearance, with police making little progress, Alan and Patricia Landers left their home in Glen Innes and moved to Sherbourne in southern England.

In the intervening decade, the police continued their investigation throughout the North Island and even overseas. They made no startling breakthroughs, but gradually built up information from interviews, and solicited help from the public. On Tuesday, February 19, 1991, the disappearance featured on Television New Zealand's *Crimewatch* programme, provoking further offers of assistance for the investigating team. A hitchhiker called to offer some new evidence. Still the case was weak against Bennett. Then an ex girlfriend made a complaint of assault against Bennett. Although it was unrelated to the murder inquiry it did allow the police an opportunity to arrest Bennett on a minor matter and separate him from Vicky, his stepdaughter.

On Tuesday 11 November 1993, more than eleven years after Yvonne Bennett vanished, Warwick Bennett was arrested at Stratford, south east of New Plymouth. Hours later, he appeared in the New Plymouth District Court charged with his wife's murder.

Bennett called me shortly after his arrest. He introduced himself on the telephone and asked me if I knew who he was. I had just been admitted to the bar at the time of his wife's disappearance but told him I read the newspapers regularly so I was aware of the mystery, but never familiar with the details.

Bennett told me he had been reading the newspapers and following current events in New Zealand for the past decade, and that he had assessed that I was the lawyer to help him out in his 'time of need'. He was, he said, absolutely innocent of the murder allegation and had not been involved in his wife's disappearance in any fashion.

On the telephone, Bennett sounded cool and measured. He was articulate and seemed intelligent. I agreed to meet him. Barrister Shane Cassidy, with whom I have worked closely for over six years, met me at the prison gate. We talked for a moment then the two of us went upstairs into the interview room where we both met Bennett for the first time.

My first impression of Bennett was that he was a tall, confident man with a gaunt face and receding hair. He projected his military background – he was clean, confident and disciplined - but he was clearly not coping well with incarceration. He wanted bail. He overflowed with nervous energy. I found the most memorable feature of Bennett to be his eyes. It was hard to say exactly what it was that was different about them but they certainly were unusual.

From this man we first heard a tale of unceasing police harassment, a decade-long nightmare for an innocent man already devastated by the loss of his wife. At our first meeting Bennett was adamant: he was the innocent victim of a campaign of police persecution. We discussed his situation in detail. We could apply for bail but it was unlikely to be granted. He was likely to spend the time before his trial in custody. From arrest, his jury trial could take up to a year to be heard. In Bennett's case because there was over twelve years of police paperwork to investigate the trial was not likely to start until late 1994.

We applied to the High Court for bail twice in December but were turned down on each occasion. Bennett was not pleased that he did not get bail. He was a man who missed his freedom.

During December 1993 and January 1994 Cassidy and I worked through a dozen Eastlight files given to us by the police as their initial disclosure to the Bennett defence. There was much more to come. Half a forest must have been cut down to make the paper needed to record every detail of the twelve-year case. It quickly became apparent that a remarkable amount of police resources had been expended over the years in an effort to try and solve the mystery of how Yvonne Bennett disappeared.

The officer in charge of the case, for all those years, Stan Keith, was now near retirement. His second in command was John 'Fingers' Flanagan. It was now or never for the police in relation to Warwick Bennett.

The police case against Bennett was not strong. It rested in part on a hitchhiker who claimed Bennett had picked her up (recalled after twelve years when a *Crimewatch* TV programme had highlighted the case) a short time after the initial disappearance, and an alleged admission he made to a woman friend that he had dumped his wife's weighted body at sea.

The police files included interviews with employers, alleged sightings of Yvonne Bennett and details of an involvement she had with another person. On the face of the material before us there was nothing that clearly pointed to Bennett as being the killer. The Crown would argue otherwise.

Agatha Christie would have been challenged to compile such an eclectic collection of relevant information, material and red herrings all mixed into one. The wealth of material supplied to the defence provided a good 'Who done it?' defence.

An unexpected admission

In February 1994 Warwick Bennett was still being held in custody at Mt Eden prison. I was still reading his files and had not yet visited Bennett in the New Year. A nervous Bennett called Peter Williams, QC to discuss his case, and Williams, as a matter of professional courtesy, informed me of the call. I promptly went up to the prison to see my restless client to explain to him that I had been reading through his numerous police files and that was why he had not heard from me.

I met him in a cramped, dingy little interview room on the upper level of Mt Eden's visitor's hall. It was little more than a cell. The room overlooked a mass of prisoners being visited by their girlfriends or wives with young children scurrying amongst them.

Bennett seemed anxious. The media had been running stories about his case and it was stressing him. His wife's parents, the Landers, were also in town and the media was having a feast.

I told him I had read his files thoroughly and that although there would be much more to come I felt I really knew him having read what I had. I referred to the ex girlfriends' statements in which they tell of Bennett putting his hands around their necks in play but making suggestive comments as to how easy it would be to kill them.

Again I told Bennett that I thought I knew him really well. I said I could understand how such a thing could happen unintentionally. I am not sure why, but all of sudden without any planning, I revealed to Bennett that once, many years before, while I was under the influence of alcohol I had tried to throttle my wife in the course of a domestic argument. I recalled nothing of the incident but I could not deny the marks around her neck the next morning.

Then my mobile phone rang.

'Harder!' I answered. I listened for a good twenty seconds without saying a word. It was my father calling from Canada. He asked me what I was doing. I quickly explained I was at the jail with a client, a man charged with murder.

Suddenly my impatient client feeling ignored, rose from his chair, stood at attention, and then sputtered out words to the effect:

'*I don't care if this compromises you or not, but I killed my wife and buried her body in the Woodhill forest.*'

I felt like a stunned mullet! My ears were ringing.

'Um, Dad, can I call you back please?' I said without explanation. Then I switched off my phone. Some statements can suck the air out of a room. For me, the background noise of the prison was gone: the hubbub of the incarcerated and their visitors had disappeared. I stared at Bennett in silence for a moment.

'Don't say another word – I have to go away and think about this. Just don't say another word,' I said. 'I have got to go and think.'

I left Bennett in the interview room then walked out of the prison and wandered dazed, to my car. I drove straight to the closest dairy to Mt Eden prison. A non-smoker for the previous three years, I immediately bought a packet of Pall Mall Menthol cigarettes (my old brand) and lit the first one up as I tried to work out what I was going to do. I called Shane Cassidy and we spoke about my dilemma. I decided to return to the prison and speak further with Bennett. I was not looking forward to the prospect.

Back in the little interview room, I heard the rest of his story. Bennett and his wife had a domestic argument. He didn't want the neighbours to hear them fighting so he put his hand over her mouth to stop her raising her voice. He explained that in the process she bit his thumb and how this caused him great pain.

Bennett went on to explain that he grabbed her by the throat with his other hand to try and make her release his thumb. Suddenly she collapsed. He checked her pulse and breathing but could find no signs of life. He panicked, carried the body to the car then drove to the Woodhill forest where he buried her. The next day he visited a lawyer for advice then went on a holiday, with his adopted daughter.

Bennett also described how after living with his deed for nearly three months he became concerned that perhaps he had not buried her deep enough. He described how he drove back into the forest, located the grave and dug up his wife's decomposing body. Then he dug a second, deeper grave, grabbing her ankles then flipping the body over into the new grave and reburying it.

Why did Bennett tell me all of this? Why didn't he just keep his mouth shut and let his lawyers proceed to trial on the basis that the police could not establish the death of Yvonne Bennett, let alone the identity of the killer? I think the reason Bennett opened up to me as his lawyer and admitted what he did, was because he was guilt-ridden and desperately needed to get it off his chest.

Bennett trusted no one. Then when I ignored him for a moment in the interview room when my father called long distance, Bennett felt compelled to interrupt us and get my attention back by blurting out to me that he had killed his wife and buried her in the forest!

Perhaps he felt genuine guilt – certainly whenever he spoke of Yvonne he claimed to have loved her. It is also possible that the sympathetic media coverage the Landers' were then receiving in relation to their desire to find their daughter's remains and put her to rest- also motivated Bennett's revelation to me.

As soon as Bennett told me he had killed Yvonne, he developed a very specific plan so far as the outcome of his trial was concerned. There would be no changing of lawyers or turning back. Bennett wanted to assist the police in locating the body. He hoped to gain some benefit for this help.

Bennett was accepting of the fact that he would be imprisoned (having killed Yvonne in some fashion, buried her, lied about it and later re-buried her to evade detection) but he desperately wanted to be convicted of manslaughter, not murder.

A manslaughter verdict would most likely result in Bennett receiving a finite jail sentence (a set number of years) as compared to murder and a life sentence although one could be sentenced to life for manslaughter. A finite sentence would leave Bennett free to travel the world after he had served his time. If he were convicted of murder he would receive the mandatory life sentence that would mean he would serve a minimum 10-12 years in jail before being released on parole for life in New Zealand.

Whatever his motives, Bennett told me that he knew where the body was buried and he wanted to see if he could find it and avoid a trial by him pleading guilty to manslaughter early in the piece.

Once Bennett had finished explaining to me what he

wanted to achieve, I decided Cassidy and I could continue to act for him because Bennett had made an informed decision when he instructed me to contact David Morris with his offer of the body for a manslaughter plea. The Woodhill forest comprises 22,000 hectares stretching from Muriwai Beach to South Kaipara Head, so without Bennett's help there was little chance his wife's body would ever be found.

I made it clear to Bennett, and he understood, that this first approach to the Crown, even if off the record, would mean that he had crossed the Rubicon. (A mythical river in Roman times, which once crossed, can never be re-crossed) Up until now the Crown did not have a strong case. Because the case had no body it was a lawyer's dream. Still Bennett wanted to help recover the body.

Bennett also wanted to make a statement to the police to tell the truth about how Yvonne really died. Previously he had told the police and the media all manner of lies about his wife's disappearance. Because of this factor I required Bennett to write his own statement to the police on his own in his cell and in his own handwriting. When Bennett had completed his voluntary statement he called us back to come up to the prison. Cassidy and I read it. Bennett claimed he killed his wife by accident trying to get his thumb out of her mouth.

Acting on Bennett's instructions I contacted David Morris. Cassidy and I met Morris in Paul Davison's legal chambers in Princess Court. At the time I suggested to Morris that Bennett might be able to assist in locating Yvonne's body. Then I asked, 'If the corpse is recovered are you prepared to entertain a guilty plea to manslaughter if there are no bullet holes in the head, no knife nicks on the bones and no broken hyoid bone?' In a manual strangulation the hyoid bone in the neck normally breaks.

After some consideration Morris went so far as to say that he would consider taking my request for a manslaughter plea to the Solicitor-General after the autopsy, depending on the state of the evidence at that time but first the body would have to be found.

Morris wanted Bennett to be interviewed by the police. I indicated that I thought that unlikely because the topic had already been discussed and Bennett had said he would rather write up his own statement.

On a one-to-one level I believed I could trust Morris even though the two of us fought like cats and dogs in and out of court. Both of us had a good wit in front of the jury – and neither was scared to stand up to a judge when it seemed appropriate. We both liked to win even though Morris will never admit it! I had dealt with Morris enough over the years to know where his boundaries lay or so I thought.

Paul Davison assisted Morris. Davison was the son of the former Chief Justice Sir Ronald Davison and a barrister on the Crown Prosecutors Panel. So far as my Bennett plea bargain suggestion was concerned, Davison was vehemently opposed to it and in a letter he sent to me several days later, he confirmed that no arrangement of any kind had been agreed to by the Crown in relation to Bennett.

Fortunately for us Davison was not calling the shots. I had the beginnings of an understanding with Morris, and that was good enough for me.

Bennett's statement was finally given to Morris together with a hand drawn map of Woodhill Forest. Bennett had marked a cross on it where he claimed he had buried Yvonne's body twelve years before.

It took the police a day to organise the trek to the Woodhill forest. Two days later a strange convoy of vehicles left Mt Eden Prison. It had not taken the media long to learn of the development in the Bennett case. A large contingent of television and news reporters followed the official police cavalcade. Cassidy sat in the back seat of the police car with Bennett.

It was a hot and sunny day when we drove to the Woodhill forest for a preliminary view. Bennett directed the police to a spot in the forest where one logging road joined another. With a policeman nearby, Bennett and I walked up and down the road first one way, then another. Bennett was trying to recall the exact spot after 12 years. Things change. After some time had passed my client walked 50 paces from the crossroads corner then he turned and walked into the forest. He counted to himself. One step, two steps, three steps, four, Bennett was the centre of attention once again. He appeared to be enjoying it.

Bennett walked about 80 paces into the forest then he stopped. He was at the top of a tree-covered hill. He pointed down towards the middle of the slope. 'If my memory is correct as to how many paces I took off the road it should be buried 10 meters down that bank.' He walked 10 meters down the bank then he turned around. He looked around then walked back up the hill. He said he was confused. His recollection was that he had buried her body beneath a large tree stump on the flat ground. The steps he paced out from the tree line next to the road led him half way down the hill. He must be wrong. He walked around on the level ground then he stopped.

Finally after a lot of looking around he pointed to a spot and said, 'Dig here.' A police officer in jeans began to dig. After a time he found nothing. Then Bennett suggested another spot closer to the road but said it did not match with the number of paces he recalled taking all those years before. A second team of policemen began to dig. People were getting excited. Had the location of the buried body been found?

The press had been kept about a mile back up the road at a fire gate fence at Walker Road. The media seemed to know almost immediately that the purpose of this expedition was for Bennett to disclose the location of where he buried his wife's body to the police. Television broke the story on the six o'clock news.

The *Sunday News* ran a big picture of my co-counsel Shane Cassidy, Warwick Bennett and myself shot from a distance with a telephoto lens. In the picture you could see Cassidy side on. He was wearing a brown leather cowboy hat that made him look like Indiana Jones. Next to him stood Bennett with his back facing the camera. A large bald spot on the top of his head was clearly visible. I was captured by the camera standing next to Bennett with a cigarette in my hand pointing into the forest.

The weekend papers and the TV news ran items that inferred Bennett had confessed to the murder of his wife when he had not. In his statement Bennett expressly stated that his wife's death was an accident. The media slant annoyed the hell out of me and Cassidy because it was not accurate – certainly Bennett had admitted killing her, but the difference between murder, manslaughter or accident as he now claimed was the legal case, was huge.

Any chance of Bennett getting a fair trial would be severely diminished if the media continued to poison the potential jury pool with speculative stories inferring the client had confessed to murder.

After Bennett had finished 'briefing' the police on where he believed the body was buried he was returned to Mt Eden prison to await the results of the search. The area was marked off with yellow police scene tape. Methodically the police officers began to dig. They dug hole after hole without success. Holes began appearing all over the forest floor. Some were shallow (three feet), others were deeper (six feet), but still there was no sign of any bones from a body.

Two weeks passed without any success. Now the designated corner of the forest looked like a moonscape covered in meteor craters. The marked off search area had now expanded to the size of a football field. After three weeks of searching everybody was getting very frustrated. The police were ready to give up the search.

My relationship with the officers involved in the search was becoming very strained. Clearly they felt my client was leading them on a wild goose chase for his own amusement Perhaps Bennett had forgotten the location, or maybe he was directing the search away from where he buried the body for his own reasons, suggested one of the police officers.

In order to demonstrate to the police that Bennett and his lawyers were serious about finding the body we hired a scientist from Canterbury University named Dr Knobbs who was skilled at using a ground-radar to locate objects buried underground. We hoped this modern technology would help us locate the body.

Over several days a number of possible sites were identified with the radar then marked with fluorescent paint on the spot. The police would follow along in their jeans and Tee shirts with their shovels. One by one a very tired team of police officers dug up each spot. Unfortunately only rocks or tree stumps were found.

After three weeks the police concluded that the area had been thoroughly searched and that Bennett was wilfully misdirecting them. After all, the police knew that Bennett was a skilful liar and a manipulator.

Just before the search was to be abandoned an ex forestry worker who had worked the area years before, showed up at the dig site. He had a number of old aerial photographs of the area. A close look at the pictures revealed that the tree line had been moved away from the road by about 25 meters some 8 years before. This meant Bennett could be telling the truth after all.

In 1982 a wide grass verge ran next to the logging road. Subsequently trees had been removed from the edge of the road as a firebreak. Even if Bennett remembered his paces correctly he would be out by 25 meters. The effect of this had been to throw Bennett off his paces during his walk into the forest three weeks before. The police decided to ignore the suggestion and continue with their methodical search of the site but from the other end of the marked off area.

The police renewed the search by digging another series of holes in the forest floor. Still no body was found. To speed up the search police had a backhoe digger brought in to excavate the remaining area.

After almost four weeks, police patience had worn out. The senior officer announced that the search was at an end.

'Harder, we're closing this down.'

'No, not yet!' I pleaded. Again I had Bennett brought back to the forest.

Bennett appeared to be distraught on this occasion with all this effort for no gain.

'They just don't believe it's here Warwick. They think you're bullshitting.'

'I need to talk to you alone,' said Bennett.

'Let's go down the road away from the police.'

A condition of Bennett's bail was that while he was in police custody during the forest search he would still have the freedom to withdraw 50 metres so that he and I could speak in private without the police listening to everything we talked about.

The two of us walked down the forestry road one last time. When we had walked nearly 50 metres we stopped. Bennett asked me to step into a glade so we could not be seen talking. He was being very careful.

'Is everything I say to you just between you and me?' Bennett asked. I replied 'Well, yes. What you say to me is privileged (confidential between lawyer and client) unless you release me from privilege at some later stage.'

Bennett then explained to me why I should believe him when he said he was absolutely sure his wife's body was buried on a particular corner.

The two of us returned to the crossroads. A group of tired police officers were standing next to the search co-ordination trailer. I spoke to the officer in charge of the site.

Then I asked the police to dig one more spot. It was the only place they had not yet dug. 'This spot fits with Bennett's first recollection.' My request fell on deaf ears. I was told in no uncertain terms that the search had been called off. I said, 'We'll see about that!' For four weeks I had been as polite, courteous and helpful to the police as one could be. Now I was getting angry.

I refused to give up. I phoned the area police commander (remember: always go straight to the top decision-maker) and advised him that since the police had abandoned the search the defence wanted the right to take over the search the next morning for a short period of time, (2 days at most).

My demand (politely dressed up as a request) to the area commander caused uproar with the police who had been working the forest dig. The defence quickly obtained the permission of the forestry company Carter Holt who owned the land to continue the search subject to us agreeing to pay for any trees that we damaged.

I used my mobile phone to organise a suction truck normally used to clean out septic tanks to come to the site early the next morning. I asked that the operator bring some extra length of hose so he could reach the site in the forest.

The area still to be searched was mostly loose sand. I thought that if a grate was positioned over the end of the suction hose and sucked up dirt at a reasonable rate, we would not have to worry about sucking up remains found in the grave when we found it. Bennett had absolutely convinced me it was definitely buried here.

The Water Tech works suction truck would arrive at 8 the next morning. I then explained to the police officers - who now had their noses out of joint because I had gone over their heads - that the defence had permission and were intending to search the remaining area the next day. With our intentions made clear the three of us, Cassidy, Robyn Harre and I left the site.

I arrived at the dig early the next morning to meet the 'sand sucking' truck operator. I could see the truck with the big Kingfisher painted on the side of it parked on the side of the road. But something was wrong.

Instead of the police closing down the site it looked like it had been reopened with twice as many policemen as there were the day before. Then to my surprise I saw acting crown prosecutor Paul Davison walking across the dig site towards me. I asked him 'what are you doing here?' He said nothing for a moment as I explained that the defence had permission to continue the search. He replied 'that will not be necessary Hards, (Hards was Grieve and Davison's nick-name for me in the Plumley-Walker case) the police have found the body.'

'You're bullshitting me' I exclaimed. Again Davison said 'No shit, Hards, the police have found the body. The remains are over there.' He pointed to the spot we had intended to search that morning. I was disappointed but glad the body had been found.

Apparently shortly after we left the site the Officer in Charge of the scene instructed the mechanical digger operator to stay back and quickly excavate the area the defence intended to search the next day. However the digger driver went through the area in such a rush he failed to recognise the grave when it was finally located. Instead he dug through the grave and only after a police officer examined the dumped bucket loads did some one yell out, 'Stop digging.'

The gravesite was covered with a large tent. The crown prosecutors were notified. The defence was not. Over the next two days a box was built around the gravesite. What remained intact would be moved in situ to the pathology lab at the Auckland Medical School. When the grave was closely examined Yvonne Bennett's high heel shoes and her nylon jacket were found.

At this stage, the full pathologist's report was not finished. We were told that due to work overload his report would not be available until after the deposition hearing had been held. The $64,000 question for me and the one I was scared to ask was, 'had the hyoid bone been found, and was it broken or intact.' A broken hyoid would support manual strangulation and murder.

At the deposition hearing Bennett pleaded not guilty to murder but guilty to manslaughter. Crown prosecutor Morris immediately rejected his guilty plea to manslaughter. The Justices of the Peace found that there was a prima facie case of murder made out against Bennett and they remanded him in custody. A pre-trial date was set for later in the year. In due course a trial date would be set for late 1994, probably December.

Pathologist Dr Tim Koelmeyer, from the Auckland Medical School was to carry out the autopsy. Some weeks later Cassidy and I visited the lab to view the remains of the recovered skeleton. When we first viewed the remains of Yvonne Bennett her skull and bones were laid out on a stainless steel table. I looked at the skull. I reacted with shock! There, as clear as day, was a hole in the side of the skull near the temple, about the size of a .22 calibre bullet.

Cassidy and I looked at each other for a moment in quiet panic. On seeing the shocked looks on our faces Dr. Koelmeyer quickly explained, that the hole in the head was not a bullet hole.

'No, no – that's an artefact. It fell out when we were working on the skull.'

'What a relief! When I next saw Bennett in jail my warped sense of humour compelled me to tell him that he was 'fucked because the skull had a .22 bullet hole in it!' He looked stunned. Quickly I explained it was only a joke, and the hole I referred to had been accidentally made during the autopsy.

It would be almost a year until the trial, but there was plenty to keep me occupied, including other interesting clients to help - such as the Collie case.

The Collie Case

In August 1994 barrister Shane Cassidy and I appeared in the Court of Appeal in relation to the Collie rape case. At his trial before Justice Ted Thomas QC, top QCs Peter Williams and Simon Lockhart defended Collie. Half a dozen street prostitutes had alleged Collie had raped, assaulted or detained them against their will. One complainant alleged that Collie had stuck a knife in her vagina and that she had to go to hospital to have it stitched. Collie was convicted of most charges.

Justice Thomas sentenced Collie to 16 years in prison describing the knife attack incident as a serious matter. The first 7 years of the sentence was made up of various penalties imposed by the judge in relation to the first five prostitute complainants. The sentence imposed for the vaginal knife attack drew Collie a further 9 years on top of the initial 7-year sentence.

Of course Collie's defence lawyers submitted their client denied the offences, especially the very serious knife attack but still he was convicted.

At Collie's appeal hearing our sentencing submissions pointed out how the police had told the prostitutes that they believed Collie had killed Leah Stephens, a fellow K road prostitute who had gone missing from Queen Street one night.

The K Road prostitutes whom Collie frequented on occasion turned on him after the police revealed they suspected him as being responsible in some fashion for Leah Stephens's disappearance. The Sunday papers ran story after story referring to the missing Leah Stephens in many of the Collie news items that were written at the time.

Collie's rape appeals were dismissed except in relation to a couple of the lesser charges Shane Cassidy and I had dismissed.

Stephen Collie's father Bunny Collie continued to search for the truth about his son's case. He said his son did not kill Leah Stephens and the police case was a complete jack up.

Sure enough a number of years later, after Collie had been convicted of various rapes and sentenced to prison, the police arrested another person for the murder of Leah Stephens. This person was subsequently convicted and sentenced to life in prison. Stephen Collie had been wrongly accused but not charged with murder in a silent whisper campaign by police, prostitutes and press that was to prejudice his chance at a fair trial.

After spending years of effort and an enormous amount of money on behalf of his first-born son for more lawyers and private investigators, Bunny Collie laid a private prosecution of perjury against the complainant who alleged his son had put a knife inside her. He alleged she lied under oath when she said she went to the hospital and had her injury stitched up. Private investigations proved the complainant had never been treated at the hospital for any injury.

Instead of denying the charge and going to trial, the complainant pleaded guilty to one count of perjury. The guilty plea did away with the need for a trial. This denied Bunny Collie one last bite at the cherry to have his lawyers question the police about how his son's case actually got started in the first place and his efforts to show that it was a conspiracy based on a wrong assumption.

Next, John Haigh, QC was engaged by the Collie family and he had the Appeal Court re-hear the 9-year sentence the trial judge had imposed on Collie cumulatively for the knife attack complaint after the complainant pleaded guilty to perjury and was sentenced to 12 months jail. To that extent the Court allowed Collie's appeal.

The 9-year sentence was reduced by only 3 years.

'This goes to prove how unfair and prejudiced the legal system can be in this country,' Mr. Collie says, (but) *'a number of people involved in this case will get their day before I am finished.'*

I was no longer involved in the case but still followed it. I was of the view that had the issue of the prejudice created by the police rumours that Collie had killed Leah Stephens plus the admitted perjury conviction of the complainant been put before the Court of Appeal at the same time, the Court would have been forced to re-assess the whole of the Collie case.

Stephen Collie is now a free man. His father Bunny Collie would have to get the Gold award for the decade he spent sticking by his son while he was in serious trouble. He has battled on relentlessly for years and years in a very expensive fight. Still he never gives up his search for that piece of information or potential witness that might finally unravel the police case made against his son.

The way certain police officers tied Collie to the Leah Stephens disappearance was unfortunate and unfair. Unfortunately in Stephen Collie's case the prejudice the police unfairly allowed to get into the heads of the K Road prostitute complainants' won out!

Hopefully this summary of my recall and assessment of the case will help remove some of the stain left unfairly on the Collie name by this case because of the way the police investigated it after making an incorrect assumption as to who was really responsible for Leah Stephens' disappearance.

Body In The Woods, Pt 2

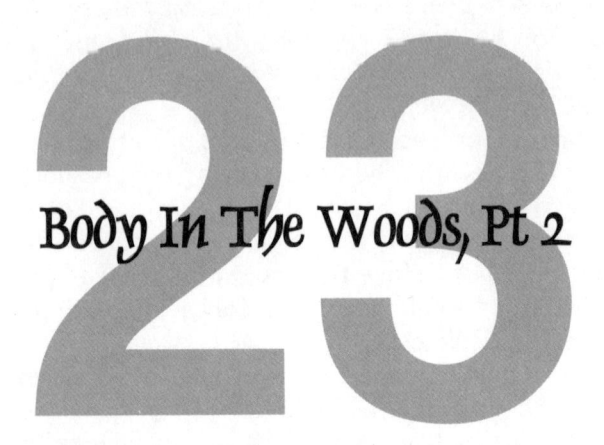

When the pathologist's report for the Bennett case was finally completed and released to defence counsel, David Morris was no longer prosecuting the case because he was now a sitting High Court judge. Simon Moore was the new Crown Solicitor at Auckland.

The Bennett trial would be the first big murder case of what was effectively a new prosecuting regime: Moore was in charge assisted by Paul Davison, QC. There would be no consideration given by the Crown to accepting any manslaughter plea from Bennett. Simon Moore said the reason the Crown maintained this stance was because they believed Bennett had lied in the voluntary statement he had given to the police and the Crown.

As I recall, in his statement Bennett claimed that his wife had been standing in the kitchen baking when they had a brief domestic argument. When the police searched Bennett's house several days later they indeed, found baking. But years later when the grave was found and searched the police found Yvonne Bennett's windcheater and her high heel shoes.

Moore asked me, 'Who bakes cakes while they are wearing a ski jacket and high heels? The trial would go ahead.

The pre-trial defence application on behalf of Bennett would be decided at a *voire dire* hearing (a trial within a trial to test the admissibility of certain of the evidence the defence challenged). This proceeding is conducted before a judge alone and normally before the trial starts so as to not inconvenience jurors with down time in court.

In the Bennett case, my very reliable and experienced junior counsel Shane Cassidy applied for a large volume of potential evidence to be excluded on the basis that its prejudicial effect would outweigh its probative value in Bennett's case.

Fortunately for Bennett, Cassidy succeeded with the application and the complained-about material was excluded from the trial.

The trial started in December 1994, in the High Court at Auckland. One of the prosecution witnesses against Bennett was a woman named Doreen Wikaira. She testified that a man who looked like Bennett picked her up shortly after his wife's disappearance in April 1982. She said she had been hitchhiking up north and had been picked up by a man driving a green Morris van. She said a little girl sat in the back seat. She described how Bennett had tried to encourage her to come and be a nanny for his daughter. He said he needed someone to help look after her. The witness said she hadn't been wearing a wedding ring, and he (Bennett) refused to believe she was married (she was). In the witness box, Wikaira told the jury how she had spoken with Vicky, who had said, among other things, 'Mummy has been bad'. The young girl had repeated this several times.

This evidence was highly prejudicial if the crown proved that Bennett had been looking for a nanny while he and Yvonne's daughter were on holiday between April 19 and 25, 1982. It tended to show that he knew his wife was dead before returning home to the police investigation What followed, however, was even worse, in a strange way for Bennett.

The witness described how her mother had given her advice to be careful of strangers when hitchhiking. She explained that her mother had always told her to watch out for their eyes.

'What did she tell you about eyes?' asked Moore, prosecuting.

'People either have sheep's eyes, or goats eyes. She told me to be careful of people with goat's eyes.' Moore paused for a moment before he asked his next question.

'What kind of eyes did Mr. Bennett have?'

'Goat's eyes!' she replied.

In the context of a big murder trial a two word answer like that is normally of no note. Here however it had a significant impact on the jury as soon as the witness said Bennett had 'goat's eyes.' With this highly prejudicial bit of evidence now before the jury the Crown ended its case on a high with what lawyers call a trial break.

All of a sudden Bennett wanted to give evidence. He wanted to refute the hitchhiker's claim that he had picked her up in April 1982. Bennett accepted that he had picked her up hitchhiking but months after he and Vicky went on holiday and after Yvonne had disappeared.

For a variety of reasons it had previously been decided that Bennett would not give evidence. Bennett knew the reasons. One was practical the other was ethical. In the end I told Bennett that if he insisted on giving evidence I would have to pull out of his trial and Cassidy would take over the case. Bennett decided that he wanted me to stay on his case and do the closing address. The question of him giving evidence was not discussed again.

I had the Crown pathologist Tim Koelmeyer examine Bennett's thumb one morning before the trial started for the day. When he gave his evidence he acknowledged he had examined Bennett's hand and that there was a scar on his thumb. This was important to the defence. The scar meant that Bennett's version of putting his hand over his wife's mouth to stop her screaming at which time she bit his thumb, and how he had grabbed her throat to try and make her let his thumb go free, now had some evidential back up.

The pathologist also gave evidence as to how the vasal vagal nerve in the neck worked and how a person could die almost instantly from light pressure accidentally applied to the nerve. The hyoid bone was found intact in the grave. Against this background Cassidy and I thought we had a good chance of a manslaughter verdict every hour the jury stayed out deliberating their verdict. Then after 16 hours' deliberation the jury convicted Warwick Bennett of the murder of his wife, Yvonne Bennett. He was immediately sentenced to life imprisonment, as is mandatory in New

Zealand for anyone found guilty of murder.

Shortly after Bennett was convicted and sentenced in 1994 he asked barrister Kevin Ryan to take on his appeal. Now my nightmare would begin. The conviction was appealed on numerous grounds. Bennett, through Ryan, alleged that his defence lawyers had been incompetent at his trial, and that the Crown had reneged on a promise to allow Bennett to plead guilty to manslaughter if he helped find the body. He also claimed I refused to let him give evidence at his trial, that I had not given him a jury list, that my instructing solicitor Robbie Harre had not made a formal application for an adjournment of the trial and that I had not visited him at the prison. It was a lengthy list of complaints.

Opposing Bennett's appeal were Simon Moore and Paul Davison QC for the Crown. Bennett had filed a number of affidavits containing a long list of complaints and criticism against myself, Shane Cassidy and Robbie Harre.

Of course, having represented the now-convicted man, everything I had been told by Bennett previously was covered by lawyer-client privilege. This meant that I could neither voluntarily reveal details, nor be compelled to reveal them without my ex-client's explicit permission by way of release of privilege. This would include the conversation Bennett had with me on the last occasion he came out to the Woodhill forest dig when police were looking for his wife's body.

However after Bennett continued his appeal points that criticized my co-counsel and myself, the Court of Appeal required him to sign a waiver of his legal privilege between each of us. Bennett made allegations of unprofessional conduct, incompetence and later perjury when I filed my reasons explaining why I refused to allow Bennett to give evidence at his trial. He later through his counsel Kevin Ryan accused Shane Cassidy, Robbie Harre and me of lying when we denied we had told him there was a deal done where the Crown would let him plead guilty to manslaughter if he helped find the body.

SEPTEMBER 1996 BENNETT APPEAL

On Tuesday 17 September 1996 *The Dominion* trumpeted:

"Convicted killer gives evidence for first time on wife's death."

Bennett said lawyer Christopher Harder failed to defend him properly and he thought he should be given another trial. To Crown Lawyer Paul Davison QC Bennett said he had "lied through his teeth" till he confessed in February 1994. Bennett said he had done a deal with police and prosecution in which he would plead guilty to manslaughter instead of murder in return for telling police where Mrs Bennett's body was. But the prosecution had not stuck to the arrangement. Bennett said Mr Harder had also prevented him from giving evidence at his trial as he wanted. Mr Harder said the prosecution had agreed to reduce the murder charge to manslaughter if there were no signs of injury on the body when it was found, but this arrangement had not been put in writing.

Asked about his fees, Mr Harder said he had originally got $40,000 on the basis of Bennett telling him he had nothing to do with his wife's death. He charged more when the $40,000 had been used up during the search for the body

Retired Auckland solicitor Robyn Harre said in evidence Bennett owed her $16,000 in fees for the University of Canterbury for a geological report needed for the case.

On 17 September 1996 *The Evening Post* said,

"Lawyers lied, claims Bennett"
The man who admitted he lied about his wife's disappearance for 12 years, has told the Court of Appeal he stopped lying in February 1994. When Bennett wanted to give evidence, Mr Harder explained that would compromise his ethical position because of what Bennett had already told him, so he would have to withdraw and junior counsel complete the trial. Bennett didn't press to give evidence, Mr Harder said.

I was called before the Court of Appeal to testify for the Crown about the manner in which Bennett's defence case had been conducted. I was to be cross-examined by Kevin Ryan. Ryan was, at this stage of his career, an icon in the New Zealand criminal law. He had practised successfully for many years and he had a track record of murder acquittals few in New Zealand could match.

I knew that Ryan's cross-examination of me would be testing. In my second year in the law I took on a change of plea application for three of Kevin Ryan's previous clients. Each had pleaded guilty to rape after advice from Ryan. All three prisoners wanted to change their plea back to not guilty. They claimed Ryan had forced them to plead guilty against their will. The Court of Appeal required my new clients to sign a waiver of legal privilege for Kevin Ryan before he would be required to respond to the allegations. In due course I cross-examined Kevin Ryan with vigour and I doubted he would have forgotten that incident, unfortunately for me.

This was my second experience in the witness box and I knew what a lawyer could do to a witness. You were left wide open to a credibility call that could destroy a promising legal career.

The cross-examination Ryan put me through was an extremely unpleasant experience. I, of all people, appreciate that it is the barrister's professional duty to regard the client's claims as truthful, but the tone of the cross-examination became downright 'nasty' as the hearing progressed with Ryan taking on all the bitterness and venom that Warwick Bennett spewed at me. To many of his questions I replied, 'I do not recall'.

On 17 September 1996 *The New Zealand Herald* said:

"Murder case lawyers face accusations"

Bennett has accused his three case lawyers of lying to cover incompetence and ineptitude. Bennett admitted 12 years of lying to his daughter, his wife's parents, friends and police about his wife's disappearance. In a sometimes testy exchange with Mr Kevin Ryan, Bennett's present lawyer, Mr Harder said Bennett had blurted out his confession that he killed his wife during a visit to Mt Eden Prison in February 1994. Bennett said he had insisted several times on giving evidence but his wishes were rejected. In the Court of Appeal dock Bennett rejected Mr Harder's sworn claims and also dismissed an accusation from Robyn

Harre that he told her of choosing a forest burial site before his wife's death.

"I never thought in my wildest dreams that three solicitors would lie in the way they have", Bennett said. "I just can't believe it."

On 18 September 1996 *The New Zealand Herald* said,

"Crown pleads on Harder's behalf"

Christopher Harder was an unconventional lawyer with an apparent lack of case notes and files, but he had represented the convicted murderer Warwick Bennett fairly, the Crown said yesterday. Mr Davison said the better evidence from Mr Harder and his junior counsel, Mr Shane Cassidy, was that Bennett had accepted the tactical approach of not taking the witness stand at the start of the trial.

Mr Ryan, Bennett's present lawyer said that Doreen Wikaira had given damaging evidence about Bennett suggesting she could be a 'surrogate mother' for his daughter. She also described Bennett as having "goat's eyes". Davison said Bennett's rebuttal of such evidence would have added little to the defence case and would have opened him up for possibly damaging cross-examination. Davison said that Mr Harder's appeal statement that Bennett had confessed presented ethical problems for a defence lawyer but none which disadvantaged his client. (Harder) "is an unconventional counsellor, he is a robust counsellor, he has secured some good results for his clients...."

Earlier, Ryan had said Mr Harder had taken Mr Bennett's $40,000 fee on top of $30,000 legal aid, and $15,000 legal aid for his junior, and had then wanted to get the trial over and done with quickly.

(On 21 November 1996 the New Zealand Herald corrected Ryan's statement. "A $40,000 fee paid by Bennett to Harder was on account of future legal services, and services to that value were provided before an application for legal aid was made.)

New Zealand Herald, 18 October 1996
"Bennett's appeal rejected"

The Court of Appeal has rejected Warwick Keith Bennett's claim that an inadequate defence meant he was wrongly convicted of murdering his wife. Mr Harder's failure to advise Mr Bennett to plead self-defence had not created a miscarriage of justice because the jury decided he acted with murderous intent, in an effort to extricate his finger from his wife's mouth. It was also open to Mr Harder to take the view that a 1.8m, well-built man would have difficulty establishing that he was defending himself against a 1.63m woman. Mr Harder said he would not wish such a 'bizarre' case on any defence lawyer. In any future similar case, he would record a client's decision on whether or not they would give evidence.

The case was appealed to the Privy Council, and at the same time Bennett filed a series of complaints with the Auckland District Law Society relating to my handling of his trial. I was subjected to a barrage of letters and numerous questions from the Law Society.

Then in late November 1999, four years after Bennett made his initial complaints to the Law Society against me, my barrister in chambers, Melanie Coxon, was sitting at her computer typing up a draft of my last response to the Law Society in relation to the Bennett complaints. As Melanie was finishing off my draft letter, all of sudden for no real reason, I picked up a cardboard box that had been sitting on top of another box behind Melanie's desk for some time. As I shifted the box I noticed a single piece of paper that had been stuck between the two boxes. I picked it up and read it. It was a press release prepared by the Bennett defence team dated 10 March 1994. This was shortly after Bennett had led the police to Yvonne's grave in the Woodhill forest. The press release extensively quoted Barry Bennett, Warwick's brother, who said in part:

'*There was no pressure on Warwick to lead the Police to the body, Warwick could have sat back and said nothing. He had a good chance of being acquitted without the body being found. No deals have been done, and there has been no plea bargaining although the defence are hopeful that the Crown will give due consideration to a plea of manslaughter once the autopsy is finished.*'

This document was prepared and given to the *Sunday News* reporter Joe Lose prior to the deposition hearing but not run in the paper. Instead it was put away. Now the document spoke for itself. It conclusively proved that Warwick Bennett's allegation that I told him there was a plea bargain done with David Morris to the effect that he would get to plead guilty to manslaughter if he helped recover his dead wife's remains, was a big lie. My life as a lawyer in the late 1990s would have been much easier if I had uncovered this press release five years earlier.

Bennett's final, wild and unsuccessful swipe at me was the following:

New Zealand Herald, 18 November 1996
$1m Bennett lawsuit 'hogwash'
By Tony Stickley
And Martin Johnston
Convicted murderer Warwick Bennett wants to sue his former lawyer, Christopher Harder, for up to $1million. Mr Harder said if anybody was going to sue anyone for $1million, it was Yvonne Bennett's parents who should be suing Warwick Bennett.

I called Kevin Ryan after the Privy Council judgement was issued dismissing Bennett's appeal.

I said 'Hey Ryan, what's it like for an Irishman to have to go to a British court to try and fuck a Canuck?'

'I feel gutted Christopher.' He replied.

'Well, we all know what that feels like,' I replied. 'I guess we should make peace.' (Holding a grudge in the law is just too much hard work)

'I'll say a prayer for you, Christopher, said Ryan. You can never have too many people praying for you!'

My dad sent me this great email recently about forgiving your enemies. It goes like this......

FORGIVE YOUR ENEMIES
In his Sunday sermon, the minister used "Forgive Your Enemies" as his subject. After the sermon, he asked how many were willing to forgive their enemies. About half held up their hands.

Not satisfied, he harangued the congregation for another twenty minutes and repeated his question. This received a response of eighty percent. Still unsatisfied, he lectured for fifteen more minutes and repeated his question. All responded except one elderly lady in the rear.

"Mrs. Jones, are you not willing to forgive your enemies?"
"I don't have any."
"Mrs. Jones, this is very unusual. How old are you?"
"Ninety-six."
"Mrs. Jones, please come down in front and tell the congregation how a lady can live to be ninety-six and not have an enemy in the world."

The old lady teetered down the aisle, slowly turned to face the congregation, and blurted out, "I outlived the S.O.B.s!"

In February 2000, the Privy Council dismissed Warwick Bennett's final appeal against his murder conviction; they held that there had been no miscarriage of justice. My trial conduct had finally been vindicated, or so I thought, and now the Law Society letters about Bennett would go away. But I was wrong.

To bring five years of torment to an end I admitted four minor charges before the Tribunal. In a surprise move the parents of Yvonne Bennett, Mr and Mrs Landers, called the Tribunal long-distance from Sherbourne, England at two in the morning their time to plead with the Tribunal to be merciful with me.

The Landers, God love them both, spoke emotionally about their ordeal during more than twelve years of sustained trauma and grief over the disappearance and death of their beloved daughter, Yvonne. They said how grateful they were to me for insisting on the search being continued after the police were ready to give up. At least they were then able to give their daughter a proper burial in a decent resting place. They also had the opportunity to say goodbye to her, finally.

In a remarkable coincidence, it happened that this very day would have been Yvonne's 43rd birthday. When my two surprise witnesses had finished what they had to say there was not a dry eye in the room.

As I stood for sentence, the Chairman said, 'Sit down,

Mr Harder, you have suffered enough.' The Tribunal ordered no convictions, penalties, fines or costs be recorded.

Warwick Bennett thought he would get a benefit for helping to find his wife's remains. In the end however it was me who gained the benefit when the victim's parents (bless them) went into bat for me.

Satisfying as the outcome of this Tribunal hearing was, it did not match the even bigger rush of my previous Tribunal hearing in 1995 when I defended myself. (I was only convicted of conduct unbecoming a barrister) The Chairman, Lester Chisholm, said:

"It is appropriate for us to indicate at this stage that the evidence, and our findings as to proved charges, are likely to persuade us that this is not a situation where Mr Harder's right to practice should be removed. In making this observation, we take into account Mr Harder's previous appearances before the Tribunal in 1992 and 1994."

I had missed suspension from practice by only one vote in 1994. Making a mockery of the charges brought against me by the Solicitor-General in relation to the Plumley-Walker and Donnelly trials.

Legal Sunscreen CD

It began with the Auckland power crisis in early 1998. I needed to drum up business and let the Auckland public know I was open. I created a series of radio adverts. These ads contained free legal advice. The response was phenomenal! In the following weeks I received phone calls and letters from mothers concerned about their children, girlfriends worried about their boyfriends and the list goes on. Their response was that the ads were becoming the topic of discussion over the dinner table and that their kids and/or boyfriends sat up and took notice. They wanted their own copy! And so began the CD.

I recorded the CD with the assistance of Revolver Records and BMG. A number of things have happened since then.

1. The Judges of the High Court and Court of Appeal have responded by saying, "Every student in every school should have a copy of this CD". Their Honours requested of the registrar that she should make copies of the CD to be distributed to each and every judge of the High Court. Since this time there have been a number of inquires made by their Honours in the District Court to defendants as to whether they 'used legal sunscreen' in their dealings with the police.

2. Various police stations have responded by playing the CD to suspects prior to interviewing to encourage them to "Be polite to the Police, don't have an attitude" and to "tell

the truth or say nothing, bullshit only grows mushrooms".

3. Rotary New Zealand have responded by using the CD for youth training sessions in an attempt to teach life skills that will prevent teenagers being 'burnt by the law'

4. Saatchi and Saatchi have responded by releasing the CD to every one of their offices around the world to promote it via a worldwide advertising campaign. Kevin Roberts of Saatchi and Saatchi impressed with my original thoughts, wrote to me and signed the letter, 'Nothing is Impossible'. Accepting that Roberts knew his business and often 'less is more' I decided to abandon the full Che Guevera quote, 'When they say it is impossible, that means there are a thousand solutions.' This did away with the negative connotation some associated with the rebel - ie; terrorist, communist etc; and in future adopt the abridged version, 'Nothing is Impossible!' promoted by Roberts.

5. The goal is to ensure every student in every school will have a copy of this legal advice.

LEGAL SUNSCREEN IN THE PUBLIC INTEREST
By *The Criminal Lawyer.*

If I could offer you just one piece of advice as legal Sunscreen, it is be polite to the police, don't have an attitude.
*Hey, What did he say?
The benefits of this have been proved time and again. Attitude can mean the difference between being nailed, jailed or bailed.
*Attitude's a two-way Street.
If you drink, don't drive, take a cab, safe driver or walk.
*Now that's for real.
In most Western countries first time drink drivers get a big fine and suspension. In El Salvador offenders risked execution by firing squad.
Bang, Bang
*Whoa, that's too heavy.
Beware of too much alcohol, it can make some people mean. Don't use it as panty remover. Play safe. Ask your date; is this a consenting kiss, touch or act? Ice breaker or jail maker. You choose. Remember, no means no unless she or he says yes. That applies to you, me, even the Presi-

dent of the United States.
*Now that's gotta be fairer.
If interviewed by the police tell the truth or say nothing. Bullshit only grows mushrooms.
*Be a magic man, not a tragic man facing doom.
Drive safely; driving is a privilege not a right. Remember that. So must I.
*Me too.
If you accept you did something wrong plead guilty early. The judge will give you credit for this. Imprisonment is not always inevitable.
*True.
Remember when they say it's impossible that means there are a thousand solutions.
*Hey Hey, there's always a way.
If you get drunk and aggressive or hit your partner, do anger management quickly and join Alcoholics Anonymous. It can save your life, your wife, and you from jail. I know.
*Yeah, I've been there too.
If you are thinking of interfering with a young child, don't. If you already have, stop! Remember children have feelings and memories as long as an elephant. So does the law.
*Innocence is a feeling you can't replace.
Dishonesty is like a cancer to your character. Cut it out. Come clean. Life will get better.
*Not like Coolio.
Treasure your job and reputation. A clean police record is your weight in gold to those who would judge or hire you in future.
*Dig it.
A drug conviction can clip your wings. Be cool. Travel.
*Yeah, be free. Fly, brother fly.
This advice is based on 16 years' experience in the criminal law. You don't have to take it, but trust me on the legal sunscreen. Be polite to the police. Don't have an attitude.
*Get up with the play, just do it one day.
_If this advice has reached your ears too late and you now find your future seemingly bleak and hopeless, have faith in yourself. Be strong. Believe in your God or Higher power. Remember, the storm will pass and the sun will shine

again.

Yeah, and don't forget the elephant

The rap words underlined above, were written by Te Kaha, Tame Iti, Chris from 'Three the Hard Way' (Maori rap group) and Bull - a gang member. Bull wrote the response to the child abuse section, 'Innocence is a feeling you can't replace.'

Every time we tried to record the rap version and Bull reiterated his retort he said it with such force that he blew the fuses of the Revolver Records sound desk, which stunned owner, George Shuouskoff. I got such a buzz from putting the CD together and Malcolm Smith did a brilliant job of mixing the tracks.

I was able to put *Legal Sunscreen* to good use in the case of Tame Iti and Te Kaha. Both had been charged with offences arising out of an incident where the two had allegedly confronted a group of Maori youths at a sleep-out who they suspected had been responsible for a number of local burglaries. A semi-automatic .22 rifle was fired above their sleeping heads to give them a fright and the main offender was taken outside, tied to the swing set and given a thrashing. Tame Iti and Te Kaha now faced serious criminal charges.

I was approached to act for and defend Tame Iti. After assessing the evidence I suggested that the two would do better if I tried to negotiate a plea bargain. Prior to trial, the Crown dropped charges against Te Kaha and reduced the seriousness of the charges against Tame Iti. On my advice, Tame Iti pleaded guilty to the reduced charges saving his credibility and I pleaded for a discharge without conviction if he did 200 hours community service.

The Chief Justice, Sian Elias, listened to my submission and the Tame Iti/Te Kaha/Harder rap version of *Legal Sunscreen* which Tame Iti was to promote in schools on his plea of mitigation. Her Honour refused to give Tame Iti a discharge without conviction saying the charges were too serious, but that she was prepared to deal with the matter by way of a suspended sentence and no community service because she believed Tame Iti had spent his whole life in public service.

This offence arose out of the Police investigation in relation to the stolen Colin McCahon painting believed taken by Maori activists from the conservation building in Tuhoe. Some months later, acting as a facilitator, I introduced Tame Iti and Te Kaha to the arts patron Jenny Gibbs. Later still, Jenny, with the help of her new acquaintances, recovered the painting intact and not seriously damaged. Te Kaha was charged with theft of the painting but was given a suspended sentence when an anonymous person paid the cost of the repairs to the painting in full. I had no doubt that Justice Sian Elias who was a director on the Colin McCahon Trust would be pleased with this outcome.

25. The Baby L Saga

My job often involves dealing with the worst aspects of human nature – the greed, the violence, the corruption and, all too often, the madness. As you may have gathered from what you have read so far, I have at times taken my professional involvement on board to a personal level. My clients' problems have become my own; I have felt their pain, voiced their outrage and fought their enemies with all the powers available to me.

The case that I describe on the following pages involved none of humanity's lower motives. Everyone I dealt with throughout the matter was, in all his or her intentions, beyond reproach. The events revolved around life, hope, and, most of all, love. Perhaps because of this, I found my involvement with the Baby L case a severe emotional trial.

At the end of July 1998, a baby was born at National Women's Hospital in Auckland. The birth of a child is usually a joyous occasion, but this one was not celebrated as it might have been. The little girl, who came to be known as 'Baby L,' was seven weeks premature. She suffered from multiple health problems, including cerebral palsy, Mobius Syndrome – an abnormality of the cranial nerves – and Poland's Anomaly, which affects chest wall muscles and limb formation. She could not see, or hear and would never speak. Doctors at the hospital did not have high hopes. They believed Baby L to be severely brain damaged and, they said, she would not survive. Treatment would prolong the baby's suffering and inevitable death, they said. They encouraged the child's parents to remove the life support systems that ensured her survival. Mr. and Mrs. L were Pacific Islanders, strong in their Mormon faith, with two sons aged three and four. They refused.

After the child had spent seven weeks in an incubator, being fed through tubes and having her breathing aided by a ventilator, the doctors at National Women's hospital formally sought court permission to turn off life support. Baby L's parents refused their consent, forcing Auckland Healthcare Services Ltd to apply to the High Court for an order making the baby a ward of court. This would allow a judge to decide whether or not to continue treatment.

Raynor Asher, QC - a good man - was appointed counsel for the child. The next thing I did was considered unusual at the time. I set up an Internet website for Baby L, requesting advice from those around the world who knew about the conditions she was suffering from, and might be able to support us in arguing that her life support should not be turned off. Many dismissed this as a gimmicky move by a publicity-seeking lawyer. It wasn't. I wanted clarification about her prospects for the future, and the prognosis for her recovery.

We received a lot of support from around the globe as a result of the website. Suddenly this was not just a huge national issue, it was also being noticed internationally. Sadly, we did not gather much hope about Baby L's long-term prospects. While the legal battle for Baby L's life was being heard in the High Court at Auckland before Justice Dame Silvia Cartwright and Justice Barry Paterson, there was no shortage of opinion outside the courtroom. A disabled rights group, the Assembly of People with Disabilities, described any attempt to turn off life-support as infanticide.

"*The disability community in this country is again forced to watch impotently as one group of people is given licence to make decisions about whose lives are, or are not, worth living,*" said the group's vice-president, Lorna Sullivan.

She believed that disability was being seen only in a medical context, 'to be discarded if no cure can be found.'

A spokesman for the Catholic Church and a lecturer in bioethics, the Rev Dr Graeme Connolly, told the *New*

Zealand Herald,

'That people should ask whether it was right to put a patient through great pain, if doctors could not 'hold out the reasonable prospect of benefit. Sound medical opinion that such extraordinary treatment is certainly futile gives a very clear indication that there is not a moral imperative to continue to use extraordinary measures.'

The leader of the Christian Heritage Party, the Rev Graham Capill, said severe abnormalities should not be a reason for terminating life.

In the courtroom, the clinical director of newborn services at National Women's Hospital, Dr David Knight, told the judges that Baby L's prognosis was hopeless and that even if she was kept on life-support and other treatment, she would 'progressively decline and die.' A pediatric neurologist and a medical ethics committee supported his prognosis. Although she could not cry, Baby L's eye movements and the colour of her face indicated she felt pain. Continuing treatment was inhumane because it was sometimes painful and there was little hope of recovery.

Raynor Asher, QC, agreed with the doctors: Baby L's future was grim. The only reason for maintaining treatment would be for her parents' sake. 'She is a beautiful little girl, who is easy to love and who reacts to the stroking and warmth of her mother. For doctors committed to the business of saving lives, all life is very, very precious indeed. But in this case the life cannot be saved,' he said.

I, as lawyer for Baby L's parents, compared taking her off life support to an execution. I said she was greatly loved and displayed signs of enjoyment when she was cuddled. I begged the court for compassion to allow the baby to die naturally: 'She is dying and they know she is dying. But like many handicapped children, they believe she has heart and spirit and it has taught them compassion and they seek that same compassion from the court and the medical people on the basis that she is dying.'

The judges cleared the court to hear submissions from Baby L's parents. Shortly afterwards, in a judgment which opened the way for doctors to withdraw life support, Justices Cartwright and Paterson made Baby L a ward of the court.

Dr Knight was given the right to manage the baby's treatment, including the withdrawal of life support. Dr Knight had a grave responsibility. He would continue to take into account the parents' wishes so far as they were compatible with his clinical judgment. But it was now his responsibility to determine whether and at what point, ventilation and other therapeutic intervention should cease. And at all times he had to bear in mind that Baby L's interests were the paramount consideration, said the judges. Three generations of Baby L's family gathered at her parents' central Auckland home to discuss the court's decision.

The historic High Court decision that gave Auckland Healthcare permission to turn off the little girl's life-support was made public just as she died. Baby L had been taken home from the newborn intensive care unit in her life-sustaining incubator. Dressed in a delicate lacy white gown with matching mittens and booties, her eyes were open as she kicked her legs and waved her hands. Family and friends lined up to kiss and cuddle the much-loved baby. Her brothers held her while last photographs were taken.

As Mormon Church leaders blessed her during a 30-minute prayer service, Baby L looked like any other child. Then, just before 10am, the humming ventilator became silent. Baby L's mother held her precious daughter, tears running down her face, as a nurse eased the tubes gently from the child's nose and the machine was turned off. Her father turned away, looked to the heavens, and sobbed. Hospital staff, including Dr David Knight, and several nurses, kissed the infant and said goodbye. Baby L died peacefully several minutes later, in her mother's arms in the back garden of their home.

Watching her being taken off life-support was the saddest thing I have ever seen. People who loved her surrounded her and Dr Knight showed more compassion than I have seen any man show. She did get dignity in death. Baby L's death was not in vain. From the volume of Internet mail to her parents, it was obvious that in her short lifespan she taught many around the world the meaning of compassion.

The baby whose plight captured the heart of the nation was buried in a tiny white coffin at Mangere cemetery, along with a Pooh Bear card, soft toys and an album of family photos. I had known Baby L for one week, but she had taught me more than most people in my entire life.

The case took its toll on me. I cried my way through a televised statement announcing Baby L's death. Sometimes tears still flow when I think of her now. I had argued to the High Court that Baby L should be left to die naturally, but in the end the two judges sided with doctors. I sympathized with their decision: It was one of those tragic, tragic circumstances where the cards fell all wrong. Depressed, I ignored my 50th birthday the next day. There was nothing to celebrate.

As for the critics who questioned my motives for taking on the Baby L case, I confirm that I was paid. I received a great big box of corned beef, a mat and a $50 bill because that was all that the parents could afford.

26
The Long Rape Case

The Howard Long rape trial was one of the most successful of what has become, contrary to a number of expectations, a lengthy career. This was due to a very specific technological advancement, still in its early stages of introduction to this country.

Watching court proceedings in New Zealand, regardless of the nature of the hearing, is nothing like *LA Law*. It is not even much like *Crown Court*, or *Rumpole of the Bailey*. Speed has always distinguished reality from television drama: real proceedings move at a veritable snail's pace. This is because verbatim transcripts of questions and answers have to be typed by typists, and the participants are forced to keep their rate of speech to a pace the court typist can manage. Witnesses are judicially instructed to speak slowly. Whenever anyone accelerates the flow of his or her speech, the typist will raise one hand and utter a little grunt. The judge hears this, even if no one else does, and asks that the witness please slow down.

Thus, even at the most climactic moments of the most famous trials, witnesses and counsel have been speaking at a practical maximum of around 100 words per minute – a leisurely pace for an after-dinner raconteur, but hardly a normal conversational speed.

I always felt that this system disadvantaged me. My

brain works very quickly, if not entirely normally, and slowing it down to transcript production pace seems to choke its efficiency. It was not uncommon for me to lose my train of thought, or even to forget the gist of the question I was trying to ask before I finished it.

During Queen v Long, however, proceedings were, for the first time in my experience, digitally recorded and typed up after the event. I could, for once, move at my own pace. I cannot overstate the difference this made: it was wonderful. I felt like I was flying in court, I made my points more effectively, and my cross-examinations were far superior to previous experiences especially with the assistance of my junior Melanie Coxon, who kept my files in order for me.

Howard Long was the best whiteware salesman in New Zealand for Kitchen Things. For eight years he had been involved in a co-dependent relationship with a woman I will call Carol, the major sticking point of which was the fact that Howard would never voice the words, 'I love you'.

One October night in 1997 he returned home to find the couple's shared flat close to empty. All of Carol's possessions had been moved out. It transpired that the best salesman for a competitive company in New Zealand had been having a secret affair with Carol for the past year. She had left Howard for his greatest rival.

Carol remained fixated with Howard after their separation. She started phoning him and leaving messages. Some were pleasant, some very nasty. They had been planning a trip to Hawaii together on 30 October, and on the evening of 29 October Carol came to visit Howard at their old apartment.

Something happened in the kitchen and something happened in the bedroom. Carol telephoned her boyfriend, a karate black belt, who immediately drove to the apartment and went upstairs where he began to beat Howard up. In the meantime Carol ran down the stairs screaming. As she stumbled past one of the startled neighbours the neighbour asked,

'Do you want the police called?'

Carol replied,

'No, I don't want him to get into trouble.' Who she was

referring to later became a crucial trial issue.

Howard went to Hawaii the next day, black and blue with bruises.

Five months later, little had happened. Howard had been trying to recover some of his property from Carol, and had progressed to suing her for it. The two bumped into each other in Newmarket. Carol wanted to speak to Howard, so they sat in his car together. Howard told Carol that he had entered into a new relationship with an American woman, who was coming to New Zealand that July. Carol was adamant: that was doomed to failure.

The details of what followed are unclear, but certainly the conversation became heated, perhaps because of Carol's jealousy. Carol lost a gold necklace that was the subject of an ownership dispute. Howard may have ripped it from her neck.

The next day, Carol laid a complaint of theft against Howard with the Newmarket police. She also showed the police a scratch on her chest, claimed it had been made when her necklace was stolen, and laid a further complaint of assault. More seriously, she alleged that in October 1997 Howard had attempted to rape her. A file was opened, but the police took no further action on the matter.

In July, Howard's new American love duly arrived in Auckland. Carol's behaviour continued to be a little unusual. She called the new girlfriend, Suzanne, and welcomed her to New Zealand, wishing her and Howard all the best together. Then she returned to the police station, following up her earlier complaints and adding that during the incident the previous October she alleged she had also been digitally penetrated while the two of them were in the kitchen of the apartment.

In October there was a function held at the Downtown convention centre to recognise the best whiteware salesman in New Zealand. The glitterati of the whiteware sales industry were there, decked out to the nines and enjoying the highlight of the year's social calendar. Howard and Suzanne were there together, as were Carol and her boyfriend.

The highlight of the evening's festivities was the presentation of the Best Salesman award. Howard won.

After the awards ceremony, Suzanne went to the bathroom. Carol followed. What was said in that room remains a secret between the two, but it developed into fisticuffs. Carol called the police and Suzanne was charged with assault. Howard and his girlfriend came to see me.

The matter was not complicated. In court the common assault was quickly dealt with by diversion, whereby instead of facing charges the alleged offender signs a contract with the police and makes reparation by way of a donation to charity or by completing some agreed task.

My relationship with the police on a day-to-day basis is pretty good, now that the old hard-liners have left, and I make the most of it. On the whole, cops are a good bunch nowadays. The charge against Suzanne was withdrawn on the same day she appeared in court when she was granted instant diversion instead of the normal two-month delay for an appointment with the diversions officer.

When Howard returned to work the day after his new girlfriend was diverted, he described to his work colleagues how the charge against her had been dropped. The following morning the Newmarket police turned up on Howard's doorstep with a search warrant. They were looking for a gold necklace and a torn, bloodied robe, among other things. Carol had contacted them complaining about Howard's girlfriend's diversion, asking what had happened in respect of the charge she had filed.

The necklace and robe were found. Howard was arrested and taken to Newmarket police station, charged with attempted sexual violation by rape and sexual violation by digital penetration. After receiving a phone call, I met Howard at the police station and was present when he was interviewed. The questioning did not go well. The officer conducting the interview, Gerry Whitley, was unhelpful, to say the least.

Howard had kept recordings of Carol's telephone answer phone messages to him, running the gamut from pleasant to outright threatening. Discussion of these was curtailed out of hand by the police officer. Seeing that Howard's interests were not of the slightest concern to him I ended the videotaping session.

The matter did not proceed to trial for a full year. In

December 1999 it finally came before a jury in the Auckland District Court. The prosecution case was that Howard had sexually violated Carol in his kitchen and that he had attempted to rape her in the bedroom. We argued that Carol and her new boyfriend - out of jealousy, bitterness and animosity - had concocted the allegations.

The prosecution called a number of witnesses who set the scene. One was an elderly woman from Remuera, who had been Howard's neighbour. 'I remember the night well. I heard these terrible screams coming from the apartment across the way. It sounded like someone was being raped or murdered.' The witness was visibly upset, crying throughout her testimony.

As the court took a brief adjournment I was faced with a dilemma. The witness had the jury's sympathy, and to browbeat her would alienate them. Moreover, she seemed sincere. How could her evidence be attacked?

Before beginning my cross-examination I spoke quietly with the guard at the door to the court holding cell, asking him to leave the cell door unlocked when the trial recommenced, 'in the interests of justice'.

When I stood to begin my cross-examination, I was idly playing with my ballpoint pen. Clumsily, I flicked it out of my hands (I'm still pretty uncoordinated, when I want to be). It flew across the courtroom and bounced off the door to the holding cells.

'Sorry, sir.' I walked across to my pen, bent down and picked it up, then without explanation opened the door and walked out of the sitting courtroom closing the door behind me.

Then I walked down the corridor next to the cells. Then I turned around, opened my mouth and let forth a series of blood-curdling screams.

'*Help!Help!Rape!Murder!Stop!Help me!*

A moment later, I walked calmly back into the court, relieved to find the cell door had not been locked behind me. The prosecutor leapt to her feet. 'I object, your honour!'

'Objection noted.' The judge was smiling.

I asked my question.

'Now witness, do you accept that unless you had seen me

walk out that door, you wouldn't have known whether that scream was real or just made up, would you?' The answer didn't really matter. I had made my point.

Carol's boyfriend was called as a witness by the prosecution. 'It was about eleven o'clock. I was at home at our flat in Mission Bay and Carol wasn't there when she was supposed to be home. I know it was just before eleven because I had a shower, changed and noticed the clock while I had a beer. Then Carol called and said, 'I'm at Howard's. Come and get me – things aren't going well,' then she hung up.

'What did you do next?' asked the prosecutor.

'I jumped in my car and drove to the flat in Remuera. I screeched to a halt outside the flat and called Howard's number on my mobile phone. Carol answered it and screamed, 'Help!Help!He's raping me!"

'What did you do?'

'I put the phone down and ran to the doorway. Carol buzzed me in and I ran up the stairs. As I was running up the stairs she was running down.'

A neighbour had given evidence that as Carol had run down the stairs, looking extremely dishevelled; all she had been saying was,

'Where are my knickers? Where are my knickers?'

'Shall I call the police?' asked the neighbour.

'No, no, no – he'll get into trouble.'

She ran back upstairs and retrieved her underwear from the pocket of Long's dressing gown – for some reason her underwear and his had been tied together. Her boyfriend confirmed these details, and continued.

He said that he gave Long a moderately serious beating before driving with Carol back to their Mission Bay flat, where she telephoned Howard's boss to tell him of the rape.

I had carefully planned his cross-examination. The boyfriend was a very big man, a black belt, so I wanted to avoid standing before him and attempting to dominate him. Better to lead him gently the way I wanted him to go. I told the judge I had a trick knee, and obtained permission, temporarily, to question the witness while sitting down.

I started by taking the witness through his statements to the police to avoid any ambiguity, asking my questions very softly.

'Let's go through this again. Just before eleven Carol called you. She said, 'I'm at Howard's. Come and get me - things aren't going well then she hung up. Is that right?'

'Yes.'

'So you're sure nothing else was said? It was just like that?'

'Yes.'

'So it took about five or six seconds, maybe ten or fifteen seconds tops?'

'Yes.'

'Then you drive to the apartment, screech to a stop outside and dial the flat on your mobile phone. Carol answers and she screams rape, and you go into panic mode. Is that right?'

'Yes.'

'And she tells the neighbour she doesn't want the police called because she doesn't want to get 'him' into trouble.'

'Yes.'

'Then after you leave, when you get home, Carol uses your cell phone to call Howard's boss, and tells him that Howard had tried to rape her, is that right?'

'Yes.'

'So she obviously wants to get him into trouble. She wanted to get him where it hurts – his job, his money, eh? You know, witness, I'm sitting here trying to figure out how I can prove that you two conspired against my client.'

'You can't, Mr. Harder, because we didn't.'

I sat for thirty seconds as if in thought. Then suddenly I stood to my feet, my trick knee suddenly better and I spoke to the witness with force in my voice.

'*Is that right? Is that right?*' I said. 'Well let's look at it. You got this phone call of ten seconds at most from Carol, then you drive to Howard's apartment and you phone his number then when you get back to your flat, Carol calls Howard's boss. Is that correct? He confirms I am correct. Well here's your phone bill. See that phone call at eleven o'clock to your number? Yes.

'So this must be the call from Carol to you, the ten second call when she said three phrases. How come the record states that the call lasted 54 seconds? Do you have any idea how long that is? Let's just stand here. Let's watch the clock . . . Five . . . Ten . . .'

I sounded off the passing time in five-second blocks as the whole court waited in silence. It really is a long time. Try it some time.

'Now that's 54 seconds. That's a long time, eh? What else was said?'

'Nothing.'

'Okay, so then you drive to Howard's and call his number on your mobile, she screams rape, right?'

'Yes.'

'Then you run upstairs as she runs downstairs.'

'Correct', he replied.

'Look at your mobile phone bill, witness! *Where's the call from your mobile to Howard's number?*'

'Ummm . . . it's not there.'

'No. You've been caught out, eh? Both feet nailed to the floor. Thank you witness.'

Then I sat down without further question.

The other crucial witness was Carol, the complainant. She told how she visited Howard Long about eleven at night, chatting with him in the kitchen as she sat on the counter. It had been, she said, 'just like the old days'. She then told how Howard had insulted her by referring to her fat stomach, and then pulled her off the bench and onto the floor, where he forcibly spread her legs and tore off her nylons and underpants. Carol testified that he then digitally penetrated her. She described how she had told Howard she needed to go to the toilet, so he had climbed off her and frog marched her to the toilet.

'Then he pushed me into the bedroom. He jumped on top of me and was rubbing himself up and down against me. He tried to rape me but he couldn't – his penis went limp and then he leaked semen all over me!'

In his interview with the police and subsequent conversations with me during the year waiting for trial, Long had claimed that he and Carol had fallen together onto the bed consensually, but that nothing sexual had taken place. As case preparation had progressed, it rapidly became clear that something sexual had happened: the removal of underwear was by itself a useful indicator of that fact. Howard wanted me to go to a doctor and get him to say that it was impossible for a man to leak semen from his penis when it was not erect. I told him that if he wanted a doctor to say that then he should go to the doctor, not me.

'You can try and find someone to say you can't leak semen from a flaccid penis, but the reality is that you probably can!' This exchange was symptomatic of our lawyer-client relationship. Carol was still in the witness box. I would have another crack at her tomorrow. After cross-examining Howard's ex girlfriend, I was satisfied my client had not told me the whole truth. I finally lost my temper.

'Listen, you son of a bitch! I don't think you did this, but there's no way you've told me what really happened. *If you don't tell me the whole Goddamn truth right now you're going to get convicted and sentenced to 8 years in jail. Now tell me the fucking truth!*'

I've been in trouble for swearing at clients in the past (X, for example), but sometimes you just have to. It worked: Long told me the truth, and I was able to prepare my cross-examination accordingly.

When I continued my cross-examination of the complainant the next day, I did so very slowly and carefully.

In a rape case the complainant often receives jury sympathy, so attacking her immediately would have been counter-productive. Better to walk her through her story again and lead the witness into demonstrating her own unreliability.

'So you left Howard on the first of October, is that right?'

'Yes.'

'And you moved in with your new boyfriend?'

'Yes.'

'And how long had you been seeing him?'

'About a year.'

'So you were having a secret relationship, and telling Howard lies, and being devious and deceiving . . . ?' I slowly worked my way through the whole scenario, climaxing with the events of the night in question.

'You were in the kitchen with Howard. You've got nice legs – did you flash them at him?'

'Oh yes!' Unbelievably, the witness suddenly stepped from the witness box and adopted a supermodel pose before the court to demonstrate how attractive her legs were, 'They are lovely aren't they!' she exclaimed. Then she stepped back into the witness box. There's a little bit of jury sympathy gone I thought to myself. I was coming to the opinion that this lady was not the full quid.

'So in the kitchen, didn't you tell the police officer that Howard said he wanted to kiss you and he pulled you towards him, and that you didn't say or do anything, and that the next thing you remember you were on the floor? Isn't that right?'

'Yes,' she replied.

'So later, you were in the bedroom. You two were a couple for a long time and you had sex many, many times in many, many places and in many, many different ways.' Fortunately for me, the judge did not interrupt what might have been characterised as leading evidence of a complainant's previous sexual history. I don't think it really was, but it was a close call.

'*But at home with Howard you only ever had sex one way.*' Everybody in court collectively pricked up his or her ears waiting for my next question.

'Witness, isn't it true that the only way you two ever had sex at home was that you would sit with your legs apart, and Howard would kneel between them and play with your vagina while he masturbated and that just before he ejaculated you would have him thrust his penis inside your vagina? Isn't that what you always did?' No response.

'*In fact, on this occasion this was exactly what was happening, but for the first time in seven years his penis went limp and he leaked semen all over your fanny!*'

'Mr. Harder!' interrupted Judge Thorburn. '*You can't say "fanny" in this court Mr Harder!*'

'Sorry your Honour. I mean your vagina. Isn't that true?' Carol was becoming visibly angry.

'Mr. Harder,' she said, 'he wasn't holding it he was rubbing it.'

'And you are twisting things. No, he couldn't hold it because it was limp, then he leaked all over you.' I said.

'*Mr. Harder, I like semen, I just don't like it all over my pubic hair!*

'Mr. Harder, can I see you and Crown counsel in chambers, please,' interrupted the judge. Settled into our chairs in the judge's chambers His Honour spoke directly to me.

'Mr Harder, I haven't done this before with defence counsel but I think you have well and truly cooked the witness and you should sit down.'

I explained that I would like to but that I still had a duty to put to the witness what Howard had said to the police in his police interview or else I was leaving myself open to criticism if I failed to put the matters to her. Reluctantly he agreed.

All the same I rushed through my remaining questions because I agreed with the judge. The complainant and her credibility were truly cooked. After some 5 hours of deliberations the jury returned with its verdicts and acquitted Long on all charges. He now lives in Australia with a new, nicer girlfriend.

27

Sami Rape Appeal

In December 2000 there was a very unusual occurrence that presented me with an amazing challenge. A Fijian Indian who looked like he had the world on his shoulders, walked into my office with an ex-client I had previously saved from disaster. He explained that his friend had just been convicted of rape and was due to be sentenced in December. The potential client claimed something had gone terribly wrong with his case. He pleaded with me to help him and agreed to pay me well if I could make his nightmare disappear.

He told me his lawyer was John Billington QC and I was gob-smacked! I had recently had a drawn-out, difficult situation involving Billington and Howard Keyte QC in relation to Bennett's ongoing complaints.

I had the Fijian Indian client (Sami's) sentencing adjourned until the New Year then filed a rare 347 application after verdict, asking the trial judge, Marion Frater, an ex Family Court judge, to discharge the accused because of a fundamental trial error.

The judge dismissed my application stating, 'If she had made a mistake, then that was a matter for the Court of Appeal'. A new sentencing date was set but when it arrived, the judge had broken her leg and the sentencing was further delayed.

After discovering fresh evidence that suggested the complainant had lied at trial, I brought an unheard of second 347 application after verdict but before sentence. By now the judge was being difficult to say the least at my persistent applications. To make my point as clearly as I could, I brought in a whiteboard in an effort to illustrate my point to the judge in that she had the judicial discretion, sufficient grounds and new material before her to justify taking such a rare step.

My second application for discharge of my client after verdict was also dismissed. She reiterated that if there was fresh evidence (not available at trial, but cogent and relevant) then it was still a matter for the Court of Appeal. She then proceeded to sentence Sami to eight years in prison.

I consoled my client in the cells and promised I would get a bail hearing in the Court of Appeal as soon as I could. Three days later I filed a memorandum in support of bail.

Bail was denied despite it being submitted that Sami had strong grounds on appeal and that being held in custody pending appeal would destroy his business.

The applicant is a self-employed businessman and runs a restaurant in Newton, Wellington and has half ownership in a taro importing business that he originally set up. His businesses would deteriorate over the next few months because he is very much hands on running the businesses. If his conviction was overturned and matters came to an end he would be left financially ruined or near it. All very hard to win back if he remained in jail. This was unfair to him and his family of five and also extended family and community responsibilities.

After a half hour of vigorous argument, the President of the Court of appeal, Sir Ivor Richardson, said the court was not prepared to grant my client bail but that there had been a cancellation and if I was prepared to proceed on short notice, I could have a hearing date the following week. I quickly accepted because I knew the case inside out having worked on it for nearly five months and that there was a fatal flaw in the judge's direction to the jury. Seven days later I was back in the court of Appeal.

IN SUMMARY – STRONG GROUNDS FOR HIS APPEAL
1. There were at least two possible abuse of process

calls, maybe three, that could have been made at trial before an experienced criminal court judge.

2. There is fresh evidence that has come into existence after verdict but before sentence that destroy the complainant's general credibility.

3. Regrettably the jury was misled by an unfortunate sequence of events involving the Prosecutor, the Judge and the defence Counsel that has undoubtedly brought about a miscarriage of justice. Although Sami gave evidence it was not led from him that he had no previous convictions.

4. With all the material now available no jury properly directed could exclude the reasonable possibility Sami had reasonable grounds to believe the complainant consented, even if she did not consent.

In less than twenty minutes I completed my submissions and made my point to the court that Sami had not received a fair trial because the judge elected not to tell the jury of the result of a previous trial involving the same complainant and where the accused in that case had been acquitted on both counts.

Unfortunately, this direction misled the jury, a fact the Court of Appeal recognised after only five minutes deliberation. They accepted there had been a fundamental trial error and a re-trial was ordered.

After Sami's appeal, I wandered down to the High Court where the Chief Justice had her office and I spoke to her personal assistant. My aim was to express my outrage at the suggestion by Chief District Court judge Ron Young, who had just been appointed to the High Court bench, that, 'New Zealand JPs were superfluous and past their use-by date and should go quietly'.

I thought this to be a most insensitive and rash comment coming from someone who no doubt had benefited in the past from the voluntary work done by these pillars of society. I wanted to go to his swearing-in and pass out buttons in protest but a Justice Department person gave me the wrong date and I missed it. And to prove 'what goes around, comes around,' a couple of weeks after His Honour was sworn in, he was issued with an infringement notice for failing to wear a seat belt.

I had a briefcase full of electioneering-type bright yellow buttons that I handed to the Chief Justice's assistant. They boldly stated in black,

"Apologise Justice Ron Young" and "Justice for JPs"

Someone needed to support the 2000+ respected JPs who in turn supported the justice system amongst other duties.

On March 28th 2001, I addressed members of the Auckland Justices of the Peace association at their annual dinner, where I played my CD *Legal Sunscreen*. In the letter of thanks that followed from Registrar, Ross MacKay, he said, *"We were all particularly impressed with the thought and wisdom that had gone into the production of your CD. I would appreciate a copy of the words and/or a disc."*

About that time, I was also asked to address the Press Club in Wellington. I thought this was a good opportunity to ask my son Josh (with commercial pilot's licence and twin engine rating) if he had time to fly me to Wellington. I had not yet had the opportunity to fly anywhere with him since he got his licence. Unfortunately he was unavailable on the day because he had university commitments.

At the Copper Room in parliament buildings, only twelve people turned up. The secretary of the Press Club Ken Little, who also happened to be the Registrar of the Royal federation of Justices Association, and a JP himself, apologised for the low attendance but said after the event, it was a bit like Woodstock in that those who *were* there would never forget the experience.

Six weeks later, Wellington Crown prosecutor, Kate Feltham phoned and advised me that the complainant in Sami's case was no longer prepared to give evidence at a re-trial and accordingly the Crown would not oppose a discharge under section 347 of the Crimes Act 1961. It was a case of 'third time lucky' for Sami.

THE END: Where My Heart Is

Much as I have a passion for conflict resolution, both internationally and on a basic legal level, (locally) what spurs me on to continue the battle in the District Court on a daily basis is the final story.

Simon Kerr was part of the 'Hole in the Wall' gang, famous for dislodging and stealing ATMs (Automatic Teller Machines) and the contents.

He faced a total of 35 charges and acted for himself on 33 of them. Because he had been personally involved, he was a master of the facts. Time and again he caught the police out because he knew the truth and won. Of 31 charges, all tried before juries, the juries preferred his version of events to that of the police.

On two minor charges, to which he pleaded guilty, he was fined. This left two major jury trials to go. But now Kerr, like me, was exhausted, so just before his case was to start, he walked down to my office and asked for my help. He said he was prepared to plead guilty to the remaining two matters but only if he did not have to spend one more day in jail.

The prosecutors were tough nut Mike Ruffin on one case and suave, determined Brian Dickie on the other. The judge was Chris Field. I spoke to both prosecutors looking for a satisfactory outcome for Kerr.

It suited them not to go to trial but they were looking for guilty pleas and five years imprisonment. Finally it was agreed that Kerr would plead guilty to the Christchurch ATM burglary that day and as his defence counsel I would accept that a prison sentence of two and a half years would be appropriate for the first offence. Because Kerr had spent eighteen months on remand, this meant that when he was sentenced and taken back to prison, he would be immediately released.

Two days later, in relation to the second charge, Kerr pleaded guilty and was sentenced to two years imprisonment suspended for two years and 200 hours community service plus pay $40,000 reparation which Kerr was expecting to be paid for one of the incredible film scripts he had written that was based on his personal experience. This result reinforced to me that when I engage my lateral thinking ability to solve a seemingly insurmountable problem, NOTHING IS IMPOSSIBLE!

Epilogue

Not all courtroom appearances are dark and dire. Some can be very entertaining and light-hearted as the following stories demonstrate:

His Honour Mick Brown is one of the fairest and most pleasant of all the judges I have ever met and appeared before. I recall a memorable day in 1984, April 2nd to be precise, when I appeared for a client at the Henderson Magistrate's Court where Mick was on the bench. During proceedings my pager went off! His Honour paused and said chuckling, 'Mr. Harder, I believe your eggs are done!' It was in fact a message announcing that my wife Philippa had given birth to our daughter Kate.

Best Courtroom Performance Award

Retired District Court judge Ron Gilbert has often been asked to comment on the performance of barristers before a jury. His most memorable recollection was not that of a barrister but of an 'individual' who provided a spectacular occasion during the infamous 1981 Springbok tour trials when a number of persons, some of them activists, some not, were jointly tried for offences or crimes against the police. There was a range of charges but most of them related to identity because most of these persons were disguised or they had motorcycle helmets on.

One of the defendants was one Hone Harawira of activist fame. Another was Ripeka Evans of similar description. Three defendants were represented, one by Russell Johnson, (now a judge) one by Alex Witten-Hannah and another by someone whose name escapes me. Miss Spain represented the Crown.

Throughout the trial the constant issue of identification from videotapes of the protest became paramount. Hone Harawira was an outstanding looking person with great demeanour who conducted himself very well. He was cross-examining a police sergeant who had identified Harawira as being a person who had been running down the right hand side of the street in certain clothing and he subsequently cross-examined a police constable who had him running down the other side of the street in different clothing.

It came to a point where I had to decide if various people

were going to give evidence. I called on Harawira to see if he was prepared to give evidence or call any evidence. He opened his evidence beautifully to the jury in glowing terms. 'I'm not a very intelligent person. I'm somewhat simple and I hear words in the course of this trial that I do not understand so I go home at night and I look them up in the dictionary. One word I heard during the course of this trial was 'supposition', I looked it up and what did it say? *All you've got left when you've got no proof!* That's what this trial is about, all you've got left when you've got no proof!

'But I have grave difficulties because the judge asked me if I wanted to call evidence. But who do I wish to call evidence about? The man on the right hand side of the street, who the police sergeant said was me or the man on the left hand side of the street who the police constable said, was me? I do not know. I am at a loss. Who should I call evidence about?

'I won't argue. I am entitled to call some evidence. Call Bishop Tutu!'

The court doors opened up and into the court room, bedecked in his purple robes strode Bishop Desmond Tutu! Straight into the witness box.

Harawira asked the bishop, 'What is your name?' He replied, 'Desmond so and so Tutu'. And where do you live asked Harawira. 'So and so Street Soweto.' Said the bishop. 'Tell us about apartheid!' Harawira demanded. Of course it was totally irrelevant, but it was beautiful stuff. The whole jury stood up, all the witnesses stood up, even the Crown prosecutor stood up!

Ron Gilbert managed to retain his seat, but was full of praise for a tremendous performance. No barrister could ever have pulled it off! Harawira was acquitted at the end of the day and rightly so.

notations

In regard to adrenalin rushes, getting the "not guilty" verdict in the third Plumley-Walker trial had to be the best, followed closely by the "not guilty" verdict handed down at the Donnelly murder re-trial. This was after having called no evidence and my client not having made a statement to the police. It was left to the Crown to make their case and there was simply too much doubt for a jury ever to convict.

My funniest experience was when one of my clients was arrested on drug-related charges and interviewed in a secure room at Harlech House, Otahuhu, by Detective Lavea. My client was left in the room to talk to me privately on his cellphone. The phone went dead and when he called the detective in to tell him so, Lavea re-entered the room, leaving the keys outside.

The door closed behind him and, without the keys, they couldn't open the door again. After whistling, yelling, banging and even barking like dogs, no one came to their rescue. They were locked in the room for four hours until they were finally discovered and released.

In return for the detective promising to be polite to me in future I promised not to put the story on the front page of the NZ Herald or the Sunday Star-Times.

The worst murder trial I was ever involved in and not mentioned in this book was the trial over the death of baby Delcelia Witika. In terms of horrific and tragic detail it was monstrous and exhibited the worst possible side of human nature. Tania Witika told police she held her baby in her arms, looked into her eyes and knew she was going to die, then put her back down on the un-sheeted bed and went with her boyfriend Eddie Smith to a party. When they came home hours later poor little Delcelia was dead.

Conclusion

I have been questioned by the FBI, and under surveillance by various international agencies, including the CIA. I have been harassed, strip searched, threatened with imprisonment in half a dozen countries, imprisoned in two, followed, wire tapped, bugged and accused of being everything from a spy to a saboteur.

I have been flat broke in some of the least desirous countries in the world, but I have never been poor. Poverty is a state of mind.

Through all my trials, travels and tribulations I have refused to sacrifice that one thin thread of belief, THAT ONE MAN OR WOMAN **CAN** MAKE A DIFFERENCE.

FEES

Unlike some lawyers, **I do not charge by the hour.** I prefer to reach an agreed fee with a client to help them make their 'nightmare' disappear. Once I establish what their goal is I am better able to assess cost. There are major cases, medium cases and small cases. For major cases where a jury trial is involved there is often a year's work before the trial starts.

The fees are agreed in such a case and yes, it can cost. After all, the client is wanting me take on their nightmare and live it until it's hopefully brought to an end.

Moderate cases range in price from $2000-$20,000. All fees are by negotiation, so if I nominate a $15,000 fee and the client indicates $10,000 is the maximum he can afford, I will negotiate, I am not that hard nosed.

Small cases range from $500-$2000

How to Deal with your Nightmare

I have found that if I get involved early enough in a case, often it can be turned around before the concrete sets. My formula with new clients is to get them in, discuss the facts of their case then endeavour to give them realistic options. These range from first trying to get the police to withdraw the charge, doing a plea bargain to reduce the seriousness of the charge, designing a sentence aimed at getting a discharge without conviction, keeping your driver's licence, a restorative justice conference, staying in the country (on immigration matters), staying out of jail by pitching for a suspended sentence, and trying instead for periodic detention (Saturday work up to 12 months), community service, (up to 200 hours work over a year) defended hearing, jury trial and conviction and sentence appeals.

Most fees are private because the client is better behaved and normally this assists in getting the best result in the circumstances. Melanie Coxon and I do legal aid for those that cannot afford to pay an affordable fee. We are available seven days a week on mobile 021 9111 33. Appointments are available evenings and weekends. Kingston Street Legal Chambers is one block from the Sky Tower, at 40 Kingston Street Auckland City.